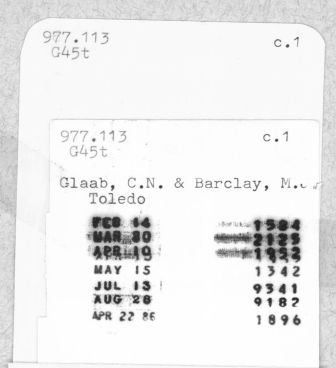

toledo

GATEWAY TO THE GREAT LAKES

BY MORGAN BARCLAY AND CHARLES N. GLAAB
PHOTOGRAPHY BY HAZEN AND SUE KEYSER

Gateway to the Great Lakes

toledo

a pictorial and entertaining commentary
on the growth of Toledo, Ohio

by Charles N. Glaab and Morgan J. Barclay
Dedicated to Randolph C. Downes,
who paved the way for this volume.

Publishers:
Larry P. Silvey
Douglas S. Drown

Managing Editor:
Kitty G. Silvey

Manuscript Editor:
Ellen Sue Blakey

Associate Editor:
Sharon Mason

Art Director:
Rusty Johnson

Designer:
James Michael Martin

Current Photograpers:
Hazen and Sue Keyser

Historical Consultant:
Fred J. Folger III

Manager of Production:
Mark Radcliffe

Project Director:
Joyce Moffett

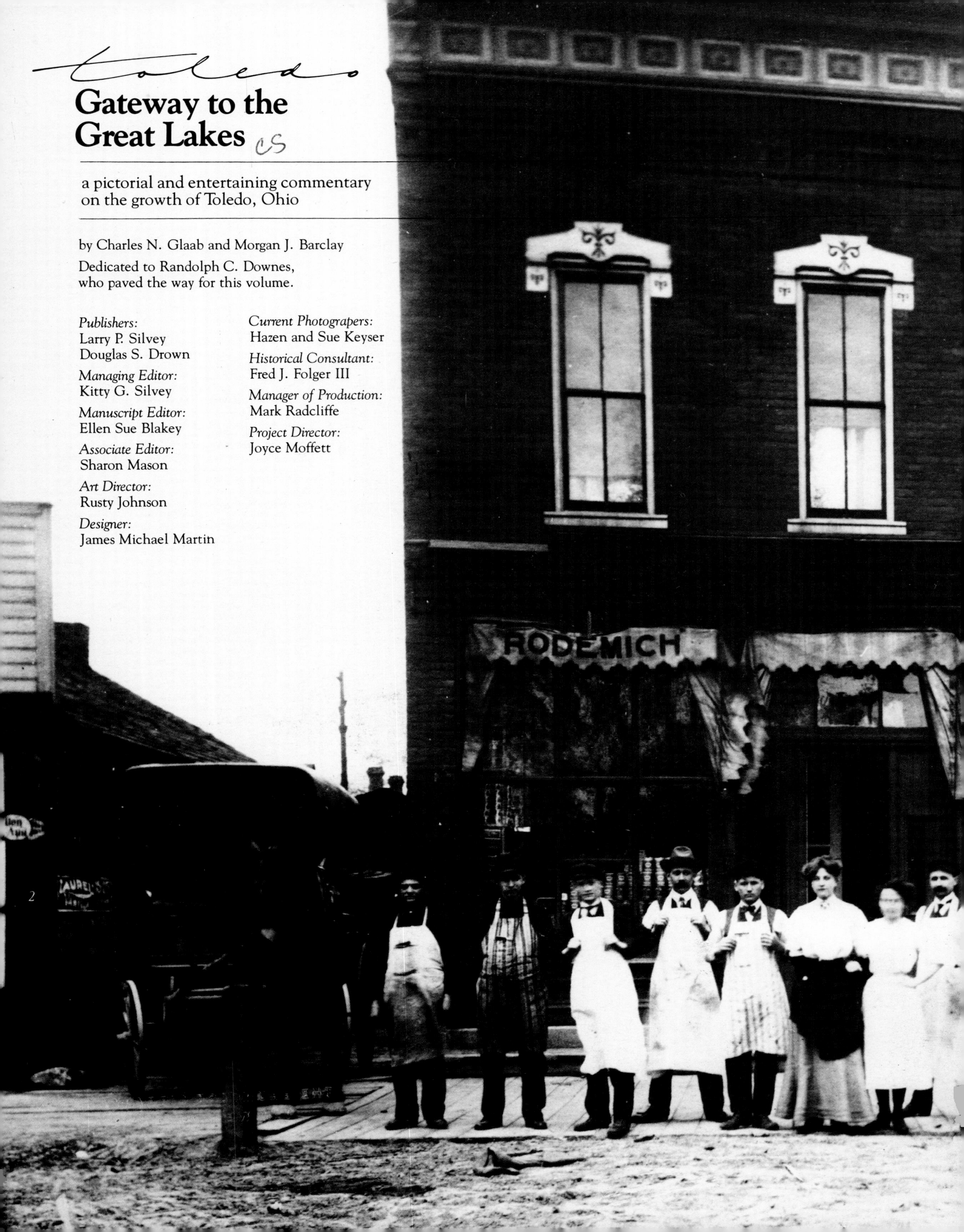

RODEMICH

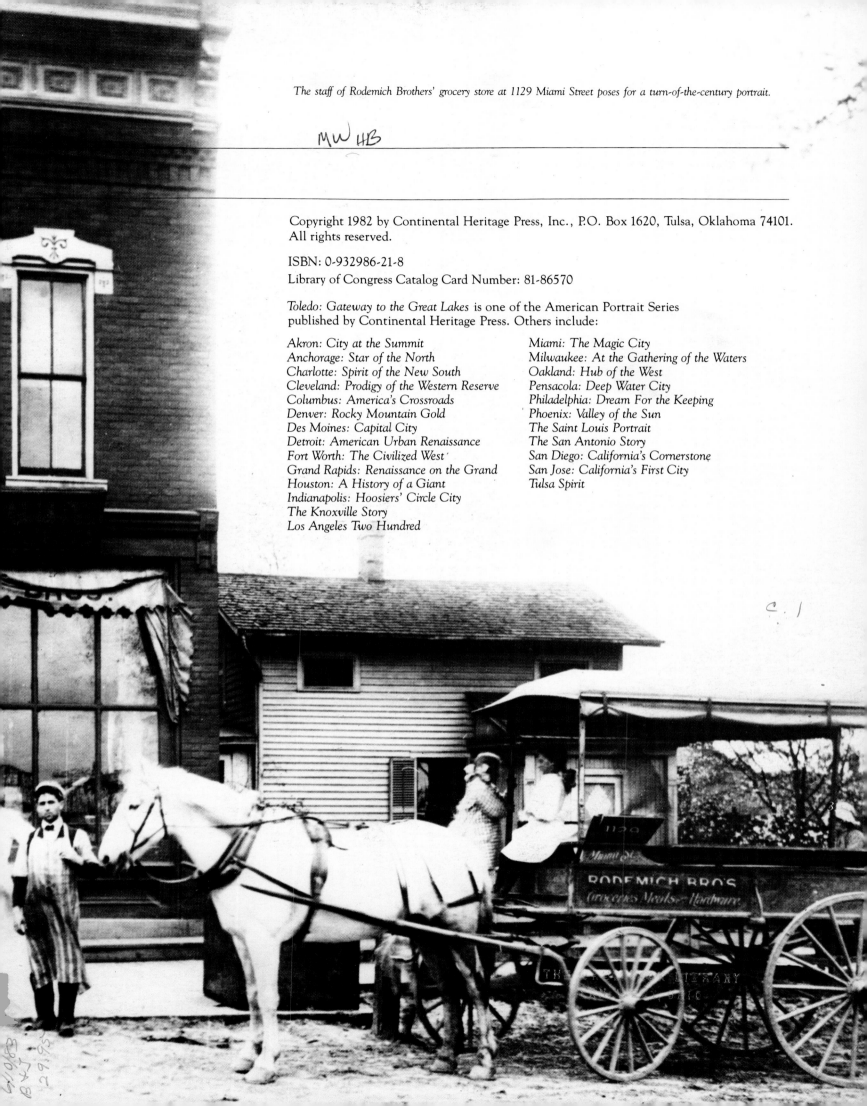

The staff of Rodemich Brothers' grocery store at 1129 Miami Street poses for a turn-of-the-century portrait.

MW HB

ISBN: 0-932986-21-8
Library of Congress Catalog Card Number: 81-86570

Toledo: Gateway to the Great Lakes is one of the American Portrait Series published by Continental Heritage Press. Others include:

Akron: City at the Summit
Anchorage: Star of the North
Charlotte: Spirit of the New South
Cleveland: Prodigy of the Western Reserve
Columbus: America's Crossroads
Denver: Rocky Mountain Gold
Des Moines: Capital City
Detroit: American Urban Renaissance
Fort Worth: The Civilized West
Grand Rapids: Renaissance on the Grand
Houston: A History of a Giant
Indianapolis: Hoosiers' Circle City
The Knoxville Story
Los Angeles Two Hundred

Miami: The Magic City
Milwaukee: At the Gathering of the Waters
Oakland: Hub of the West
Pensacola: Deep Water City
Philadelphia: Dream For the Keeping
Phoenix: Valley of the Sun
The Saint Louis Portrait
The San Antonio Story
San Diego: California's Cornerstone
San Jose: California's First City
Tulsa Spirit

4

Visitors at Fort Meigs catch a glimpse of the spirit that protected the Maumee Valley settlement from British invasion in 1813.

Maumee Valley fishermen stand solitary vigil (above and inset).

Sponsors and benefactors

The following Toledo area firms, organizations and individuals have invested toward the quality production of this historic book and have thereby expressed their commitment to the future of this great city and to the support of the book's principal sponsor, The Maumee Valley Historical Society.

Airtite Inc.
W. J. Albring Services, Inc.
Alexander-Patterson Associates, Inc.
Aluminum & Zinc Die Cast Company
Mr. and Mrs. John D. Anderson
A-1 Schmidlin Plbg. & Htg. Co.
Arnold Industries, Inc.
*BancOhio Corporation
*Bauer, Stark and Lashbrook, Inc.
Bell & Beckwith
Ben-E-Lene Exterminators, Inc.
*The A. Bentley & Sons Company
Binkelman Bearings, Inc.
B-Jay Advertising-Distributing Co., Inc.
Blue Cross and Blue Shield in Northwest Ohio
Bostleman Corp.
*Bostwick-Braun Company

Brell, Tebay, Turner, Holt & Dettinger, Inc.
The Broer-Freeman Company — Jewelers
Bud & Luke Restaurant
Capital Tire Inc.
*Champion Spark Plug Company
Clarklift of Northwest Ohio
*The Collaborative Inc.
Covenant House, Inc.
Dana Corporation
*The Sam Davis Company, Inc.
*Davis Junior College of Business
Deloitte Haskins & Sells
DiSalle Real Estate Co.
*Doehler-Jarvis Castings
Doyle, Lewis & Warner
Drew Cartage Co., Inc.
*Dura Corporation
Eagle-Picher Bearings
Ecolotreat Process Equipment Corporation
Entelco Corporation
Finkbeiner, Pettis & Strout, Limited
First National Bank of Toledo
Judge Joseph A. Flores
*Flower Hospital-Crestview Center

Freightway Corporation
Frisch's Big Boy Family Restaurants
The General Engineering Company
*General Mills, Inc.
George Ballas Buick-GMC Truck, Inc.
Gilbert Mail Service, Inc.
Girkins Electric Co.
Glasstech, Inc.
Grogan Chrysler-Plymouth-Charlies Dodge
Ron Hemelgarn
The Historical Society of Grand Rapids, Ohio
Holiday Inn — Southwest
Holland Inc., Building Services
*The Huntington National Bank
Industrial Printing Company
J-C Pratt & Associates
The Jobst Institute, Inc.
Jones & Henry Engineers, Limited
*Kuhlman Corp.
Kiemle-Hankins Company
Kistler Ford, Inc.
Knauer Supply Company
Lamb Enterprises, Inc.
*The Lane Drug Company
The Lathrop Company

6

Lopez International Steamship Agency, Inc.
Louisville Title Agency for N.W. Ohio, Inc.
Beckie and Bob Lumm Sr.
*The Mather Company
McDonald's Corporation
McManus/Troup Company
Medical College of Ohio
*The Mellocraft Company
Miller-Zamis, Inc.
A. Mindel & Son, Inc.
National Institute of Technology
Ohio Belting & Transmission Co.
*Ohio Citizens Bank
The Ohio and Michigan Paper Company
*Owens-Illinois, Inc.
John G. Packo Family
Delos M. Palmer & Associates, Inc.
*Parkview Hospital
Peerless Molded Plastics, Inc.
Peters Stamping Company
Pexco Packaging Corporation
*Plaskon Products, Inc.
*The Prestolite Company, An Allied Corporation Company

*Riverside Hospital
William J. Ross
R. S. Electronics, Toledo, Inc.
*Rudolph/Libbe/Inc.
The Ruth Corporation
Fred and Ray Saba
*St. Luke's Hospital
*St. Vincent Hospital and Medical Center
*Schindler Haughton Elevator Corporation
Schoen Investments, Inc.
Sears, Roebuck and Co.
*Seaway Food Town, Inc.
*Seeger Metals and Plastics, Inc.
Seyfang Blanchard Associates Inc.
Sheller-Globe Corporation
*Sisters of Mercy
*The Standard Oil Company
Steger-Showel Corporation
*Storer Broadcasting Company
*Sun Refining and Marketing Co., Toledo Refinery
*Surface Division, Midland-Ross Corporation
*The Sylvania Savings Bank Co.
The Tackle Box, Inc.

*Teledyne CAE
*Toledo Area Chamber of Commerce
*The Toledo Blade
Toledo Board of Education
Toledo Deburring Company
*The Toledo Edison Company
*The Toledo Hospital
Toledo Industrial and Maintenance Supply, Inc.
The Toledo-Lucas County Public Library
*The Toledo Museum of Art
Toledo Refining, Inc.
Toledo Stamping and Manufacturing Company
*The Toledo Trust Company
Touche Ross & Co.
24 Toledo
*The University of Toledo
Valley Farm Foods, Inc.
VARTA Industries, Inc.
WDHO-TV
The Welles-Bowen Company
West End Management
Willis Day Management Inc.
*WSPD Radio
*WTOL-TV

*Denotes Corporate Sponsors. The histories of these organizations and individuals appear in a special section beginning on page 185.

7

CROSSING THE RIVER:
Construction of the Fassett Street
Bridge about 1895; Lake Shore
Michigan and Southern Railroad
bridge in the background (left).

Toledo's only suspension bridge at sunset.

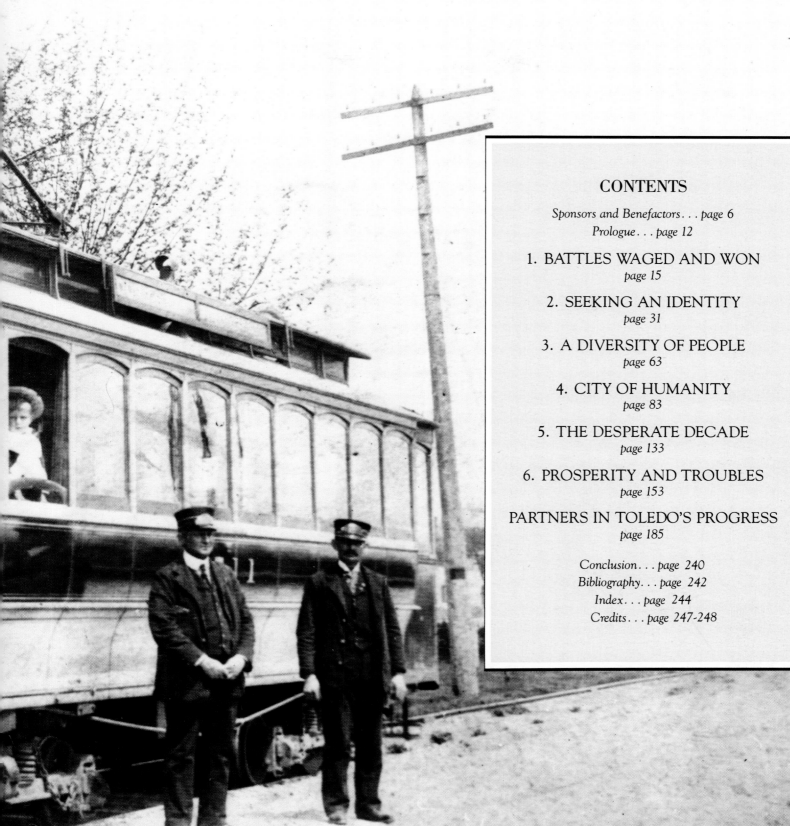

CONTENTS

Sponsors and Benefactors. . . *page 6*

Prologue. . . *page 12*

1. BATTLES WAGED AND WON
page 15

2. SEEKING AN IDENTITY
page 31

3. A DIVERSITY OF PEOPLE
page 63

4. CITY OF HUMANITY
page 83

5. THE DESPERATE DECADE
page 133

6. PROSPERITY AND TROUBLES
page 153

PARTNERS IN TOLEDO'S PROGRESS
page 185

Conclusion. . . *page 240*

Bibliography. . . *page 242*

Index. . . *page 244*

Credits. . . *page 247-248*

The Dorr St. Streetcar reminded 1910 passengers of the local baseball games.

*L*and—it was the dream of thousands of Americans,
and when the West began to open,
adventurous souls sought out places in the wilderness
to start fresh.
In the Maumee Valley, entrepreneurs marked out lots
and began a dream they called Toledo.

It was a jumping-off place to the West,
and canals and narrow-gauge railroads grew up.
There was plenty of hard work, mud and malaria,
but the swampland soon gave way to farms,
and the town became a center of commerce.

Citizens touted Toledo
          as the metropolis of interior America.
It was always the future great city of the world.
Those who believed in the town
called it a giant awakening from slumber.
Something was always going to make the city great—
bicycles or natural gas or glass.
But the city only yawned, turned over and
returned to more pleasant dreams.
It remained a good solid city—
          but not the leading metropolis.

Many families found that solidity attractive.
Thousands who stopped at the end of the lakes and
the railroad on their westward move went no farther.
The new immigrants formed neighborhoods
that maintained old-world charm
          reminiscent of their diverse homelands.

Thus Toledo expanded.
Streetcars, trolleys, automobiles linked new suburbs.
When the hard times of Depression hit,
many who had worked behind desks
found themselves peddling apples on the street.
War rescued prosperity as businesses
          cranked up production,
but the pangs of growth erupted
          in urban problems in mid-century—
racial and labor strife, slums and strip suburbs.
Good sense and community concern preserved
          the city's integrity.

But Toledo has never become the big megalopolis.
Instead, it remains a city of good taste and comfort.
And a heritage of colorful citizens gives the city
a very special flavor.

Frogtown residents are reminded of the
nineteenth-century nickname by the mosaic
rendering in the Courthouse floor (below); in all
seasons, Toledoans take advantage of the water,
whatever its form (right).

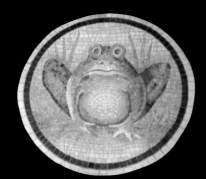

13

14

Turkey Foot Rock, commemorating a fallen Indian chief, once resided along River Road and now rests at the Fallen Timbers Monument.

BATTLES WAGED AND WON

15

The early history of Toledo, Ohio, is not the history of a single city. Any account of Toledo's founding and first years must include the history of the Maumee River valley. In the early part of the nineteenth century, the valley became the site of a booming urban frontier as a new region of the Midwest was opened to settlement. The rivalry and accompanying boosterism among competing villages and towns—a common occurrence in the early American West—fundamentally shaped the spirit and character of the town that emerged as Toledo.

The Maumee River flows northeasterly from Fort Wayne, Indiana, about a hundred miles to its mouth at Lake Erie. Long before the onrush of white settlement, it had been a main transportation artery through the wilderness. The fertility and lushness of its valley was a product of glacial erosion and had been noted by Europeans throughout the eighteenth century. The Ottawa Indians were the largest and most settled native group along the Maumee. By the time the region opened to pioneers from the East, the Ottawa had cultivated much of the area into fields of corn, but there was still a rich natural vegetation. A private soldier, who served in the area during the War of 1812, described the countryside as the "most delightful" he had ever seen. An observer could view, he wrote,

natural plains of many miles in extent. . . apparently as level as the ocean, seemingly bounded only by the distant horizon and interspersed with a few small islets, or groves of oak and hickory timber and hazel bushes, and here and there a solitary oak tree or two, standing out in open expanse. These isolated trees and groves contribute much to the beauty of the scenery. But this is not all. These plains are covered with a most luxuriant growth of grass and herbs, and an endless variety of beautiful native flowers—Cardinal Flower, Lady of the Lake, Blue Flag, Honeysuckles, Red Lobelia, Wild Fox Glove, Wild Iris, and Wild Columbine, representing all the hues of the rainbow and loading the atmosphere with their perfume.

But such a description applied mainly to the country on the northwest bank of the river. Swampland in much of the river basin contributed to the valley's fertility but also provided the geographic feature that most affected the early history of the northwest Ohio and lower Michigan region. The Black Swamp was a tract of land about 40 by 120 miles covered by dense forest extending along the western end of Lake Erie. There was no way to reach the Maumee Valley or Michigan overland from the East except to cross the Black Swamp. This obstacle contributed to the relatively late settlement of northwestern Ohio. Travelers continually told of their dread of the crossing, of wagons embedded in mud and horses dropping dead in their tracks. "My great terror, the Black Swamp is passed," wrote William Woodbridge in January 1815 on his way to assume the administration of Michigan Territory.

As late as 1829, when town builders had been at work in the valley for several years, Zophar Case recorded his journey from Cleveland to Vandalia, Illinois, in more prosaic, down-to-earth terms than those of most travelers.

THE MAUMEE

On Maumee, on Maumee,
   Potatoes they grow small;
They roast them in the fire,
   And eat them—tops and all.

There's Bass and Mullet, too;
   They run from Spring till Fall;
They take them by the tail,
   And down them—tail and all.

There's 'Possum, Coon and Fox,
   So poor they scarce can crawl;
They catch them in a trap,
   And eat them—fur and all.

There's Crows upon the bank,
   So lean they never squall;
They shoot them through the eye,
   And take them—down and all.

The soil is rich and black;
   The Corn it grows quite tall;
They take it from the field,
   And eat it—cobs and all.

On New Year's holiday
   The chaps they have a ball;
'Tis whisky in a gourd;
   They drink it—gourd and all.

The girls are plump and fair;
   The Babes know how to bawl;
The boys they always court
   The Girl, Mam, Dad and all.

On Maumee, on Maumee,
   'Tis Ague in the Fall;
The fit will shake them so,
   It rocks the house and all.

There's a funeral every day,
   Without a hearse or pall;
They tuck them in the ground,
   With breeches, coat and all.

Maumee City Express
June 24, 1834

Artist William Machen portrayed his sons fishing in a view of the
lush area surrounding Ten Mile Creek near what is now Central Avenue.

Folk hero Peter Navarre was an American scout during the War of 1812. William Machen painted his portrait in 1867, when Navarre was 80.

On December 11, he and his companion left from the eastern edge of the Black Swamp. "Mud from 8 to 12 inches deep," he wrote. "Started on foot. . . about 11 o'clock A.M. walk steadily the remainder of the day and got 13 miles." The next day they had a "hard days travel" the remaining eighteen miles to Perrysburg, one of the town settlements below Toledo. "Started about 10 o'clock mud as deep as yesterday. . . . Nothing to talk about or see but the mud in the Maumee Swamp, a good grassland, very rich, timber black ash elm hickory and basswood with occasionally a berch ridge and some lime stone."

The Black Swamp hampered early movement into the Maumee Valley and required extensive drainage before the area could be farmed. It also contributed to the region's long-time reputation for unhealthiness. "I want work," wrote a printer turning down a job in Toledo in 1839, "but I could not think of risking my life on the Maumee River. They tell me they have ten funerals a day there and not enough people to bury the dead." Late in the nineteenth

century, Toledo promoters were still unable to discredit the view that the Maumee Valley was a land of fevers and plagues that came from the swamp. But these health problems were mainly a result of the contagion spreading within compact urban settlements.

NESTS OF VILLAINY

For generations, the Maumee Valley had been occupied by Indian groups who hunted and farmed and used the river for trade and transportation. The Ottawas had long lived in the valley. The Eries had once occupied the valley but were destroyed when Iroquois from the East invaded the area several times in the mid-seventeenth century. They left few remnants of their occupancy. Miami Indians had lived in the valley before 1700 but were driven westward into Iowa and Wisconsin by the Iroquois. After the French established a fur-trading post at Detroit in 1701, the Miami returned to the valley under French protection. They provided the name of the valley. The word Maumee was a corruption of Miami, customarily attributed to the American soldiers in the region during the War of 1812. The Maumee River was called the Miami of the Lake well after 1800.

In the eighteenth century, the Maumee Valley and surrounding region became an important site in a great war for empire—an imperial struggle for economic and political control of vast territorial regions of North America. The struggle included England, France and, late in the century, the new republic of the United States of America. At the end of the French and Indian War (as the American stage of this world-war-of-sorts was called in the colonies), the region passed from the French to the English by the Peace of Paris of 1763. During the American Revolution, the Maumee Valley was the site of military action against the British and their Indian allies, especially the Ottawas who sided with the British after 1763. George Rogers Clark was the hero of western operations. As a result of his victories at Kaskaskia and Vincennes, he was able to gain control of the Illinois and Wabash river valleys in 1779. However, he could not pacify the "nests of villainy," as he called them—the towns and fortifications of the Miamis and the Ottawas. Clark was therefore unable to achieve his primary objective to move northward and capture Detroit, the seat of British operations in the western region.

The Maumee Valley was part of the territory that the United States acquired at the end of the war, but Great Britain continued its influence in the region in an attempt to maintain and extend a vast Indian protectorate in the West. In 1794 (eleven years after the Peace of Paris), the British erected Fort Miami (officially Fort Miamis) a few miles upriver from the later site of Toledo near the major rapids of the Maumee. This was one of several northwest posts in American territory that were in dispute between Great Britain and the United States after the war. By the time Fort Miami was built, the British government had begun to seek better relations with the United States because of war with France in Europe. As a result, Britain abruptly abandoned its Indian allies. The armies of the

Chief Pontiac (above) led an alliance of Indian tribes in 1763 to defeat nine English garrisons, winning better trading terms for Maumee Valley Indians; the Shawnee Chief Tecumseh (inset) fought to expel the white men from the valley, particularly during the War of 1812.

19

General Anthony Wayne.

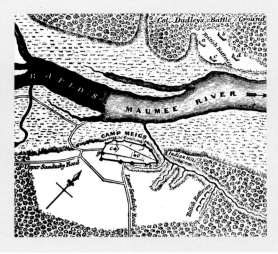

Fort Meigs was hastily built during the winter of 1813 to protect the valley from British and Indian invasion.

American general "Mad Anthony" Wayne moved down the Maumee and decisively defeated the Miamis and other Indians at the Battle of Fallen Timbers, fought near present-day Toledo in August 1794. By the terms of Jay's Treaty negotiated the next year, the British withdrew from Fort Miami and its other posts in American territory.

The Treaty of Greenville of August 3, 1795, was negotiated with 88 chiefs representing seventeen tribes. The defeated Indians relinquished sixteen tracts of land in the region including a twelve-mile square at the foot of the Maumee rapids and another six-mile square at the mouth of the river. (Sections of both tracts were to become part of Toledo.) These military and diplomatic events opened the Northwest to American settlement; and by 1803, Ohio was sufficiently populated to be admitted as a state.

The Maumee Valley remained sparsely settled for the next several years even though part of the Twelve Mile Tract was sold to land developers in 1805. Seven years later, the Maumee Valley was still an area of trading posts, farms and a few very small villages. There were only 67 families scattered around the main settlement called Maumee at the foot of the rapids. It was the first urban concentration in the region. Fort Industry—located at the juncture of Swan Creek and the river in present-day downtown Toledo —served as a post where government annuities were distributed to Indians.

The continued competing imperial ambitions of Britain and America in the American and Canadian West helped trigger the War of 1812. The Maumee Valley again became a major site of military operations. William Henry Harrison was in command of northwestern armies. As part of his strategy after the British captured Detroit in 1812, he constructed an immense fortification below Toledo. Called Fort Meigs, it became the center of a vast defensive operation against British invasion. Fort Meigs withstood two major British sieges. The first lasted from April 28 to May 5, 1813, and was one of the most critical engagements in the West. Later in the year, Commander Oliver Hazard Perry defeated the British navy on Lake Erie at Put-in-Bay. Since Britain could no longer support a land invasion by water, this secured the valley from further attack during the war.

LAND, LOTS AND CANAL ROUTES

Land—it was the dream of thousands of Americans. When the War of 1812 ended, the government abandoned Fort Meigs and offered to sell the land around it—along with the remainder of the Twelve Mile Square Reserve, only part of which had been sold in 1805. The great urban land boom was on. The auction at Wooster, Ohio, in February 1817 attracted many professional speculators and their representatives. Investors bought land, platted towns and sought future profits in urban real estate. These town promoters were the first pioneers, betting their fortunes on the arrival of settlers.

Between 1817 and 1840, the Maumee Valley was an urban frontier. The town of Maumee—the site of the first English and American settlement at the foot of the rapids—was laid out in 1817 on the northwest bank of the river. It was the first real urban community in the area. (Today it is a substantial Toledo suburb.) Perrysburg (which has also retained its identity) was platted just across the river. Manhattan was located at the mouth of the Maumee on its northwest bank; Utah and Oregon were nearby below the river. At least fifteen towns were platted along a fifteen-mile strip of the valley, including such places as Austerlitz, Marengo, East Marengo and Orleans, which were never anything other than paper towns. Eventually, these speculative town plats became part of Toledo or its metropolitan area.

The promotional enterprise that led most directly to the creation of Toledo was the establishment of Port Lawrence. At the 1817 government land auction, two Cincinnati companies purchased tracts in the Twelve Mile Reserve. They merged as the Port Lawrence Company and laid out a town at the mouth of Swan Creek and the Maumee River (the site of Fort Industry). Before their project got underway, the company encountered the problem of all western promoters—the possibility of the collapse of credit and bank failures. The Panic of 1819 and the severe depression that followed forced the Port Lawrence syndicate to default on its payments and to return portions of its holdings to the government. By 1823, Port Lawrence

Commander Oliver Hazard Perry sent the now-famous message when his smaller ships outmaneuvered the British fleet at the Battle of Lake Erie: "We have met the enemy and they are ours. . ."

21

*H*arriet Whitney Collins (1814–1903) came to the early Toledo settlement of Port Lawrence with her parents in 1824. She is credited with being the first woman schoolteacher in the city. With considerable family wealth, she became a social and civic leader in the community. In 1940 the new Harriet Whitney Vocational School was dedicated in her honor.

Her straightforward memoir, compiled when she was in her 80s, is one of the better accounts of life in early-day Toledo:

Previous to going to Painesville the last time I had met Mr. Sanford Langworthy Collins and our acquaintance had resulted in an engagement to each other, so he accompanied me on the way as far as Cleveland. He was engaged in the dry goods business and was going to New York for supplies. . . . His stock consisted of a general assortment, with Indian goods as well.

After a term of three months in Miss Sherman's school I started for home in a stage, in company of Mr. Converse, a friend of the family, with whom I had been making my home. We left Painesville at two o'clock in the afternoon and rode all night, reaching Cleveland at an early hour in the morning. We remained there one day on account of some trouble with the coach, when we started on our journey again with four horses, riding all night. After reaching Fremont, then Lower Sandusky, we were obliged to take an open wagon with a high box, which contained all the mails coming this way, besides a number of passengers. Mr. Converse was obliged to leave me at Fremont and I was to look to Mr. McDonald for care during the rest of the trip.

After we had entered the Black Swamp we found the mud to be very deep, almost impassable, and the wagon was very uncomfortable on account of the constant motion, so I requested the use of one of the horses which was being brought there for stage purposes. The horse was brought to the side of the wagon and I mounted, much to the surprise of my fellow passengers. I rode fifteen miles in this way, until midnight, when we stopped at Portage River for supper. I was very tired when we took the wagon again and proceeded on the wearisome journey.

When near Perrysburg, one of the leading horses fell down and died, so the men had to walk and I rode alone in the wagon, peering through the darkness, which was without starlight even to bring a ray of cheer. We reached Perrysburg about midnight and stopped at a hotel kept by Mr. Spafford. Then we took a coach for six passengers and crossed the Maumee River in a scow boat, proceeding down the turnpike (present Detroit Avenue) for home. When near what was called Halfway Creek the driver passed over a log of a tree which had fallen over the road and broke the tongue of the wagon. The lamps went out and the darkness prevented the damage being repaired, so we waited very impatiently until morning, when we once more started on our way.

Toledo pioneer-merchant Sanford L. Collins married Harriet Whitney (above) in 1834. He became the first county treasurer in 1835.

Finally we reached the home of my brother Ashley, who lived on what is now Detroit Avenue, near Monroe Street, where I found a safe haven at last. . . .

The stage passed on until it came to the house kept by Mr. Parks, where the passengers partook of breakfast. As this was near the store of Mr. Sanford Collins (he made his home there) and while at breakfast he learned that a young lady had come on the stage from Painesville, he at once surmised whom it might be. This was the tenth of December, 1833, and the intervening time between this and our marriage passed quickly and happily away, not quite a month before my nineteenth birthday anniversary.

At early evening, on the nineteenth of January, 1834, there were assembled by invitation some twenty or thirty of our family and close friends to be present at our wedding. . . . I wore a white bishop lawn, cut low in the neck and with large leg-of-mutton sleeves, a long plain skirt with a deep hem. My hair was done high on the back of my head, and the front was rolled at each side, two rolls on each side and three on the other and finished with a large shell comb reaching from ear to ear. I wore black velvet slippers and white silk gloves. A set of jewels, earrings and brooch of topaz set in gold filigree, which was the gift of my husband-to-be, completed my costume.

Mr. Collins wore a black broadcloth suit and velvet vest, white necktie and white gloves, and "he was the handsomest man I ever saw."

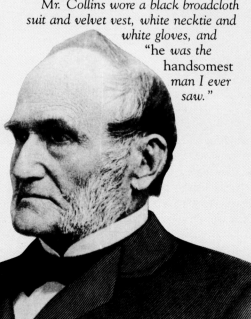

An 1803 drawing by Major O.J. Hopkins exaggerates the bluffs upon which Fort Industry stood.

consisted of a handful of log warehouses and a few small houses. As the country began its recovery from the depression, the syndicate tried again and in 1827 replatted its town on a more modest scale.

By this time, the principal advocate of Port Lawrence was Benjamin F. Stickney who had purchased the largest number of lots from the Cincinnati land companies when they had first put them up for sale. Stickney had been an Indian agent at Fort Wayne during and after the War of 1812, traveling among the Indian tribes along the Maumee and Wabash river valleys. According to his own accounts, he became absorbed in the possibility of a canal connecting the two rivers and Lake Erie and establishing a city at the terminus.

The building of the Erie Canal between 1817 and 1825 provided efficient transportation from the Great Lakes to the port of New York. Its tremendous success intensified a canal boom in the West. In advancing his proposal, Stickney argued that the swampy plain that lay between the headwaters of the two rivers and from there to Lake Erie permitted the relatively easy building of a canal connection. DeWitt Clinton, the governor of New York and the leader in promoting the Erie Canal, was impressed with Stickney's plan. He wrote to Stickney, "I have found the way to get into Lake Erie, and you have shown me how to get out of it."

Initially, Stickney's proposal involved Indiana and its canal plan. But as a part of its program of the 1820s, the state of Ohio had endorsed a canal to be built into the same area—from Cincinnati and Dayton to the Maumee River and Lake Erie. In 1824, the route was surveyed from Cincinnati to Defiance and from there along the

northwestern bank of the Maumee to the lake—a distance of 301 miles. After complicated negotiations involving Stickney, Indiana surrendered its Congressional canal land grant to the state of Ohio to build a second regional canal project called the Wabash and Erie. It would run a distance of about 242 miles to Lafayette, Indiana.

With these two canal projects underway, Stickney grew unhappy with the slow development of Port Lawrence and joined a group of investors from Lockport, New York, to set up a rival town project in 1832. Called Vistula, it was located slightly downriver from Port Lawrence. The next year, in order to compete for the site of a federal post office, the two rival investing groups joined to form a new town and chose the name Toledo, after the city in Spain.

Why they chose the name is uncertain. It was commonplace in the period to name an aspiring new town after the great cities of ancient times or those of Europe, Asia and Africa. Few of the Madrids, Constantinoples, Balbecs and Palmyras of the period ever got beyond the status of paper towns. In the nineteenth century, the name Toledo was not inappropriate and probably was selected without much thought, perhaps because there was no other Toledo around. But it was one of the few grandiosely named communities to achieve metropolitan status in the twentieth century. The exotic implications of its name (reminiscent of cathedrals, the masterpieces of El Greco, warriors in armor) were in sharp contrast with the traditional image of the midwestern manufacturing city (lunch pails, bowling leagues and ethnic celebrations). Sometime in the twentieth century, Toledo became a symbol—particularly in entertainment and some cultural circles—of midwestern boosterism, drab everyday life and

23

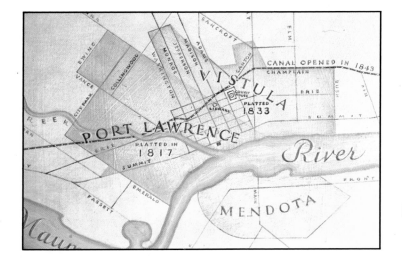

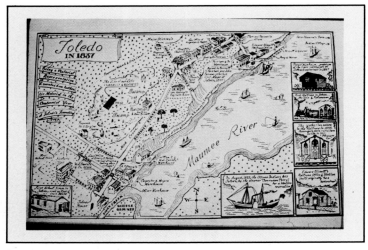

TWO BECOME ONE: WPA-commissioned map (top) showing the villages of Port Lawrence and Vistula; by 1837 the two rival towns had joined to form the new town of Toledo (above). It was mostly swamp—only Summit Street was above water.

dismal urban vistas. The image was inaccurate—Toledo fared well in any cultural comparison with other regional manufacturing cities and was more livable than most. But the image persisted.

In the mid-1830s, the Maumee Valley town boom entered a stage of frenzy. Jesup W. Scott, the most influential and the most articulate of the early Toledo city fathers, wrote that in 1835 "commenced that memorable speculation in wild lands and wild cities, which culminated in 1836. The whole Maumee Valley was filled with fortune-hunters. Congress and state lands were raced for entry, and the shores of the river from Fort Wayne to the foot of the Maumee Bay were alive with city-builders. From the foot of the rapids to the bay, land was all that was considered necessary for three-story brick blocks; and after the canal was located on the north side, all the shore . . . was held as city property."

The Maumee Land and Railroad Company instantly laid out the city of Manhattan with 5,000 lots at the mouth of the river. When it was discovered that the main channel of the Maumee ran near the southeast bank, promoters platted Lucas City opposite Manhattan. But the hopes of Lucas City were doomed from the start since the canal route lay on the northwest bank of the river.

Not content with canals alone, Toledo interests in 1833 launched one of the early railroad projects in the West, a narrow-gauge line that ran a short distance into Michigan. The Erie & Kalamazoo—which never reached Kalamazoo—used horse-drawn cars to Adrian, Michigan, until two small locomotives were delivered in June 1837. The road did not survive the depression after 1837 and went bankrupt in 1842.

THE BATTLE OF THE BORDER

The most spectacular episode of intense town-booming in the early 1800s was the Toledo War of 1835, a boundary dispute between the state of Ohio and the territory of Michigan.

The Toledo War involved 468 square miles of land seven miles wide at the Indiana border and eleven miles wide at Lake Erie resulting from conflicting northern boundaries of Ohio, one stemming from the lines in the survey of the Northwest Territory and the other submitted at the time of Ohio's admission to the union. The disputed strip included Toledo and the mouth of the Maumee River but not the town of Maumee and some of the other upriver town promotions. It had been of little interest until the canal plans were formulated. If Michigan won its claim, Toledo investors feared the loss of the canal terminus to upriver rivals. Other groups throughout Ohio feared loss of the Great Lakes trade to Michigan. The Ohio legislature authorized the organizing of an Ohio county in the disputed area with Toledo as its seat.

This dispute, a satirical contemporary observed, produced "a fearful war, and the destruction of many lives of chickens and honey bees, and occasionally a turkey." The "war" had comic-opera features which regional folklore emphasized over the years. But it also had serious aspects. The promoter Benjamin Stickney made the point. Stickney initially supported Michigan's position in the dispute but shifted sides to Ohio. "Interest," he wrote, "was at stake—our pockets were touched."

The mobilization of 10,000 Ohio militiamen to protect the strip infuriated Michigan authorities, particularly Stevens T. Mason, a 21-year-old acting territorial governor who tried to prevent Ohio law from being enforced in the strip. A series of minor confrontations and incidents followed. A party of Ohio surveyors was attacked, and Stickney was arrested and jailed briefly in Michigan. Benjamin's son, Two Stickney, drew the only human blood of the war. (His other son was named One Stickney.) When a Monroe, Michigan, deputy sheriff came to arrest Stickney, Two struck at him with a penknife, wounded him slightly and then fled the scene.

Just before 1,200 Michigan troops were set to occupy the area, a group of Ohioans sneaked into Toledo from neighboring Perrysburg. An advance party of 100 Michigan militiamen were already on the scene. The Ohioans organized a county government after midnight then fled back to Maumee to celebrate. On the way, they had to retrace their steps in order to retrieve vital documents lost in the woods during their flight.

At this point, two federal commissioners negotiated a

Quaker businessman Richard Mott served Toledo as mayor and congressman in the 1840s and '50s. He was well-known for his antislavery views and support of the Suffrage movement.

PROPHET, PROMOTER AND LEADER:
JESUP W. SCOTT

Jesup W. Scott was the preeminent leader who most vigorously asserted the argument of Toledo's magnificent destiny. His effectiveness as Toledo's booster contributed to the city's victory in the Maumee Valley rivalry. The wide dissemination of his writings about Midwest cities focused national attention on Toledo and the Great Lakes area. As editor, promoter, writer and—above all—land speculator, Scott was the one man who best reflected the spirit of Toledo during its urban frontier days.

Born in Ridgefield, Connecticut, in 1799 into a well-to-do family, Scott had begun his career in South Carolina at the age of 20. There he edited a newspaper, the Columbia Telescope. He also practiced law which he had earlier studied briefly in the North and taught at the South Carolina Female College. He was not particularly successful. The reason, he asserted, was that he was disliked as a Yankee. In the years before the Civil War, he became a dedicated and intense critic of the Southern system and way of life. In 1830 he returned to the family home in Connecticut and the next spring went west to the booming area of northwest Ohio to look after the land investments of his father-in-law, Jessup Wakeman.

Like most such land buyers, Scott did not confine himself to a single site. He bought property for himself or for others around Florence (later Huron, Ohio), Maumee and other spots in the region. Wakeman was a sometime partner with Elisha Whittlesey, a Whig Congressman who was instrumental in opening the whole Maumee Valley region to land developers. They were active in various enterprises including Ohio banks. Wakeman warned Scott of the danger of speculation in western town lots and town sites and indicated why so many were willing to take the risk. He wrote that nine out of ten of his friends had been ruined, most of them through the purchase of wild lands. "Yet," he continued, "some may succeed—wherever your great city is located the fortunate holder of land will make a great profit. Toledo, Miami [Maumee], the foot of the Rapids & Put-in-Bay—all say it is I—but all must be disappointed but one & . . . all the fond expectations of the others [will be] gone to the winds."

After spending a brief period in Florence where he turned out a promotional periodical, Scott became closely identified with the town at Maumee and edited the first newspaper there, Miami of the Lake. He also did so well buying and selling land during the boom that he retired to Connecticut with holdings worth $400,000. But the panic struck. He had to liquidate most of his investments and returned to the valley to try to recoup.

Again he initially backed the most promising settlement—Maumee—and presented an elaborate argument asserting its splendid future. But in 1844, he assumed the editorship of the Toledo Blade and became an advocate of that city's fortune. This evoked a cry of treason from former associates in Maumee. But Scott, like Benjamin Stickney earlier, argued that self-interest justified changing sides. Besides, what was really at stake was the future of an urban valley. Scott succeeded magnificently in rebuilding his fortunes, chiefly because of a tract that he had purchased between the early towns of Vistula and Port Lawrence. His holding was not a part of either town, but after the two settlements joined as Toledo, Scott's property gradually became part of the downtown as the city expanded northwestward away from the river. (By the time of his death in 1873, Toledo was thriving and Scott was a city hero and one of its major benefactors.)

Scott's principal contribution was the donation of land for an educational institution that eventually became the University of Toledo. The gift reflected and shaped an essential aspect of the city's culture—a hard-headed belief in the practical. During his years with the Blade, Scott became a great admirer of the "learned blacksmith," Elihu Burritt of Boston, a self-taught scholar and folk hero proclaimed as the equal of the professors of Harvard. To provide the possibility of self-improvement for all, Scott began advocating the establishment of "manual labor schools" in the mid-'40s. There workers "with stout hearts and good hands" could thoroughly educate themselves.

The Toledo University of Arts and Trades did not get underway until after his death and had hard going for many years. Early plans not realized included establishing professorships of Food Preparation, the Arts of Building and Mechanical Drawing.

In 1874, Frank Scott, Jesup's son, wrote that graduates of schools of cooking "have a marked advantage, other things being equal, over those who spend time in classical courses, in finding steady employment." After World War II, the University of Toledo became a full-fledged municipal and later a state university. But Frank Scott's view still stands as the wisdom of the community.

As editor of the Blade between 1844 and 1847, Jesup Scott began to write frequently about the economy and growth of the Midwest. Between 1843 and 1860, he published well over a dozen articles (some unsigned and not clearly identifiable) in the popular national commercial journals, Hunt's Merchant's Magazine and De Bow's Review. In his writings, he emphasized the importance of midwestern cities and reflected a faith in their material growth. It became a dominant theme in Toledo's history.

As early as 1832—and perhaps even while he was still

in the South—Scott had begun to develop the view that the great metropolises of the future would spring up in interior America. Initially, he argued that Cincinnati would be the first city of the heartland. When he moved to the Maumee Valley, he began to predict that Maumee would soon have this preeminent rank. When he shifted his interests to Toledo, he moved the site of his great city slightly down the river. By the end of the Civil War, it was clear that Chicago, not Toledo, would be the great metropolis of interior America, and Scott knew this. But he continued to present Toledo's case. His most famous work on Toledo as The Future Great City of the World published in 1868.

Late in his career, Scott reflected on whether an excessive promotional zeal and a preoccupation with real estate profits might be hampering city development. He echoed Henry George and other reformers of the era who saw the source of urban problems in unearned land values. "I have been, and I yet am, a land monopolist," he wrote in 1869 on the need for a workingman's university. "The law permitted it and public opinion sanctioned it. . . . There had been a selfish desire to monopolize. Now I wish, if land monopoly is continued, that it shall be devoted to public ends. . . . Whether I shall make due reparations for my share of unjust appropriation, may depend on the extension of a life, now near its end, and being able, in time, to come to a definite conclusion as to the best mode of doing it."

But more characteristic were his reflections a few years earlier in a letter to a cousin. "I think I am in exactly the best climate—on the isotherm of 50° in heat. It is the isotherm on and near which mankind have chosen to congregate in greatest numbers and built up nearly all the great modern cities. It is the climate of the best grasses, the best grain, the best fruits and—and—and the best men." Scott went on to say that in 1828 and 1829 he had foretold that the great cities of the nation would grow up in the interior plain. He had picked Cincinnati, St. Louis, Chicago and Toledo as sites for the great central metropolises at a time when Chicago and Toledo were nothing but villages. Now they were magnificent cities still in the first stage of becoming continental metropolises. Land that he had bought in Toledo for $12 an acre was worth $12,000 an acre, and lots that had sold for $25 when he had first gone there brought $25,000. The surrounding country was being converted into the richest fields in the world; more buildings were going up every year; soon Toledo's greatness would be fully realized. But in piling up token upon token of growth, he recognized overexuberance. "Hello, there," he whimsically commented, "where is my pen carrying me," and shifted to family subjects.

Scott's buoyant optimism and faith in material urban growth were shared by those who built the cities of the Midwest. It was an outlook vital to the spirit of Toledo.

truce. This enabled Congress to settle the dispute the next year. As part of a compromise worked out among Democrats in Congress and the administration during a presidential election year, Ohio received the disputed territory and Michigan was granted its upper peninsula.

Toledo celebrated the great victory June 25, 1836, with cannon fire and bells at sunrise, a parade, all-day speech making and a gala evening party with 26 toasts proclaiming the victory. The cannon for the occasion had been borrowed from a steamboat in port, and turpentine balls were substituted for the rockets customarily used on such occasions.

With the boundary dispute settled, the Ohio Board of Canal Commissioners in August decided to settle the conflicting claims of the rival communities vying for the canal terminus. The canal would be built all the way to Lake Erie with "side cuts" provided at three sites— Maumee, Toledo and Manhattan.

THE LAND BOOM FIZZLES

The frontier land boom did not continue long. On July 11, 1835, the Andrew Jackson administration took an action that curtailed land and real-estate speculation—the issuance of the Specie Circular which required that public lands be paid for in gold and silver.

Panic hit in 1837, and only the towns of Maumee, Toledo, Perrysburg and Manhattan survived the depression that followed. Places such as Marengo—characterized during the boom by a Toledo newspaper as "that bubble of an hour. . . that bare and solitary city, known to paper, known to high prices, but unknown to population"—simply disappeared. The depression stopped all internal improvements in the country. The Wabash and Erie Canal was not completed to Toledo until 1843; the linkup to Cincinnati (the Miami and Erie) opened two years later. By that time, Toledo—which had the advantage of the best natural port facilities for the transfer of cargoes between canal boats and lake ships—had begun to outdistance its nearby rivals.

Hard currency was nonexistent on the Ohio frontier and local banks issued their own.

The Erie and Kalamazoo Railroad connected Toledo with Adrian, Michigan, in 1836. The trip cost $1.50 with 50 pounds of baggage allowed.

Colonel Dresden W. H. Howard, a friend and student of the Ottawa Indians in the Maumee Valley, supervised their tragic removal in 1838. In 1837, he accompanied some friends on a hunting trip into the Oak Openings between Sylvania and Toledo. They were joined by a party of young Indian hunters:

The party of hunters accompanied us, and we travelled on north, and late in the afternoon, while riding slowly along, sounds reached us like distant thunder, and continued to approach, until we called a halt to listen, when we saw a black object, apparently about the size of a large horse, rapidly passing through the trees. Its rumble was like low and distant thunder, and we were nearly half a mile away from it, and could make out nothing definite about it until one of the Indians said it was an "iron horse," a "hot water horse, that spit hot water," and this explanation enlightened us. We all knew of something they called a railroad, but we supposed the wagons were drawn by horses of flesh and blood, but they had just made the exchange for a "Pa-si-go-gi-she Pe-waw-bick," a horse of iron. This locomotive, the first that any of us had ever seen, was running on the first railroad of this country, the Erie & Kalamazoo strap rail.

After the "Chim-mi-chim-min-i-too" (the devil of the woods) has passed, we all ventured forward and took a good look at this innovation of the Indian trail, composed of two streaks of strap iron spiked to four-inch stringers.

We had intended to go on further north and go into camp for the night, but our ponies to a "man" refused to cross this new invention, and we turned our faces south, and being on good horses reached the Indian encampment in the evening.

The Erie and Kalamazoo issued its own money through a railroad bank.

The effect of the canal on Toledo's fortunes was not immediate. In a sense, Toledo was a city with an unoccupied hinterland. "Toledo was a young city in the wilderness with high expectations, but with nothing or next to nothing to live upon," Jesup Scott perceptively wrote. "The great body of lands which surrounded it, had been entered for speculation; so that, up to the time of the canal being completed to Toledo, in 1843, there were not over 200 families out of the city, which resorted to it as their principal place of trade." The depression had brought this "airy fabric into ruin."

But within a few years after the coming of the canal, trade expanded. Merchandise shipments passing through Toledo jumped from four million pounds in 1843, to eleven million in 1848 and to thirteen million in 1850. By 1851, Toledo had become the leading Ohio center of lake imports with a total of $23 million compared to second place Cleveland's $22 million. Wheat production in northwestern Ohio increased rapidly as the drained lands of the Black Swamp and surrounding areas were turned to farming. As late as 1845, no grain passed beyond the immediate Toledo market. But by the close of the decade, the export was substantial—$400,000 annual value.

A canvass of 1849 listed an array of businesses in the city—twelve forwarding establishments, over a dozen retail dry goods stores, two jobbing warehouses, over twenty attorneys, nine hotels, five churches, over 200 carpenters and joiners, two lumber yards, six blacksmiths and seven physicians. The U.S. Census of 1850 recorded a population of 3,870. By this time, Maumee and Perrysburg downriver together contained about 2,500 people. Manhattan would be absorbed into Toledo with a major expansion of its limits in 1874. But it remained an important center for several years, with many of its business functions passing to Toledo.

In 1852, after a protracted political and legislative fight with leaders of rival Maumee, Toledo captured the county seat of Lucas County. Toledo was now the governmental as well as the commercial center of the Maumee Valley. The urban rivalry in the valley had been won. The spokesmen of the city could now begin to assert Toledo's claim to be the great metropolis of interior America.

OPENING THE GREAT LAKES

The canal boat Legal Tender at Waterville around 1890.

Canal fever swept the nation in the 1830s and 1840s. Promoters thought the canals would bring instant prosperity to the state with improved transportation for both passengers and bulk cargoes.

Ohioans joined in the fever, and canal systems spread rapidly. Once a canal system was established in eastern Ohio, people in the western part of the state lobbied for their own canal system. The Miami and Erie Canal began in Cincinnati and headed northward. As the canal reached the Toledo area, many small towns along the Maumee competed to be the end of the canal. Waterville, Maumee, Perrysburg, Port Lawrence, Vistula, Marengo, Manhattan and other towns all battled to be the major city on the Maumee. In a daring move, Port Lawrence and Vistula pooled their resources, changed their name to Toledo and became the commercial center of the Maumee Valley. The Wabash and Erie Canal connecting Toledo with Fort Wayne, Indiana, opened on May 8, 1843, and the Miami and Erie Canal linked Toledo with Cincinnati two years later on June 27, 1845.

The canals did not bring instant prosperity, but they did aid growth until the city developed a stable commercial base.

The port of Toledo in 1846.

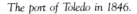

29

CHAPTER TWO

SEEKING AN IDENTITY

Employees of General Foundry and Machine Shop pose with owner Colonel Nathaniel Haughton (center with jacket and tie) around 1879. The Huron Street firm later became the Haughton Elevator Company.

The first task in early Toledo was to found the basic institutions of community life. There was little innovation in these matters in the West; new places copied what had been done earlier on the Eastern Seaboard. But the recorded "firsts" in each city are important; they become the benchmarks and the sources of local legend by which later residents find direction and meaning in their community's history.

Those who owned the city lots in new towns held that a newspaper was most vital. Without systematic promotion, no town enterprise could thrive or even survive. Journeymen writer-promoters—and this was a main part of Jesup Scott's early career—moved from place to place hiring on to advance the interests of new and aspiring cities.

In the fall of 1834, the first Toledo newspaper, the *Toledo Gazette*, was published. The city's most famous newspaper, the *Toledo Blade* (which retains its role as advocate of civic enterprise in the late twentieth century), appeared on December 19, 1835. As a counterpoint, Toledo folklore does not emphasize a success but instead a heroic loser—old Benjamin Franklin Smead who founded the *Manhattan Advertiser* in 1836 to promote that bay settlement. He confronted the depression after the panic of 1837, fought against the "ague" destroying his health and lamented the loss of Manhattan enterprises to rival Toledo. On June 3, 1840, he regretted that "the Advertiser is late this week, which may possibly be its last under our jurisdiction. Poor old horse, let him die!" A week later he was gone, and his paper and the hopes of his chosen town soon followed.

Government agencies were established after Toledo incorporated as a city on January 7, 1837. Until then it had been the seat of a county. The first important city ordinance of April 24, 1837, instituted a tax—the first certainty of society—a levy on personal property. To meet

the second certainty of all societies, a graveyard had to be provided. A site at Seventeenth Street and Madison on the road out of town leading to the nearby community of Tremainsville served as a kind of informal burying ground for ten years. The land was eventually built over and some of the remains were moved. But many others were disinterred during later construction in the area. In 1839, the city established the municipal Forest Cemetery on eight acres purchased from B. F. Stickney.

Next, there had to be a place for the sick. Local history recounts the saga of the Grey Nuns, five Sisters of Charity who came to the city from Montreal, summoned by Father Campion of the St. Francis de Sales Catholic Church in 1855. They heroically ministered to the ill in a time of flood and plague and, two years later, helped workmen construct a hospital at a wooded country site some distance away from the city (today's St. Vincent Hospital on the 2200 block of Cherry Street).

"Nurseries of learning" for the young were essential. The four early public elementary schools were badly underfinanced and remained a problem for years. The first

The Blade Building stood at 150 Summit Street. Wooden plank sidewalks kept pedestrians out of the mud in the 1870s.

Toledo High School in the 1870s; abandoned canal and shanties share the foreground.

*O*ne of the first activities of the newly formed city council was to establish fire protection for the struggling community. Equipment was purchased and the first engine house was built in 1837. A second engine house followed in 1838.

Volunteers provided the manpower for the fire department, and many volunteer companies were organized. These companies often had strong ethnic or political ties. The Neptune Hose Company was, in the early days, a strong Whig political organization. Davey Crockett No. 2 and later Franklin No. 2 were Democratic organizations. Erin Engine Company No. 2 was an Irish organization. Croton Company No. 2 was an Irish Catholic temperance company. Germania No. 4 and the Teutonic Fire Guards were strong German organizations. Independent Relief Hook and Ladder Company was made up of Toledo merchants.

Each company had a particular role in extinguishing fires. The engine companies were made up of 40 to 70 men who used hand pump equipment to suck water from the river, canal or the fire cisterns located on various street corners. The hose companies of ten to 30 men wheeled the hoses to the scenes and connected the lines to the water supply. Hook and ladder companies dragged their heavy equipment to the fires and placed the equipment in proper positions.

Rivalry between the different companies often led to rowdyism. The chief offender was Erin Engine Company Number 2. On August 17, 1852, during a fire at the Toledo House, several members led by John Mulhenny refused to join their hose with that of Engine Company Number 3. A riot ensued in which Assistant Engineer Joel W. Kelsey was kicked and beaten. As a result, several members of Erin Engine Company No. 2 were expelled.

The city relied upon an antiquated system of cisterns and wells for water, and often pressure was inadequate to fight major fires. The Chicago Fire of 1871 jarred Toledoans into accepting the need for a city water works system. It began operation in 1875.

Steam pumpers replaced the manual labor of volunteer companies, and by 1873 Toledo had a paid fire department. Fifteen fire stations served the city in 1900. The current number of fire stations has risen to eighteen.

Horse-drawn hose reel (top) in front of Station No. 7 at Bancroft and Franklin streets, around 1890; Engine House No. 2 firemen in 1888, with an 1873-model Clapp and Jones fire engine (center); fire destroyed an entire block in 1894 at Summit and Madison (bottom).

33

high school of sorts, the Union School, also struggled along during its early years. It had even more trouble when George F. Ball, the first principal, fled town with an advance on his salary and several gold watches borrowed from city dignitaries. There were at least ten private and church academies or "select schools." Many of these were run by a single person. In 1841, Miss Howlett's school offered to teach the alphabet for $1, spelling and reading for $1.50, arithmetic for $2 and higher subjects for from $3 to $4. Two of the best schools were the Sylvania Academy (1844) and The Young Ladies Literary Institute and Boarding School of the Sisters of Notre Dame (1845).

Churches, the "seats of piety and grace," were fundamental to a God-fearing community. In a time when most people had a church affiliation, the major faiths —particularly those of New England or upstate New York from which so many early residents came—were represented in the community from the first days of settlement. A Presbyterian group began holding services in 1833 and built the cradle of organized religion—an unpretentious wooden building at Superior and Cherry dedicated on May 3, 1838. A schism developed in the congregation, and the church was reorganized as the First Congregational Church in 1841. A new pastor from a famous American family, William Henry Beecher, the brother of Harriet Beecher Stowe and Henry Ward Beecher, brought the Presbyterians back into the fold. But he left soon after a quarrel with a deacon who operated a hotel containing a tavern. Beecher's successor, Anson Smyth, succeeded Ball as principal of the Union School and later became the city's first superintendent of schools.

The Presbyterian-Congregational building served as the site of services for an Episcopal group in the early 1840s and, for a time, a Universalist Unitarian group. When the First Congregationalists erected a new building in 1843, the old church was sold to St. Francis de Sales. They erected a more substantial brick structure between 1862 and 1869 (today a city landmark at Cherry and Superior streets) and moved the old wooden building to the back of the new church lot. (It served as a parochial schoolhouse until it was demolished in the summer of 1943.) The Episcopalians who had used the Congregational building constructed Trinity Episcopal Church (at Adams and St. Clair) between 1863 and 1865. (Trinity Church survived a major renewal of downtown Toledo begun in the late 1970s and stands in the heart of the city as a splendid example of mid-nineteenth century Gothic Revival architecture.)

CELEBRATIONS AND SWAMP SICKNESS

Basic social institutions were essential to any community. Public celebrations provided another means of unifying the new city. The great Fort Meigs Celebration of June 11–21, 1840, was a spectacular, mass political rally during the famous log cabin campaign of the Whig presidential candidate, William Henry Harrison. Attended by 35,000 people, it commemorated the triumph of white civilization in the Maumee Valley region.

Washington's Birthday was a major nineteenth-century holiday; and in Toledo, it was the occasion of the Firemen's Ball. During this principal social event of the year, the competitive volunteer fire companies of young men demonstrated the finery of their uniforms. The Fourth of July was the great community public celebration. The *Toledo Blade* editor in 1849 reported on a customary day of picnicking and speech-making during the course of which a "Bonfire Committee" of 500 boys—"the most noisy and snappish that the city affords"—collected brush, lumber, barrels, crates and boxes. At nightfall, the huge woodpile stacked near the post office (on Summit Street between Adams and Jackson) was set afire. The editor noted that there had been no accidents, only a few people "beautifully blue" and "some with black eyes and some with vermilion noses." "This America," he declared, "is truly a great country."

Famous men seeking office were frequent and well-publicized travelers to American cities. Daniel Webster—one of the giants of the U.S. Senate in

PAINTER OF HUNTING DOGS AND COUNTRY LIFE

Toledo's most famous painter was Edmund Osthaus (1858–1928). The local contention that he was the "world's greatest painter of hunting dogs" is probably valid. A native of Germany, Osthaus was trained at the Royal Academy of Arts in Dusseldorf. He came to the United States by way of Mexico with his father who was part of the ill-fated effort to make Archduke Maximilian of Austria the country's emperor. After Maximilian's execution, the family fled, settling in Oshkosh, Wisconsin. Osthaus came to Toledo as director of the Toledo Academy of Fine Arts

but left the post in 1886 to devote full time to his successful painting career. Osthaus was one of the founders of the Toledo Museum of Art. George W. Stevens, the museum director after 1903, portrait photographer Charles L. Lewis and Osthaus constituted a trio of "kindred spirits" in Toledo art circles. As one obituary writer put it, Osthaus "was the last of the trinity of gay spirits who found that life was worth while in a tramp up the Maumee valley, sketching now and then, the great outdoors beckoning with an insistence they could not deny."

"DON'T GIVE UP THE SHIP!"

FOURTH OF JULY PLEASURE EXCURSION.

THE STEAM-BOAT

COM. PERRY,

DAVID WILKISON, MASTER,

Will leave Perrysburg, Maumee, Toledo, and Mahattan, on a Pleasure Excursion, to the Battle Ground, on Lake Erie, where Com. O. H. Perry obtained his splendid victory in 1813.

She will leave Perrysburg at 8 o'clock, Maumee at half past 8, Toledo at half past 9, Lower Toledo at 10, and Manhattan at half past 10 o'clock.

An oration applicable to the occasion, will be delivered on board the boat by A. Coffenbury, Esq.

A national salute will be fired, at the time of reaching the battle ground.

The Bands of Music of each of the towns are invited to attend.

A cold collation will be furnished on board. $3 a couple. Tickets to be had on board, or at the offices of

JOHN HOLLISTER & CO. Perrysburg. BALDWIN & CO. Toledo. CORNELLA FOX Manhattan

*An 1838 advertisement in the Miami of the Lakes offered excursions
at $3 per couple—a large sum when wages were less than $1 a day.*

*A*rtist, architect, musician, linguist and naturalist— William Henry Machen (1832–1911) was one of the most gifted immigrants ever to settle in Toledo. Augustine Machen, his father, came to America with his family from Holland in 1847. The Machens had five sons and two daughters. Both girls died of scarlet fever during the voyage.

The family purchased a farm west of Toledo and built a house on what is now the site of the empty State Theater on Collingwood Avenue. The family's adversity continued. The oldest son Constant died while studying for the priesthood. Augustine was struck down during the great cholera epidemic in 1854. The next year, his wife Agatha died. After eight years in America, only four of the nine who had set out from Holland survived—William, then 23, and his three younger brothers.

By this time, William Machen had taken responsibility for raising his brothers and had become a familiar figure in the religious life of Toledo. He played the organ at St. Francis de Sales church and composed religious music. He had also begun his career as a painter which eventually resulted in approximately 2,500 oils and 500 watercolors.

Machen's realistic view of Toledo in 1852 is his most famous local painting. But he also painted religious subjects, picturesque nature scenes (such as his painting of Ten Mile Creek where it now joins Central Avenue), seascapes, still lifes and numerous portraits (including a famous study of Peter Navarre). Although he was primarily a nineteenth-century American realist, late in his career he adopted the techniques of Impressionism, a French import in the late nineteenth century.

In his 60s, Machen found another career. After a disastrous investment in Toledo's Pluto Oil Company, which went under during the Panic of 1893, he moved to Washington and became a translator for the State Department. In a competitive examination for the interpreter's position with the new International Postal Union founded in 1896, Machen—then 64—placed first in a test over seven languages. (He had studied Spanish for only six weeks.) He also continued his painting career, completing studies of birds and fish for the U.S. Fish and Game Commission. He died on June 19, 1911, and is buried in Toledo's Calvary Cemetery.

Self-portrait of artist William Henry Machen.

ante-bellum times—was the first dignitary to visit early Toledo. Seeking support in the West for a try at the presidency, he came into town unannounced from Adrian, Michigan, on the new Erie and Kalamazoo Railroad on July 8, 1837, apparently because he wanted to ride on the new train, a transportation innovation in the West. After making a speech in Detroit, he returned for a formal celebration. He spent the day visiting the valley settlements and toured Fort Meigs. The evening banquet at the American Hotel required six toasts before the meal and Webster's speech got underway. People watched through the windows, waiting to get in afterward. At the end of his 90-minute oration, Webster closed with a hope that reflected the central sentiment of the valley—"the continued prosperity of the four beautiful Towns—may I say, Cities—of the Maumee River."

Accounts by those who lived in early-day-Toledo—most of them in reminiscent form—recorded the simpler pleasures of the past. There were sleigh rides, card parties and quilting bees. The men hunted deer, wild turkeys and other game at a time when passenger pigeons still darkened the sky. (Not until 1867 did any game laws apply to northwest Ohio.) Residents made excursions on steamboats on Lake Erie and attended the annual military ball sponsored by the Lucas County Guards. And they rarely missed a fire, eagerly following the volunteer brigades.

But life in a nineteenth-century town could be unpleasant, harsh and unhealthy. Early-day Toledo, built on its inhospitable swampy site, was no exception. Its terrain led to good-humored satire. The nickname Frogtown caught on. Newspapers continually printed tall tales of horses, wagons and trains sinking out of sight in local mud, such as the play "Swamponia—A Tragedy in One Act" by Theodore Theodolphus Mudhen. (The seemingly strange name of the city's long-time professional baseball team, the Toledo Mud Hens—for many years a member of the American Association—is more appropriate than most team names from the animal kingdom.)

Rains brought floods that drove people from their homes and left mud. A writer at mid-century typically wrote of "the glory of mud; mud on the right of you, mud on the left of you, mud right in front of you, mud everywhere. Incomparable mud, yellow and blue, here and there green, sometimes stiff, generally soft and always greasy." An early resident watched Judge H. D. Mason—a local jurist and city leader always distinguished in his appearance—fall in the street. His elegant black broadcloth suit was covered with mud. Slowly taking off one glove and throwing it, he said, "Damn the mud!" Then taking off the other and flinging it with even more vigor, he shouted, "Damn Toledo!" and walked on with whatever dignity his appearance would allow. (Despite many drainage improvements over the years, every substantial rain still produces widespread street and basement flooding, and many twentieth-century Toledo residents have been heard to express Mason's sentiments.)

Partly as a result of the swamp-like conditions, early residents suffered and died of ague, the shakes and a variety of bizarrely named fevers. At the same time, local promoters assured everyone that Toledo's unhealthy atmosphere was a rumor thought up by jealous rival towns and cities. Most of these ailments were part of the group of infectious diseases generally called malaria spread by a variety of mosquito that serves as their carrier. And, of course, mosquitoes—like mud—were a part of life during much of the year. But at that period, scientists as well as laymen generally attributed the cause of epidemics and many everyday ailments to the presence of "miasmas," cloud-like contaminations generated in the atmosphere by a variety of conditions including decaying matter and swamp fumes. Thus, people in Toledo closed up their houses early in the evening to guard against night air, and those who could slept late to avoid being exposed to the frequent morning mists.

Asiatic cholera was the most terrifying disease to strike early Toledo during national epidemics in 1832, 1849 and 1854. Cholera had nothing to do with swamps, poisonous fog or imbalances in the atmosphere. Although these were accepted as causes at the time, Asiatic cholera was actually a bacterial infection of the intestines. It was spread primarily through water contaminated by feces. The high mortality rate and macabre symptoms—radical and sudden changes in skin color and continual vomiting—were comparable to those of acute arsenic poisoning. Fright may have contributed to many sudden deaths. During the epidemic of 1849, 80 people died in the city. Postmaster Israel Titus was well when he went to work in the morning, got sick at 10 a.m. and was dead by eight that evening. The most severe epidemic in Toledo occurred in 1854 when Asiatic cholera claimed the lives of at least 400 in Toledo at a time when the population was only around 8,000. Utah (a settlement across the Maumee now called East Toledo) was particularly hard hit and nearly depopulated by the epidemic as 34 people died during a three-day period. Many of those who fled were barred from neighboring communities and had to return to their homes in the plague area. During the course of the epidemic, the *Toledo Blade* expressed the common opinion shared by the leadership in American cities—cholera mainly struck down the immoral, the intemperate and the unclean. The disease, the paper asserted, was confined to those "who violated all the laws by which human beings exist." In July, at the height of the epidemic, the paper asserted that cholera could not be considered particularly "dangerous to the temperate, cleanly, well fed, well clothed and unterrified portions of the population." Businessmen, rest assured, could come to the city without fear.

But the disease did not spare the well-to-do and the upright. Jarvis Spafford, proprietor of a hotel in Perrysburg; the Reverend Mark Jukes and his wife in nearby Maumee; the physician Calvin Smith who supposedly had the largest medical practice in Toledo at the time; Samuel Wright who had become pastor of the First Congregational Church in 1851—all died during the epidemics.

During the epidemic of 1854, Dr. John Snow of England demonstrated how the disease actually spread. Snow studied the areas from which people drew their water in London and discovered the mechanism of contagion, the importance of a clean water supply and the dangers of sewage. Toledo and American cities began to clean up the sources of contamination. Rigorous sanitary measures were imposed by newly created boards of health. A new sewerage

Located at the mouth of the Maumee River at the terminus of the Miami and Erie Canal, Toledo quickly became a trading center. The Middlegrounds—a strip of land between the river and Swan Creek—served as a stopping point for canal boats. Lake boats sailed upriver to reach this point. When the Toledo, Norwalk and Cleveland Railroad located a station on the Middlegrounds, this fostered hotel development. Several small hotels emerged during the canal boom of the 1840s. The Island House opened in 1885 and remained a major hotel until the railroad depot was relocated in 1886.

The early zenith of the hotel industry was reached in 1859 when the Oliver House opened. Located at the intersection of Ottawa Street and Broadway, the hotel boasted 170 elegant rooms. It was designed by the nationally recognized hotel architect, Isaiah Rogers. Today it is one of his last surviving buildings.

The Oliver House and the Island House fought for the local depot business. Each hotel tried to stage the top social events of the year. During this period, hotels hired runners who met incoming passengers at the docks, solicited their hotel business and transported them to the hotel. The runners often fought among themselves and tried to run each other down with their carriages. The practice became such a nuisance that the city council finally outlawed it.

During the post-Civil War boom, several hotels were built along Madison Avenue and St. Clair Street. The Boody House, completed in 1872 and located at the corner of St. Clair Street and Madison Avenue, became the most renowned hotel between New York City and Chicago. It

The Boody House (left and inset) was the gathering place for many famous guests; the Oliver House (top) was Toledo's first grand hotel in 1859; the Island House (above), about 1870, was its main competitor.

was named for Azariah Boody, the New York railroader who was credited with bringing the Wabash Railroad to Toledo. The Boody House had the first elevator between Buffalo and Chicago and a bath on every floor.

As Toledo developed into a rail center during the early twentieth century, it became a stopping-off point for railroad men and salesmen. The Secor Hotel opened in 1908; the Waldorf in 1917; the Angelo in 1922; the Lorraine in 1924; the Fort Meigs, Park Lane and Commodore Perry hotels in 1927 and the Hillcrest in 1929.

The Depression hit the industry hard, and many hotels closed their doors. Some rebounded during the 1940s. The downtown Holiday Inn, erected in 1964, and other motels reflect current trends in hotel facilities; but the days of elegance and luxury for the night are gone.

system was started and new artesian wells drilled for a municipal water system in 1855. Work on a sewerage pipe system did not begin until 1863 when the city established sewer districts and passed a special assessment for this purpose. In 1854, a *Blade* editor greeted the new era of public health in American cities; "We must bid adieu to the frogs and tadpoles, and eat no more of the delicious mud-turtle soup, manufactured out of the denizens of that unsightly swamp hole, and drink no more of that pure Lager poured out of its depths. The time will come when Mud Creek will be forgotten in our history."

A CAPITAL GRAIN OF MUSTARD SEED

P erhaps the best insight into the character and quality of life in early Toledo was supplied by the letters of Pierre M. Irving (1803–1876), a nephew of the famous American writer Washington Irving. Irving had spent a year in New York City working as a research assistant on his uncle's book, *Astoria,* when he wrote in 1836 that he had become interested in a place in the West "which some with a modest and inventive taste in names have called Toledo."

Like most others, his primary interest was to make money. Before returning to New York, he had lived in the frontier town of Jacksonville, Illinois, where he had practiced law and bought real estate, becoming well acquainted with opportunities on the urban frontier. John Berdan was the oldest brother of Irving's wife who had died in 1832. Berdan had negotiated an agreement to buy a one-twelfth interest in the new town plat of Toledo and offered Irving one-fifth of his deal. The arrangement fell through, but the two were struck by the prospects of the place that Irving felt would become "a second Buffalo." Both men were quickly caught up in the new town boom. (Berdan would be elected the first mayor of Toledo after its incorporation in 1837 and would become permanently identified with the city.)

The country, Irving wrote, echoing Jesup Scott's retrospective account, "is alive with the all-pervading mania for speculation. Speculators are scouring the country in all directions, and entering all the wild lands they can lay hold of with indiscriminated rapacity." Later he added, "The spirit of speculation has been busy with me ever since my arrival, and I am full of sanguine hopes that my little capital will yet turn out like unto a grain of mustard seed." In this environment, he advised, Toledo offered great opportunities to those "willing to take the risk of fever & ague & billious fever." Irving bought town lots and other kinds of property for himself and also invested $20,000 on behalf of his uncles Washington and Ebenezer Irving. But his paper profits diminished sharply the next year as hard times hit. Still he managed to do well at his law practice—mostly involving real estate—and incurred no significant debt. Even during the depths of the depression, he retained his faith in the destiny of his chosen city.

Irving described a town whose chief initial activities were land transactions and its own promotion, a place where stumps stood all over the streets, where woods ran solid to the river in uncleared areas. It was a town where it was

*Toledo grew dramatically between 1860 and 1870.
The waterfront in 1876 included a railroad bridge across
the Maumee River.*

often hard to get through the day without boredom, a place "without books, with few or no means of diversion." He finally obtained some reading material when a carton of books and papers left in Illinois arrived, having gotten there by way of the Illinois, Missouri and Ohio rivers, the Ohio Canal and Lake Erie. On a trip to the East in October 1836, he married his cousin, Helen Dodge. Upon returning, he became deeply involved in the affairs of the young town. He assumed editorship of the *Blade* in the summer of 1837, worked on a committee to establish common schools and was instrumental in organizing a Young Men's Association, primarily to establish a library and reading rooms. He and his wife participated in the cultural activities of the city—the meetings of the Mozart Society, the debates at the Toledo Lyceum and the performances of peripatetic entertainers and lecturers. Irving was particularly impressed by a Mr. Russell who conducted experiments in animal magnetism—demonstrations of hypnotism which became popular in the 1830s.

The couple had clearly put down roots in the town. They lived in a boarding house, as many did, since there were neither "comfortable houses nor good servants to be procured." They found themselves "so *perfectly* happy" that they could "afford to dispense with these luxuries." But in June 1838, everything changed. Irving's own words best record his turmoil and anguish over his wife's illness and reflect an experience many shared in the new city. "Bilious fever, that malady so inseparable from the progress of population in the West, and which has raged there this year with unexampled fatality had laid its heavy hand upon her only to be succeeded by fever & ague, which continued with occasional intermissions until toward the commencement of August when she was brought almost to death's door by a second severe and protracted infliction of bilious fever. I have rarely witnessed prostration more entire. For four days it seemed as if nature were constantly verging nearer and nearer to her last struggle." As she slowly began to recover, Irving took her back East to the Atlantic shore to regain her health in air made pure by ocean breezes. When she recalled her illness, there "came a fixed and rooted repugnance to return to Toledo." Irving tried to persuade her to spend only the healthy seasons there, but she unequivocally refused any arrangement which called for long absences from her husband's side. Irving reluctantly decided after "a violent struggle to cut adrift from Toledo." He established a law practice in New York where he lived out a distinguished career, closely involved in managing the business and literary properties of his uncle.

Pierre Irving, John Berdan, Jesup Scott and the others who put their stakes on the future of early Toledo succeeded well in the years after 1850. The city grew and property values increased. Nineteenth-century promoters found population statistics the most satisfactory measure of urban success. On this score, Toledo was doing well. In 1850 its population stood at 3,820; by 1860 it had grown to 13,768. Shortly after the end of the Civil War, the 1866 city census counted 24,877 residents, and the 1870 federal census showed continuing rapid economic growth to 31,584.

In the years after 1850, Clark Waggoner (an editor and an important early city historian) and a number of other local spokesmen developed the view that a magnificent economic future was virtually predestined for Toledo. Their argument became almost an official community ideology echoed by scores of politicians and civic leaders. In his articles on Toledo and midwestern cities in the '40s and '50s, Jesup Scott supplied the main emphasis. He argued that the nation's expanding railroad and water transportation system would follow the paths of the interior rivers. Therefore, Toledo's location in relation to the Great Lakes and to the Mississippi River and its tributaries would make the city a central lake-to-lake transfer point.

By 1860 Toledo had become the hub of six railroad lines. Initially, Toledoans argued that it would not be profitable for railroads ever to haul goods eastward from the city; cargoes would be shifted at that point to the more economical lake transport. Once Toledo had become the main point and commercial depot of the Great Lakes, manufacturing would gravitate automatically to the city. Manufacturing, Scott wrote, followed commerce as naturally as "teeth in the mouth of an infant child."

This view was correct up to a point. Between 1860 and 1920, Toledo established itself first as an important American commercial city and subsequently as a major manufacturing city. Manufacturing essentially provided the base of the city's continued growth through the twentieth century. But Toledo never became the "future great city of the world." By 1890 several regional cities—including Detroit, Cleveland and Chicago—had clearly eclipsed Toledo in importance.

Local sentiment, embodied in much of the city's popular history over the years, held that this outcome resulted from the failure of Toledo leaders to take advantage of opportunities. The leaders assumed, it was argued, that Toledo would inevitably become great and therefore moved too slowly to bring in manufacturers. In addition, they were swept up in promotional schemes—a legacy of the frenzied land booms of early years—that were clearly destined to fail.

The mistakes of Toledo leaders can be seen with hindsight, but similar mistakes were found in aspiring cities everywhere. In this period of booming economic and urban growth, the quality of community leadership and the character of community decisions were important. But numerous other factors over which community leaders had little control—changing technology, patterns of national and regional economic development, the decisions of the

BUSINESS EVOLVES WITH THE AUTO: *William J. Walding started his wholesale drug business in 1877 (top); by 1910 two partners and an automobile had been added (center); a delivery crew (above) in the early 1940s, when the firm was serving the entire Midwest with medical supplies.*

41

entrepreneurs who controlled the great national corporations arising on the scene, and just plain luck—also affected the fortunes of individual communities.

The tug Florida *breaks up an ice jam in Lake Erie in the 1920s.*

42

TIED TO THE RIVER

*T*he struggling village of Toledo depended upon the Maumee River as a means of transportation. During the canal boom of the 1840s, the city underwent its first real expansion. By the late nineteenth century, Toledo was known for its port facilities, particularly for the shipping of bulk cargoes. When the St. Lawrence Seaway opened, Toledo competed vigorously with other Great Lakes ports. Today it is one of the nation's leading inland ports.

The steamer City of Toledo (top right), launched in 1891, carried passengers between Toledo, Put-In-Bay and Middle Bass Island; the Arrow (bottom right) made the Sandusky-Toledo Sunday excursion run around the turn of the century.

43

The Wabash Grain Elevator Number Four in 1898. Built of wood, it was one of few that did not burn to the ground; it was torn down in 1907.

During the Civil War, the expanded national demand for food and the closing of the Mississippi River to trade stimulated Toledo's grain trade and led to general expansion of port activities. After the war, however, several rapid changes kept Toledo from realizing further potential from its emergence as the "Corn City" in the 1860s. First, railroads proved more efficient than expected in handling heavy freight, and there was a quick transition from rail-to-lake shipping to all-rail shipping. Second, the center of wheat

raising moved westward as the northern Great Plains were opened to agriculture, and much lake shipping passed to the port of Duluth. Third, grain and flour milled in the western cities of Kansas City and Minneapolis went directly to eastern market by rail. Fourth, Chicago's proximity to the developing western regions and its ties to the newly built transcontinental railroads to the Pacific made it the rail center of the Great Lakes cities and the metropolis of interior America. In 1879, Toledo was still the nation's

General James Blair Steedman, one of Toledo's best-known and most picturesque characters, posed in full Civil War regalia for a portrait about 1864.

A New York Central Railroad carpentry gang, about 1901.

46

This little piggy went to market (below) at the Jacob Folger Packing Company on Phillips Avenue; Folger employees (above) link and tie sausages prior to smoking. Folger became one of the largest meat-packing firms in Ohio.

greatest winter wheat market and remained the fifth largest grain market in the country in the late twentieth century. But this economic activity alone could never be the base for regional urban supremacy.

As a consequence, Toledo leaders shifted their effort from the promotion of lake-port trade to lake-port industry by the 1870s; they pushed to become the meeting place of coal and iron ore from America's "Great Inland Empire." This aspiration was only partially realized. Toledo did become a main shipping point for coal and iron. In the twentieth century, the city became the world's greatest coal-shipping port. But changes in technology kept Toledo from being the center for processing iron ore. As new methods of refining steel were developed, the industry concentrated to the east in the Pittsburgh-Cleveland-Youngstown triangle because it was closer to the Connellsville coal found near Pittsburgh. (Connellsville was a variety of anthracite essential to produce the coke required in steel production.)

THE OLD RELIABLE.

A Little Help now will Long be Remembered.

The Old Reliable, manufactured in 1876, established the reputation of the Milburn Wagon Works.

Despite the hopes of local promoters, the second important industry created by the new technology of the post-Civil War period—petroleum refining—did not center in Toledo either. As John D. Rockefeller absorbed or eliminated hundreds of independent producers and refiners of petroleum in the mid-1870s, he decided to concentrate the refining facilities of his emerging Standard Oil "trust" in Cleveland. Toledo interests bitterly resented this decision, and for years accused the trust of discriminating against the city. Still, Toledo's economy benefited from the new industry as it became an important secondary refining center. In 1889 the first of four petroleum refineries was constructed, and by 1939 the industry ranked first in local manufactures based on product value.

The depression that followed the panic of 1873 had a severe impact on Toledo. City leaders launched a program of attracting manufacturers when such programs were becoming a standard aspect of urban policy throughout the country. Until then, local manufacturing had consisted of such primary production as lumber and grist mills, breweries and tobacco-making and carpentry shops. The new promotional program's first important success was the Milburn Wagon Company, which moved from Mishawaka, Indiana, (near South Bend) to Toledo in 1873. The company built a large plant and quickly became a major employer. By 1875, the Milburn works—supposedly the largest producer of farm vehicles—turned out 65 different kinds of wagons. Its famous plantation wagons were painted in bright scarlet, buff and green and were found throughout the world. During the Spanish-American War, the firm was a principal supplier of military vehicles.

The establishment of the Milburn works indirectly led to the most spectacular local industrial boom in the late nineteenth century—the emergence of the Toledo bicycle industry. The Tubular Axle Company, a subsidiary of Milburn, initially developed a method of making a light hollow axle; tubular steel was vital in constructing the frame for the new lightweight bicycles. In 1880, another local manufacturer, Peter Gendron, began producing wire wheels for baby carriages and developed techniques for using ball bearings in wheel hubs—technology that he later applied to the bicycle. The Gendron became a popular standard bicycle in the 1890s when demand for the light,

48

Peter Gendron (above) manufactured
the first wire wheel and ball bearings,
paving the way for the Gendron (left),
a popular model in the 1890s.

safe new vehicles boomed throughout the country.
Joseph L. Yost, who had managed a bicycle company in
Springfield, Massachusetts, and had invented the
Springfield Roadster, founded the first bicycle company in
Toledo, the Lozier and Yost Bicycle Works. The company
became famous for its Falcon. By 1898, there were at least
22 bicycle manufacturers and nine makers of accessories in
operation in the city.

The "Future Great City of the World," the "Corn City,"
now became the "Coventry of America." (Coventry was
the bicycle manufacturing center in England.) Local
newspapers called it "the most prosperous and thriving city
in the United States" and saw the bicycle creating
permanent prosperity for Toledo and a grand and glorious
future for the country. "What a blessing it will be—when
everyone has a wheel and almost every means of
transportation is mechanical. . . and men can live miles out
of town and get home at night quickly and economically on
their bicycles," wrote one enthusiast in 1896 who
anticipated the new dimensions of life in twentieth-century
America. "The suburbs of every city, town and village will
be extended."

Toledo's bicycle boom was short-lived. The automobile
came into use in the first decade of the century, and its
unexpected popularity virtually caused the complete
collapse of the bicycle industry in Toledo and throughout
the country. Historians of Toledo criticized local
entrepreneurs for a lack of foresight in promoting the
bicycle. But what occurred seems more a result of the
unlucky circumstance of simply being in the wrong industry
at the wrong time. In a time of rapid economic change and
growth, this circumstance happened frequently in
American cities.

The American Bicycle Company advertised its Toledo
steam auto in 1904.

The Milburn Wagon Company, which had begun
Toledo's era of wheeled vehicles, attempted to
accommodate to changing circumstances. During World
War I it began manufacturing electric cars and trucks. But
electrified vehicles never proved competitive with the
internal-combustion gasoline engine. After a major fire
swept the plant in 1922, the famous Milburn company
—once seen as the means to Toledo's manufacturing
success—went out of business.

51

The B.H. Holtgrieve and Son grocery at 11 Superior Street; note the pipe-smoking elephant in the advertisement at right.

THE GREAT NATURAL GAS BUBBLE

Even more than the bicycle boom, Toledo's "Great Natural Gas Bubble" of the 1880s and early 1890s evoked the spirit of the early land booms on the Maumee and intensified Toledo's reputation as a place where urban enterprisers were swept up in frenetic, chimerical community schemes. It began with the discovery of a large natural gas field at Findlay, Ohio, about 50 miles south of Toledo. The tapping of a major well on December 5, 1884, led to widespread drilling throughout the region. Eventually, four private pipelines were constructed into the Toledo area.

Local promoters asserted that natural gas would be the basis for Toledo's industrial supremacy in interior America. They argued—fallaciously—that fields of natural gas were self-generating and therefore inexhaustible. "'Future Great' no longer," the *Blade* proclaimed in May 1887. "Toledo has become the 'Present Great'. . . . Toledo has awakened, and like a giant refreshed by slumber, her power is being felt in all directions. . . . The eyes of all America are turned toward Northwestern Ohio as the Mecca to which all good Americans must make a pilgrimage."

On September 7, 1887, after gas reached the city, Toledo held the customary "Grand Gas Celebration." Former President Rutherford B. Hayes addressed the assembled crowd as natural gas standpipes—"beacons of light" —studded the city. "By burning jets of natural gas," the *Blade* reported the next day, "by brilliant flames from mammoth gushers, by the roar from the combined force of forty wells, thousands of strangers and citizens read last night the destiny of Toledo. . . . Toledo the queen city of the lakes, goes forth conquering, one hand bearing a torch with light for the world, with fire for a nation's forges, with heat for a million looms, with fuel for thousands of factories." Toledo real estate boomed as outside investors, especially from Chicago, began buying center-city property in anticipation of Toledo's greatness.

But all this bright promise soon faded. Opposition grew to the rates charged by the private companies, and in 1889 the city populace voted for bonds to build a municipal pipeline to the Findlay fields. Although the line was

completed and gas turned on on April 11, 1891, the project was doomed from the start. By 1890, geological reports made it clear that the fields would soon be exhausted. During the late months of 1888, even before the city election, there had been an evident dwindling of supplies. By 1895, the city system had run out of gas, and it was clear that it was not feasible to drill more wells. Efforts to get the voters to support the passage of further bond issues to convert the system to artificial gas made from coal failed, and the debt that had already been incurred proved a long-time substantial burden to Toledo voters.

The gas bubble had burst, but promoters had won a victory in their struggle to gain an industrial base. Industries—including one of Toledo's most important, glass—had been attracted to the city by the promise of the new fuel. When the gas ran out, these manufacturers stayed and converted their plants to coal or to producers' gas generated from coal.

By the time of the natural gas boom, a new theme had intruded into the promotional rhetoric of Toledo. Spokesmen for the city still argued that Toledo would be the future great city of the world. However, some of them recognized that Toledo might well remain a city of second rank but an attractive and livable city. That might even be more desirable than achieving the position of a large metropolis. Toledo had "recently come to be one of the most delightful of the secondary cities," the *Blade* observed in 1890. It was a natural resort city on the lake with notable recreational advantages. It was a place where the "wind blows round everybody's house." In his annual message of 1890, Mayor James K. Hamilton declared that Toledo was "a prosperous city" which each year was "becoming more and more attractive as a place of residence." The mayor emphasized the main aspect of the new image—it was "especially a city of homes." As the writer of a prize essay on the meaning of Toledo put it in 1891: "Toledo in its residence portion eclipses all other cities in America for beauty, neatness, care, good taste and real comfort." This new theme, which modified the viewpoint of 60 years, shaped and anticipated an essential aspect of the spirit of Toledo in the twentieth century.

GLASS CENTER OF THE WORLD

By 1900, the country had recovered from the severe depression of the 1890s. It had become clear that large-scale manufacturing sustained urban growth, and Toledo had clearly fallen behind other cities. Between 1870 and 1900, its million-dollar industries (those producing products over that amount in value during the year) increased from two to eight. But in the same period, Chicago went from 22 to 96, St. Louis from 33 to 45 and Milwaukee from three to 27. In Ohio, Cincinnati's million-dollar industries increased from twenty in 1870 to 31 in 1900, and Cleveland's from six to 31. This reality caused local promoters in the twentieth century to shift their emphasis from Toledo as the future great city of the world to Toledo as a prosperous secondary city—a good place in which to work and live.

Although lagging relatively behind other places, Toledo's

Edward Drummond Libbey (above) established his Libbey Glass Company plant (right) on a 4-acre plot on Buckeye Street. Hand blowing of 500-watt light bulbs (top) continued until 1910.

53

Michael J. Owens, with cap and ankle-length coat, (above) about 1903 with the men who helped him develop the automatic bottle-making machine.

industries did expand. Among the notable successes were industries based on new technological processes, particularly in glass production. A new city title was applied in the 1890s. Toledo—"Glass Center of the World"— acquired a measure of permanent validity in the 1900s. As part of the campaign to attract industries, local leaders presented their wares to a number of Eastern glass companies. In 1887, they induced Edward Drummond Libbey and his New England Glass Company of Cambridge, Massachusetts, to move to the city. Libbey would become one of the most famous names in Toledo history.

The move was a fortunate consequence of the ill-fated natural gas boom. The high temperatures in glassmaking required large amounts of fuel, and the inexpensive new power source in Toledo particularly impressed Libbey. The city also offered the customary inducements—a four-acre plot for his factory and 50 lots for workers' houses. Although the natural gas supply soon ran out, Libbey was there by then. Utilizing Toledo's abundant coal resources, the company was able to convert to the relatively economical producers' gas. "GLASS IS KING," ran a *Blade* headline in 1888 after a reporter inspected a Toledo exhibit of Libbey's cut glass made in Cambridge. "The specimens are undoubtedly the finest ever exhibited in this city and hundreds of persons have been examining them all day at Bell & Powell's Monroe street store. Some of the pieces cost as high as $30 and shine with the brilliancy of diamonds."

In its early years in Toledo, however, the Libbey company had problems manufacturing and selling its cut glassware products—mainly vases, bowls and lamp stands. Libbey borrowed heavily from local investors to stay afloat. Among the glassworkers recruited from the Wheeling area was the mechanically able Michael J. Owens. Initially he was employed to blow glass shades for oil lamps, but he became foreman of his department three months later. In 1891, he went to Findlay to supervise a temporary factory Libbey had set up to make light bulbs. Libbey had agreed to supply Edison General Electric with light bulbs, normally supplied by the Corning Glass Works. The New York firm had been shut down by a labor dispute. Next, Owens successfully superintended the Libbey glass exhibit at the 1893 Chicago Columbian Exposition.

54

The Libbey Glass Company promoted the faltering glass business at the 1893 Chicago Worlds Fair.

THE TOLEDOAN'S CREED
"I Serve—I Conquer"

I BELIEVE IN TOLEDO, the City of REAL VALUES—the Nation's natural gateway of commerce and travel: in the heart of great resources and markets: with unsurpassed railway, dock and harbor facilities, and the near-centre of population of the United States.

I BELIEVE IN TOLEDO, the City of REAL OPPORTUNITIES—with its great institutions of art, education, religion and business: a "Going concern" in industry, government and social uplift: a Home city with rest and recreation for all, by river and lake; where it is worth while to live, rear children, invest money and life.

I BELIEVE IN TOLEDO, the City of REAL PROGRESS—modern in municipal equipment and spirit, aggressive in commercial activity and achievement, with inspiring visions and plans for tomorrow and a big chance for every man.

Toledo Handbook, 1912

Employees of the Smith Bridge Company, 1910. Robert W. Smith (fifth from left) invented the famous truss bridge and contributed much to the growth of Toledo as a port city.

After he moved to the Toledo plant, Owens worked out the techniques to use machines in glass production instead of the costly hand-blown method, first for light bulbs and in 1901 for bottles. It was a revolutionary development in the growth of the beverage and food industry. A second major innovation in glassmaking was developed after 1910. Using a machine invented by Irving M. Colburn, Owens and others produced sheets of glass in a continuous flow, a fundamental contribution to the flat-glass industry. A third innovation occurred in an effort to develop new products during the 1930s' Depression. The manufacture of practical glass threads in various sizes—today's familiar and widely used fiberglass—fulfilled a long-time dream.

By the 1930s, the formation of new companies, mergers

and government action against some of Libbey's licensing arrangements resulted in the three large independent glass corporations that today justify Toledo's title as "The Glass City." Libbey-Owens-Ford, founded in 1916, combined the Libbey-Owens Sheet Glass Company with the Edward Ford Plate Glass Company. Ford had followed Libbey to Toledo in 1898 and had built a large plate-glass factory outside the

city in what would become the suburb of Rossford. Libbey-Owens-Ford became particularly important in the production of glass for automobiles in the twentieth century. Founded in 1929, Owens-Illinois was the result of a merger of the Owens Bottle Machine Company with an Illinois bottle firm. The company expanded into a variety of fields, including a range of containers. (By 1981, it was

Employees of the DeVilbiss Company in 1903. Physician-surgeon Allen DeVilbiss invented a spray atomizer which became the foundation for the company organized in 1888.

The internationally known Toledo scale (right) was developed by Allen DeVilbiss Jr. It was the first springless automatic computing scale, shown ready for delivery (left) on a Toledo Scale truck about 1920.

Toledo's largest corporation and the 95th ranking corporation in America.) In 1936, the original Libbey Glass Company became a division of Owens-Illinois. Owens-Corning Fiberglas was founded in 1938 to take advantage of that new glassmaking process.

In addition to imaginative technology, imaginative promotion characterized the Toledo glass industry. At the 1893 World's Columbian Exposition in Chicago, Michael Owens set up an expensive glassblowing operation with 40 glassblowers. It was one of the fair's most popular exhibits. The most spectacular creation was a spun-glass and silk gown for actress Georgia Gayvan. Princess Eulalia of Spain, who visited the fair, received a copy, and in the presentation ceremony, the Spanish government bestowed on Libbey the title "Glass-Cutter in Chief to Her Royal Highness, the Infanta Eulalia." The company also provided a lavish exhibit of glass at the St. Louis World's Fair of 1904.

Several other Toledo industries built on the technological innovation that characterized late nineteenth- and early twentieth-century economic growth. A Toledo physician, Allen DeVilbiss, invented a nose and throat atomizer for his patients. It proved so popular that he founded a company to produce it in 1888. The principle of the atomizer was utilized in a paint sprayer, and the DeVilbiss Manufacturing Company was organized in 1905. It became a major American manufacturing firm. DeVilbiss's son, Allen Jr., devised the first springless automatic computing scale. The Toledo Scale made the city known worldwide. In the 1880s, Homer T. Yaryan developed an apparatus for rapid dehydration and evaporation which was widely used in the sugar, glue, wood pulp and related industries. Herman Doehler obtained early patents in diecasting beginning in 1905, and his company made the city one of the early centers of this new industry.

CITY ON WHEELS

The manufacture of iron products, other metal items and machinery all became important in Toledo's economy in the twentieth century. But next to glass, the most significant development was the city's rise as a secondary automobile center. For a time, local leaders (as was customary) predicted that it would be the primary center. Albert A. Pope of Hartford, Connecticut, was America's largest producer of bicycles in the late nineteenth century. He diversified into producing electric cars in 1896. Reluctantly, he converted to gasoline vehicles at his large plant on Central Avenue in Toledo in 1903. The factory turned out a luxury gasoline model—the Pope-Toledo. It was priced from $2,800 to $11,000 (in contrast to Ford's well-under-$1,000 cars of the era). He also produced a less expensive Pope-Hartford in Hartford and the Waverly Electric in Indianapolis.

The Toledo company employed between 1,200 and 1,500 workers. When it faced strikes in 1906 and 1907, Toledo's reform government under Brand Whitlock did not provide the customary support manufacturers usually received in employing strikebreakers. As a result, the union received highly favorable settlements that drove the Pope company to the wall. It sold its Toledo plant to John North Willys'

FROM TWO WHEELS TO FOUR: The Pope Motor Car Company plant (above), about 1905, formerly housed the Yale Bicycle facilities; Pope went bankrupt in 1907 and was bought out by John North Willys. Employees in front of the Willys-Overland plant (top) around 1915.

59

Overland Company in 1909, and the national Pope company went into receivership in 1913.

After acquiring the Pope plant, Willys moved all his operations from Terre Haute and Indianapolis, Indiana, to the Toledo site. Willys became a major automobile producer. In 1915 the company's 91,780 units were exceeded only by Henry Ford, and by 1923 its plant was the largest single automobile factory in the world. Willys-Overland employed 12,000 workers and had a monthly output of 22,000 cars, including the Willys-Knight and the Overland, both well-known models of the day. A serious strike after World War I hurt the company, and it failed during the Great Depression. Reorganized in 1936 after a period of receivership, the Willys company prospered from the manufacturing of the Willys Jeep, the famous military vehicle of World War II. First as a part of the Henry J. Kaiser industrial empire and later as a division of American Motors, the production of Jeeps became one of the most important manufacturing activities of postwar Toledo.

Because of Toledo's automobile industry and the proximity to Detroit, a number of companies were organized to make auto parts and accessories in Toledo. The city acquired yet another title, "Auto Parts Capital of the World." Electric Auto-Lite Company produced electrical equipment. Champion Spark Plug was well-known nationally. Spicer Manufacturing produced shock absorbers and transmissions. Its successor, Dana Corporation, produced a number of major automobile parts, such as universal joints, clutches and axles. AP Parts manufactured shock absorbers and exhaust pipes. They were only a few of the early established large automotive companies. Many others followed.

Toledo became highly dependent on the automobile industry. Today it is estimated that from 35 to 40 percent of the city's employment in manufacturing is directly related to automobiles, and there are several hundred companies of various sizes that are a part of the industry. Automobiles contributed to the city's prosperity after World War II. But because of great fluctuations in the demand for automobiles, dependence on the industry has intensified the local effects of recessions and depressions in the national business cycle.

Some people feel that Toledo could have played Detroit's role as the national center of the automobile industry. When Pope came to Toledo in 1903, there were 53 independent automobile manufacturers in the country, and it was clear that there would be great consolidation in the highly competitive industry just as there had been in petroleum refining. Detroit had advantages in becoming the American Motor City. Unlike entrepreneurs elsewhere, Detroit businessmen survived partly because they could draw on large amounts of local capital accumulated from developing Michigan's vast natural resources. In addition, Detroit's factories that had been producing rolling stock for railroads supplied the technology for making automobile bodies, frames, wheels, axles and bearings. Even more important, the city's ship-building industry had developed the technology for building internal combustion engines to move vehicles. Toledo's relatively strong unions—in a time when few unions could really be considered strong—and a number of devastating strikes that occurred beginning in the late nineteenth century may have discouraged automobile investment in Toledo, but no concrete evidence sustains this view.

One brilliant individual played a part in this outcome. At the time John North Willys built his Toledo operation, Henry Ford had already located his plant in Detroit. Ford had perfected the assembly-line production of automobiles that was to revolutionize the industry and contribute to Detroit becoming its permanent center. Toledo's geographical proximity made it the automobile industry's most important satellite city.

SALES AND SERVICE: Bliss Auto Sales (below) on 21st Street kept Toledo supplied with Fords between 1912 and 1919; entrepreneur Fred J. Edler in his 1919 delivery truck (inset).

61

A Hamilton Street home in Toledo's German community around 1895. Youngsters can remember wearing out their roller skates on the plank sidewalks.

A DIVERSITY OF PEOPLE

Toledo's German community was large enough by 1856 to support a German-language newspaper.

In the nineteenth century and throughout much of the twentieth, cities grew because people migrated to them from the American town and countryside and from Europe. The great waves of migration transformed American urban life, and Toledo became home to the Irish who fled starvation in the 1840s and 1850s, the "new immigrants" from southern and central Europe after 1870 and rural blacks from the South who came north as a result of opportunities created by World War I.

As a rapidly growing manufacturing city, Toledo's character was particularly shaped by the diverse ethnic groups that began arriving after 1870 from the Austro-Hungarian Empire, the Balkans, Poland, Russia, Italy and the Near East. By the turn of the century, Toledo was a cosmopolitan place, and it remained so in the twentieth century even when foreign immigration was drastically restricted after World War I. Between 1870 and 1940, the U.S. Census identified 43 distinct nationality groups in the city, eight of which (German, Polish, Canadian, Hungarian, Irish, Russian, English and Austrian) were represented by more than a thousand foreign-born residents.

Although there are discrepancies in the available census statistics of foreign population in Toledo, the overall extent of immigration is clear. Several American cities were more than 50 percent foreign-born in the late nineteenth century. Toledo's high point was 35 percent in 1870. The total percentage of the foreign element (foreign-born and those with one foreign-born parent) reached 65 percent in 1890 and fell slightly over the next two decades. Some experts on population feel these statistics may even underestimate the extent of foreignness in Toledo's population.

Nineteenth-century public policy stressed the necessity and the desirability of quick "Americanization" or "acculturation" of the immigrant—that is, the adoption of what were considered standard American values and mores. But all immigrants retained many old-country ways in their communities, and these, in turn, reshaped American ways.

Even Germans who moved quickly into all levels and activities of urban society organized diligently to preserve homeland traditions.

Toledo's ethnic communities reflected many of the general characteristics that were part of the life of urban immigrants in America. Some groups lived in distinct neighborhoods such as Hungarian "Birmingham" in East Toledo across the Maumee. But in any ethnic neighborhood, there were always a number of residents not of the dominant nationality. (Only the black ghettos of the large Northern cities in the twentieth century reached an extremely high homogeneity. This was true also in the 1920s and '30s of Toledo's smaller black neighborhood, Pinewood.)

Life in the ethnic community tended to organize around the church—St. Patrick's for the early Irish, St. Louis' for the French colony of East Toledo, St. Hedwig's for Poles or, later, Holy Trinity for Greeks. When there were few governmental agencies to assist newcomers, a variety of self-help ethnic organizations flourished—lodges, benefit societies and patriotic groups. Hungarians established the King Mathias Sick and Benevolent Society in 1897. The small Yugoslav group of 132 had two such agencies in 1930—the Serbian Beneficial Union and the Slovenian Beneficial Union. By 1930, several Polish military organizations—including the Hussars, Sharpshooters and Cherry Pickers—were associated with St. Hedwig's.

Large ethnic groups, such as Poles and Germans, established foreign-language newspapers. Anthony A. Paryski, a Pole, came to Toledo in 1886 supposedly with $32 after a brief career as a Knights of Labor organizer. In 1887 he started a semiweekly publication called *Gwiazda*, which changed its name to *Ameryka* two years later. His daily paper *The Echo* started in 1902 but was relatively unsuccessful. It combined with *Ameryka* as the weekly *Ameryka-Echo*. By 1906, the new paper had achieved a national circulation of 42,000. Paryski employed 59 workers in his large plant and had 49 agents on the road selling subscriptions to his paper and other Polish publications. In 1898 Paryski began publishing an

Main Street in East Toledo hums with activity in July 1896 (above); the Edward W.E. Koch family raised twelve children in their Oliver Street home (below) in the Old South End. It was torn down in 1921 as Summit Street was expanded.

Children of the Stickney School
stare soberly into the camera in this 1888
photograph.

67

HOLY TOLEDO!

Billy Sunday claimed, in 1911, that he would lick the devil in Toledo.

*T*he origin of the exclamation "Holy Toledo!" is the subject of much speculation. One suggestion is that the name came about because of the heavy concentration of churches located on Collingwood Avenue. The city of Toledo, Spain, after whom the American city is named, is often called "the Holy City of Toledo."

Other suggestions of origin are not religious, but may be more likely. Holy Week has always been the worst week at the box office for show business; old-time vaudeville actors contended that any week in Toledo was Holy Week. Toledoans Joe E. Brown and Danny Thomas popularized the term as they became nationally known performers.

Another colorful possibility comes from a former policeman who joined the city police force in 1931. At that time, there was an alleged agreement between the police and underworld safecrackers (also known as box blowers and nitro men). Safecrackers would not be harassed if they would refrain from their activities in Toledo. Consequently, they could complete a job in Detroit, Cleveland or elsewhere and then retreat to Toledo—the "Holy Land."

A retired policeman said he first heard the expression as a small boy around 1911 when Billy Sunday preached at the Armory on Spielbush Avenue.

Others say that "Holy Toledo" was a sarcastic expression resulting from the high proportion of bars to churches. In the pre-World War I period, it was a standing joke that you could walk out of a church on one corner and enter a bar at the next. Regardless of the origin of the phrase, Toledo—with its many churches—has a rich religious heritage, and many of the churches have been instrumental in preserving ethnic communities.

illustrated monthly, the *Dictionary of English and Polish Languages,* which gained considerable popularity in the national Polish community. He also published religious newspapers in Polish from time to time and printed and marketed several Polish books.

OF TAVERNS AND TOLERANCE

In ethnic communities the neighborhood tavern was a source of information as well as a place for recreation. Germans had their beer halls; in the late 1870s and early '80s, there were at least nine spread throughout the city. Nationalities opposed to the use of alcohol established the Turkish-style coffee house, such as the Bulgarian Steriff's Ohio Smoke Shop on Front Street in East Toledo, which served much the same purpose.

Toledo ethnic communities tended to differ in at least one important regard from those of the larger manufacturing cities. The groups remained more cohesive and for a longer period of time. Their neighborhoods did not experience the rapid population turnover of cities such as New York, Chicago, Detroit or Cleveland. This was particularly true of the foreign enclaves in East Toledo where large-scale industrial sites and the Maumee River, bridged relatively late, limited customary residential expansion. (Hungarian Birmingham still retains many of the characteristics of the old ethnic community.) Some ethnic communities remained stable because Toledo's black population stayed relatively small in the twentieth century. The black community did not sweep out rapidly over the old ethnic neighborhoods as it did in many Northern cities.

Most important, the rate of home ownership among immigrants was the largest of American cities above 100,000 in 1900—58 percent in contrast to New York's eleven percent. People who owned their own homes were much less likely to move than those who did not. This stability was viewed differently by different groups. Toledo's nationally famous reformers associated with the Progressive Movement of the turn of the century frequently decried the city's "village mentality." This, they argued, severely hampered their efforts to build the City Beautiful or the City Efficient. (Narrow neighborhood loyalties and positions still affect Toledo politics.)

The migrations from southern and eastern Europe of the late nineteenth and early twentieth centuries transformed Toledo most dramatically, but several earlier immigrant groups also fundamentally influenced the city. French and French-Canadians were particularly important in the region's early years. Peter Navarre (whose famous namesake cabin has been much moved about the metropolitan area over the years) is a local folk hero of pre-Toledo days. He has given his name to Navarre Park and also to the city's most unpretentious monument, Navarre Triangle in East Toledo. Irish immigrants arrived in large numbers in the 1850s to work on the canals and later the railroads. Although there was a distinct Irish neighborhood around St. Patrick's Church, they tended to disperse throughout the city. By 1870 the number of foreign-born Irish had reached 3,032. The Irish provided their own early folk hero, Father Edward Hannin of St. Patrick's. Father Hannin worked with the poor and was well-known along the waterfront where he sought donations from the habitues of the saloons.

Germans—including German Jews who began arriving from Cincinnati in the mid-1840s—came to Toledo in large numbers as part of the great wave of German migration into the Midwest in the mid-nineteenth century. Toledo has not

69

*Father Edward Hannin, a fiery Irish priest, was also
an ardent temperance man; he was known to drag some of his
parishioners out of the local saloons.*

70

The Jewish congregation Anshei Sfard purchased their building from the Zion Reform Church in 1912. The Jewish community, though small, provided Toledo with many civic leaders.

been identified as a German city in the same fashion as St. Louis, Milwaukee or Cincinnati, but Germans shaped the institutions and character of community life. A visitor in 1873 noted an openness and freedom that he attributed to the Germanic influence. "The social life of the Toledoans, like their business life, moves with the greatest freedom," he wrote. "No trace of the puritanical austerity which has cramped and restricted the social ability of other great cities can be found here." (Toledo remained a tolerant place in the twentieth century; "clean-up-the-vice" campaigns were usually half-hearted; and during many periods of its history the city was reputed to be a "wide-open town.")

From the early years, Germans were community leaders. They were well-represented among the early land buyers and town promoters. Peter Lenk, an early arrival who had learned wine-making and brewing in his native Bavaria, founded the important Brand & Lenk Wine Company in 1849. In 1854 he started his own brewery, the City Brewing and Malting Company. As part of a new site for his operations, Lenk platted a city addition south of downtown; Lenk's Hill became important in the city's early growth. He also sponsored the building of Lenk's Park, later purchased by the city and renamed City Park.

A second leading German entrepreneur, Rudolph Bartley, arrived in 1867 to establish Toledo's largest wholesale grocery house. Four mayors were German-born— Guido Marx, Jacob Romeis, George Sheets and the Jewish community leader, William Kraus. (The failure of the Kraus and Smith bank in the Panic of 1873 was one of the major financial disasters in Toledo's history.)

In 1870 when Toledo was Ohio's third largest city and the percentage of foreign-born reached its height, the number of Germans had increased to 5,341. Combined with the Irish, the two groups constituted 75.3 percent of the city's foreign-born population. Until 1920, Germans were the largest foreign-born group; they reached their peak in 1910.

After 1880 the new immigration began to affect life in Toledo. Poles began arriving in particularly large numbers after 1890. They established two distinct neighborhoods— one along Nebraska Avenue to the south of the old Lenk German settlement and the other to the north along Lagrange Street. By 1920, the city's 10,283 Poles had displaced Germans as the largest foreign-born group.

When the National Malleable Castings Company built a plant in East Toledo in 1892, the company brought about a hundred Hungarian families of skilled foundry workers from Cleveland. This provided the nucleus for the Birmingham settlement near the plant. By 1920, shipping and rail companies had lowered their rates for individual passage from Budapest to the United States to $57, and the number of Hungarians in Toledo reached 5,470.

In the twentieth century, Toledo became known as the "capital of Bulgars in America" as large numbers fled the Balkan wars. The Willys-Overland automobile plant employed an estimated 500 Bulgarian workers just before World War I. Alexander Kochanoff came to Toledo in 1916. He ran a general store on Front Street and established himself as the "king" of the Bulgarian colony near downtown East Toledo. During the Great Depression of the 1930s, the Bulgarian soup kitchen was set up in the Bul-

A group of Polish parishioners gather at St. Adelbert's Church for the traditional food blessing in April 1943.

garian Front Street shopping area and became a center for the advocacy of Communism.

An old fashionable residential section that had been part of early Vistula attracted large numbers of Greeks, Syrians, Lebanese and Near Eastern groups in the early twentieth century. The switch from upper-middle class neighborhood to tightly packed immigrant/ethnic neighborhood demonstrated a process of transition that occurred in all large cities.

Toledo established many identifiable ethnic neighborhoods in the early twentieth century. In the 1920s, Syrians settled northeast of Cherry Street. Another ethnic enclave was established by Czechs near Collins Park in East Toledo. Russians and Italians arrived in substantial numbers in the twentieth century, but like the early Irish and to a lesser extent the Germans, they tended to disperse throughout the city.

As the neighborhoods changed in Lower Town and other sections, one of the most distinctive neighborhoods—the Old West End—emerged as the new enclave of the very well-to-do who had profited from industrial growth in the post-Civil War period. Platted in 1866, the area was built up between 1875 and 1915. It was consistently promoted —with considerable accuracy—as a neighborhood of "velvety lawns, shaded streets, and numerous and costly mansions of the rich."

71

BUILDING BLOCKS OF THE CITY

*L*ike most cities in the Midwest, Toledo has many ethnic roots. The German, Irish, Polish, Hungarian, Bulgarian, French, Italian and other ethnic peoples clustered in neighborhoods throughout the city. Toledo also developed neighborhoods along geographic and economic lines, including the North End (Vistula), South End, East Side, Old West End and West Toledo.

A 1902 lawn fete at Walnut and Erie streets raised funds, probably for a church or lodge. The fine Gothic Revival home was owned by Judge John Hardy Doyle, an Ohio district judge.

THE OLD WEST END: Edward O. Fallis designed a French
Renaissance chateau (above) for Toledo grocer Rudolph A.
Bartley; elms create a graceful archway over Winthrop Avenue
in the 1940s (below).

ADDING TO AMERICAN HERITAGE

The immigrant groups that created new neighborhoods and transformed old ones encountered little of the hostility from older residents that they faced in larger nineteenth-century cities. Toledo was too new to have an established old-line aristocracy. Partly because of its late settlement, the city escaped the Nativist and anti-Catholic rioting in the 1840s and 1850s that plagued many places such as Cincinnati.

Newspapers, however, were often critical of immigrant ways. Their comments emphasized the stereotyped images that were a part of the general nineteenth-century conception of race and nationality. Germans were inherently industrious, Irishmen were drunkards, Poles were riotous and violent, Jews were miserly. The new immigrants continually encountered harsh ethnic satire. Much of it was intended to be good-natured and reflected an accepted style of ethnic and racial humor now considered distasteful if not cruel. In one newspaper account, two "Polanders" (itself a derogatory term) named Szperski were arrested for stealing wood in February 1875. "At the Police Court this morning it took three or four Germans, an Irishman, two negroes, and a civilized Polander to decipher their names. After wasting a ream of fools-cap, they came to the conclusion that the nearest approach they could to it was John and Joseph Schypaski." Similar observations were made about other ethnic groups. "They say that the Servian General, TCHERNAYOFF was once a resident of this city," the newspaper recorded the next year. "But the first time he was arrested for drunkenness the reporters glared at him so balefully while trying to spell out his name he fled the city in terror."

By early in the century, however, little of this denigration remained. Newspapers and city spokesmen portrayed all foreign groups as eager to be Americanized, people who were taking advantage of the opportunities of society through industry and thrift. The immigrants provided outstanding examples of the reality of the self-help ideal in American society. "All the leading citizens in this Polish-American community are 'self made' men," the *Toledo Blade* typically commented in 1920. "They have re-enacted the lives of the pioneers of this country. Born and reared in the most moderate circumstances, these men have hewn their way to positions of affluence and prominence solely by their own efforts often battling against great odds."

Toledo's ethnic groups shaped the institutional and cultural life of the city. The history of Toledo's German organizations provides just one example of the pervasive and enduring character of ethnic influences. As early migrants, the first Germans established a wide range of cultural activities. The newspaper *Ohio Staats-Zeitung* of December 1853 was followed by three other German-language newspapers before 1900. There were several churches, and German-language instruction was offered in the schools. Michael Schonnacker's Hall on Water Street served as an early center of German dances and other social activities. By 1887, there were five German musical groups

in the city. Louis Mathias was a German immigrant from Philadelphia who came to Toledo on a concert tour in 1853. He decided to stay and organized the most important of these groups—an orchestra called the *Musicverein*. In 1867 a traditional male chorus, the *Teutonia Männerchor*, was founded with twelve members. (It is still an active social and singing group.)

A *Turnervereine* first met for gymnastics in 1854 in a hall on Oak Street. Toledo's American Turner Club zealously maintains the sport, exercise and gymnastic traditions of the old-country *Turnervereine*, including such bits of exotica as demonstrations in ribbon dancing and traditional floor exercises. The organization was disbanded during the Civil War. In 1866 it was revived and joined with another group, the *Saengerbund*, to form the *Deutsche Gesellochaft* in 1866. The new organization erected the famous German Hall on South St. Clair Street. The hall served as a center for balls and concerts as well as *Turnervereine* athletics. "The Turners"—as they were known in German-American communities around the country—reorganized as the American Turners in 1926. They bought a large building in the Old West End in 1934 and named it Turner Hall. It remains a major center of German ethnic activities.

By World War II, at least 35 separate German societies and clubs had been organized. Many represented the provincial loyalties or traditions that preceded the uniting of the German states in the late nineteenth century, such as Swabian, Bavarian or Swiss-German groups. (Derogation of "Swabs," "Barbarians" or "Pruskies" is part of a good-humored interplay within today's German organizations.)

Two groups achieved notoriety before World War II when

An organization called The International Institute introduced ethnic newcomers to their new home in Toledo in the early 1920s.

the local German community received national attention as a center of pro-Nazi influence. In 1935 an enterprising photographer shot a secret meeting of the "American League of the Friends of New Germany." It showed a packed hall of men, women and children surrounded by the panoply of the Third Reich and delivering the traditional Nazi salute. In 1938 a chapter of the German-American *Volksebund* (known generally as the Bund) met surreptitiously around the city, probably including gatherings at

Turner Hall. But with the coming of war, this pro-German sentiment disappeared immediately, and Toledo's Germans faced little of the anti-German hostility that had been a part of their experience during World War I.

After World War II, German ethnic activity in Toledo was affected by the two trends that transformed American urban life in general—large-scale organization and suburbanization. For many years, there had been no centralized direction of German-American activities in the city. For a time after 1900, a local chapter of the national German-American Alliance had coordinated some of the groups. But the federal government had revoked that organization's charter in response to the anti-German hysteria of World War I.

From then on, Toledo's German groups remained independent. In 1965, six of the major German organizations formed the GAF (the German-American Festival) to run a united German-American summer festival. After the festival that year, the GAF—consisting of the Turners, the old *Männerchor*, Swiss-German and Swabian societies, a Bavarian benevolent society, a Bavarian sports club and the general German-American insurance agency (all of which maintained nineteenth-century German ethnic traditions)—remained intact as a centralized German agency. One of the GAF's most important projects was the purchase in 1969 of a 35-acre suburban tract east of the city in Oregon. Named Oak Shade Park, it had expanded to 57 acres by 1982 and had become the site for German cultural and recreational activities. Oak Shade Hall provides a suburban counterpart of the nineteenth-century's downtown German Hall. The activities include touring players and singers from the old country, formal German balls, concerts and choral presentations.

The main activity of the GAF remained the organization and operation of the three-day German-American Festival in August. By the 1970s, it had become a major business enterprise and the largest of the city's many traditional ethnic festivals. In 1981, 40,000 people attended the

NEIGHBORHOOD SCENES: The Rodemich Brothers' neighborhood grocery (left) carried a myriad line of merchandise at the turn of the century; many Toledoans remember the sulphur water drawn from suburban West Toledo pumps (below) around 1915. David Marleau's hardware was located at 412 Phillips Avenue.

festival and spent $250,000 devouring 24,900 pounds of sausage, 275 gallons of sauerkraut, 7,560 ears of corn, 1.5 tons of potato salad, a ton of potato pancakes and drinking 854 half-barrels of beer. It is probably the largest nonprofit all-volunteer ethnic festival held in America.

SOLIDIFYING THE BLACK COMMUNITY

The black migration was part of the general movement of people from the countryside of Europe and America to the cities. The black communities formed in Northern cities, primarily after 1900, shared similar experiences with the European nationalities. But there were significant differences. The existence of black slavery and American attitudes toward race led to much more hostility between races than ever existed between ethnic groups or between old residents and white newcomers. Moreover, the black "ghettos" of the twentieth-century city were much more homogeneous and did not experience the continuing changes that characterized old ethnic neighborhoods.

Toledo was not among the very large Northern manufacturing cities, and it had a relatively small percentage of black population compared to such places as Chicago, Detroit or Cleveland. For that reason, Toledo's black community developed differently. But there were important similarities to such better-known black communities as New York's Harlem or Chicago's "Black Metropolis."

Before the Civil War, the Toledo area was part of Ohio's famous Underground Railway, and a number of fugitive slaves seeking freedom in Canada passed through, stopping in Perrysburg and East Toledo. The history of the Underground Railway is filled with legend; most Ohio towns have old houses where slaves were allegedly hidden. It seems reasonably certain that a museum operated by

Charles N. Dixon at 46 South St. Clair Street provided a sanctuary for slaves in a secret basement to which underground tunnels led.

In Toledo's early years, a small community of free blacks developed. Most of them came from Ohio. In 1840 the U.S. Census enumerated 54 blacks, and the number had grown to 115 by 1850. In 1853 the city established a separate school for 27 black students, and its desegregation after the war in 1871 came only after an intense political battle. Churches, which played a particularly significant part in black urban life, formed early. What later became the Warren African Methodist Episcopal Church was organized with 23 members in 1860. It was the first black church founded in northwest Ohio and one of the earliest in the Midwest. The Third Baptist Church followed in 1868.

Several Toledo blacks, like those in other Northern cities, joined the Union armies during the Civil War. But as in most major American wars, this did not alleviate the racial hostility that led to wartime urban race riots. On July 8, 1862, fighting broke out on the Toledo docks between black and white workers over wage scales and the hiring of blacks. A group of mainly Irish workers moved through black neighborhoods, beat several residents and damaged and demolished houses. It took a hundred police, including a number of citizens sworn in that day, to quell the disturbance. Thirty rioters were arrested.

Between 1870 and 1910, Toledo's small black community produced a number of civic leaders, and one major black figure in the arts gained recognition during the time he lived there. In 1894, the famous black poet, Paul Laurence Dunbar (honored on a U.S. postage stamp in 1975), came to Toledo as a young man from Dayton at the encouragement of Dr. Henry Tobey, a superintendent of the Toledo State Hospital. Tobey was an admirer of his work which, until then, was largely unnoticed. In 1896, while working as an elevator operator at the Nasby (now the Security Building) at the corner of Madison and Huron,

Civil War veteran Caswell Sampson, an engineer, joined the local Grand Army of the Republic organization.

BLACK VETERANS COME HOME: After the Civil War, Toledo's black community grew as veterans settled in the northern city. Artilleryman John Brown (top); William Miles (center), a brickmason; and Infantryman John Spencer (above).

79

Dunbar published his masterwork *Majors and Minors: Poems*. When the book came to the attention of William Dean Howells, the noted writer and critic, Dunbar became an overnight sensation in the United States, but particularly abroad in England.

A second black artist who achieved national prominence—the famous jazz musician Art Tatum—was born in Toledo in 1910. Well-trained in the classics, the nearly blind pianist became a staff musician for radio WSPD. During Prohibition he played in such Toledo nightclubs as La Tabernella, Chicken Charlie's and the Chateau La France, and in Cleveland and Detroit before moving his trio to New York in 1932. At the time of his death in 1956, he was generally recognized as the most technically brilliant jazz pianist of all time.

Until after 1900, the small Toledo black community was made up largely of migrants from Ohio and other parts of the upper Midwest. Black migration from the rural South began to affect Toledo as it did other Northern manufacturing cities during World War I. Between 1910 and 1930, the number of blacks in the city rose from 1,877 to 13,260—an increase of 336 percent—while the overall city population was growing by 64 percent. By 1930, blacks composed 4.6 percent of Toledo's population.

The pattern of black migration into Toledo differed somewhat from that of many larger cities. A number of blacks from the South came to Toledo after first living in larger industrial cities, particularly Chicago and Detroit. Many of these newcomers indicated that Toledo offered more "elbow room" and was a good place to "put down roots and raise a family."

More Toledo blacks owned their own homes than in many cities. Many rural blacks tried city life for a time and then returned to farming in a nearby area called Spencer Township.

Probably because the number of newcomers was not that great, the growth of black Toledo during World War I did not lead to open racial violence as it did elsewhere. In 1917, however, there were threats and incidents stemming from the efforts of blacks to move into the Bulgarian and Birmingham neighborhoods of East Toledo.

During the summer of 1919—a time of great racial strife everywhere—146 East Toledo residents filed a restrictive covenant with county officials. (Such covenants had been outlawed two years before by the U.S. Supreme Court.) The petitioners pledged their "moral support toward ridding the community of undesirable characters especially Colored people. . . . We refuse," said the East Toledoans, "to rent or sell property to them. . . . We believe that every self-respecting Colored person will take advantage of this opportunity to find a home elsewhere among those who do not object to their presence."

Confronted by such hostility during the great housing shortage of 1918 to 1921, many blacks were forced into the dilapidated downtown "tenderloin" where people lived, according to one investigation, like "rabbits in a warren, Colored and whites all mixed up together." "Based on what they get for their pitifully scanty dollars," Toledo's *City Journal* observed in 1918, residents there "are paying the highest rents for squalid vermin-ridden quarters that in many cases are not fit for the housing of animals."

The housing shortage resulting from conditions during World War I was alleviated to some extent by the mid-1920s. As a result of white neighborhood resistance to black migration into their areas, blacks eventually moved from small enclaves scattered throughout the city to one large section south of downtown called Pinewood. By 1930 when the area was in the eighth ward of the city, 44 percent of the ward's 12,886 population was black. Four years later, the heart of Pinewood—bounded by Fifteenth Street, Indiana Avenue, Collingwood Avenue and Hamilton Street—was 87 percent black.

The movement into the old middle-class German Lenk's Hill neighborhood resembled that of the black movement into New York's once highly fashionable Harlem as churches, businesses and professional offices followed people into the area. As the *Toledo Blade* observed in 1923, a black Toledo was being created comparable—but on a much smaller scale—to the famous black Chicago which became the subject of popular and scholarly attention in the 1920s and 1930s. "Negroes no longer live in a few houses in a widely separated section," the *Blade* commented. "They have come to constitute in themselves a good size city."

Although some blacks coming in the early 1900s found employment as iron molders, founders and casters and as mechanics, in general they were confined to lower-paying jobs. They held a high percentage of menial occupations, and their overall job status in the city actually declined between 1920 and 1930. By 1930, more than a fourth of all employed black females were servants. They filled 61 percent of the servant jobs in the city, and they held 62 percent of the city's elevator jobs. In 1930, black males—who by then constituted five percent of the city's labor force—filled 82 percent of the porter and 31 percent of the janitor jobs. Only one percent of the blacks held clerical or professional jobs.

In 1899, George W. Anderson, a black who worked on a city street construction crew, wrote a letter to Samuel "Golden Rule" Jones, the famous Toledo reform mayor. Anderson, who died shortly after writing, reflected the attitude and position of blacks in early twentieth-century Toledo, a time of troubles for blacks throughout America. "I'm almost driven to desperation and despondency when I think of the cruel social condition that exists in this 'the land of the free and the home of the brave.' It is indeed a white man's country. Do you not know that there are colored men who are not willing to remain forever at the bottom of the ladder? You men of standing and influence, forsake your ways and give such an individual a chance to rise whether he be white or black."

Only the social changes that followed the Great Depression and World War II would substantially improve the circumstances of blacks in Toledo and in urban America.

Black leader Charles A. Cottrill (facing page), around 1900.

Early 1900s members of the Toledo Newsboys Association.

CHAPTER FOUR

Golden Rule Park was a turn-of-the-century gathering place for Sunday afternoon speakers.

CITY OF HUMANITY

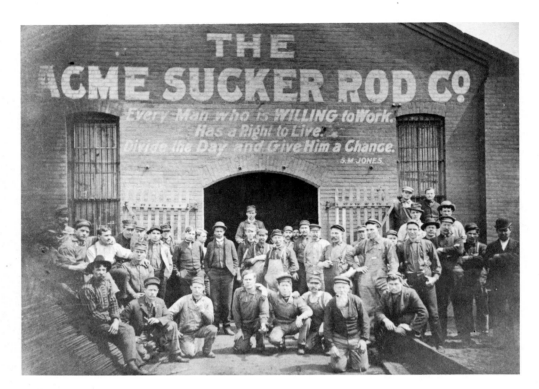

Employees of Samuel Milton Jones' Acme Sucker Rod Company, around 1902. Jones treated his employees with dignity and respect and paid them fairly.

The appeal of George W. Anderson and the black community for social justice reflected a new era in Toledo politics. From 1897 to 1915, Samuel M. Jones and his successor Brand Whitlock molded Toledo into an exemplar of municipal Progressivism at a time when a reform movement swept the country. The city won national attention as a place of humane and honest government where the poor would always have a voice.

The new era began in a smoke-filled auditorium in Toledo's Memorial Hall on February 25, 1897, during the Republican mayoralty convention. The incumbent mayor was Guy Major, a linseed oil magnate who had failed to gain renomination because of allegations of corruption and association with the anti-immigrant American Protective Association. For five ballots, the convention remained deadlocked between the supporters of the Republican bosses, Marcus Hanna and Joseph Foraker, who controlled the two wings of the state party. Finally, a compromise emerged. James M. Ashley Jr., son of the famous Civil War congressman from Toledo, nominated a political unknown, Samuel Milton Jones. After the customary long and loud demonstration, Jones won on the next ballot.

"Who is Sam Jones?" asked the headline on a newspaper the next day. Jones had only lived in Toledo for five years and had not been active in politics. Born in North Wales in 1846, he had migrated to America with his parents at the age of 3, grew up in New York State and went to work in the new Pennsylvania oil fields. He began leasing and drilling wells with considerable success. Depressed by the death of his first wife and other members of his family, he sought a change, moved to the Ohio fields and made his big strike—the Tunget Well—near Lima in 1886. He met Helen W. Beach from a prominent Toledo family the same year, married her in 1892 and moved to Toledo. Jones had invented a type of metal drilling rod with special couplings which replaced hickory rods. These "sucker rods" permitted deep-well drilling. He patented them and began production at a small facility in East Toledo. Then in 1894, he started his Acme Sucker Rod Company at an urban location across the river.

GOLDEN RULE JONES

Jones had demonstrated characteristics not usually associated with the self-made industrial leaders and politicians of the era. He embraced the physical culture movement, practiced vegetarianism and advocated temperance. He also wore a cowboy hat on public occasions.

His labor practices were much more unorthodox. It was probably the belief that he could win the votes of labor and quiet the resentment of ethnic groups against the Republicans that had led to his nomination. Jones had opened his Toledo factory during a time of depression. Hundreds of jobless Toledoans sought work there. Jones was accustomed to good wages and plentiful jobs in the booming oil fields of the prosperous 1880s, and he frequently referred to the experience of seeing the great hardships in the city as his "first awakening."

He began to question the effectiveness of the American economic system and to argue that change was necessary. He started in his own factory where he declared the teachings of Christ would apply. He said that he disliked the long lists of employee rules found on the walls of business establishments and would enforce only one rule at his company—the Golden Rule. A metal plaque inscribed with the Golden Rule was mounted on the factory wall. Jones acquired a lifetime title—"Golden Rule" Jones. He eventually carried this principle so far that he abolished the

Golden Rule Playground, around 1902, on the Segur Avenue grounds of Golden Rule Park.
Mayor Jones believed that recreational facilities would reduce juvenile delinquency,
an advanced thought for the time.

foreman-timekeeper system and allowed workers to keep their own time.

Jones believed that "every man is entitled to such a share in the products of his toil as will enable him to live decently." He instituted a number of concrete programs for his employees that were far ahead of their time and which became part of enlightened labor-management relations —paid vacations, a plant cafeteria where meals were served at cost, company insurance plans and profit sharing. He built a park, a playground and a workers' hall by his factory. "Golden Rule" Park provided the site for lectures sponsored by Jones on Sundays, and prominent reformers such as Jane Addams and Graham Taylor came to speak at "Golden Rule" Hall after it opened in 1898.

The hard-fought mayoral campaign exposed Jones to the realities of urban politics. Jones preached his Christian message of the need for brotherhood and equality in public affairs and attempted to deal with issues facing Toledo and other cities—unemployment, non-partisan government, boss rule, street railroad franchises and public ownership of

utilities. But the opposition Democrats primarily emphasized Jones' role in the Young Men's Christian Association, portraying him as a temperance man out to destroy the saloons. They hoped, of course, that this approach would alienate the large ethnic vote of the city. The election of April 5, 1897, gave Jones a margin of 518 votes or 2.5 percent of the total. Jones wired his friend Washington Gladden (a Columbus minister famous in the national Social Gospel movement) that he had won, "in spite of six hundred saloons, the streetcar companies, and the devil."

Historians of the Progressive Movement have asserted that Jones introduced into urban government a simple version of the Social Gospel and of Christian Socialism, both of which had become a part of the reform tradition of the late nineteenth century. Actually, Jones drew on long-standing traditions of reform in Toledo. Early Quaker settlers who assumed community leadership had brought a tradition of independent thinking to the early town, and reform ideas were a part of the heritage of the German

85

RAMPAGING RIVER

*T*he ice-swollen Maumee River has constantly been a problem during annual spring thaws. Major flooding took place in 1832, 1847, 1867, 1881, 1883, 1904, 1912, 1913, 1918, 1924, 1929 and 1943.

In 1867, a reporter of the Perrysburg Journal waded through the water to the Middlegrounds, out to the Island House Hotel, climbed in a second-story window and reported the event to Toledoans.

"About 10 o'clock an immense field of ice came rushing down the river, plowing its way at the rate of five or six miles per hour, and following in its wake there came with irresistible force of ice thrown up in every conceivable shape, together with timber and driftwood," he reported. Ice hit the Cherry Street Bridge. The steamer City of Toledo broke away from its moorings and the barge Crosby Express was carried away. "The yielding of the bridge produced the greatest excitement from this side," the reporter continued. "Several persons could be seen on the broken structure and as the timbers were quickly separated and all were compelled to take to the ice, the most intense degree of feeling prevailed. There were reports of many being drowned, including one female. . . . Ten thousand watched from the shore," the reporter said. "After passing the bridge, the ice gorged at the foot of Elm Street. The water rose very rapidly, at least three feet in half an hour, overflowing the dock and creating quite a respectable channel on Water Street." Water covered the Middlegrounds from two inches to five feet and trains loaded with cars were placed on the railroad bridge in hopes of weighting it down to resist the force of the ice.

The February 1883 flood also proved formidable. Ohio sustained million of dollars of damage, and Toledo lost both the Cherry Street and the Wheeling & Lake Erie Railroad bridges. Ten feet of water covered Water Street along with ice, driftwood and wreckage. In 1941, the Blade reported that some of the flood-marks could still be seen on the Water Street buildings.

migrants who had fled the failed German revolutions of 1848. The labor unions numbered at least 50 by the 1890s and had long advocated many of the same ideas of municipal socialism. There is solid evidence that Toledo attracted more than its share of dreamers and idealists in the post-Civil War era. Francis Ellingwood Abbot, a Unitarian minister, came to Toledo in 1869 and brought the publication Index with him. Abbot sought the support of Christians, Jews and atheists in the pursuit of a non-sectarian religious faith.

The women's movement emerged at about the same time. In 1869, shortly after the formation of the National Woman's Suffrage Association, Toledo organized a local chapter. Rosa L. Segur and Sarah R. L. Williams led this early campaign for equal rights, and Toledo Quaker businessman Richard Mott supported the effort. Williams published the Ballot Box, a suffrage newspaper that became a national publication. David Ross Locke—publisher and editor of the Blade—created the famous character Petroleum V. Nasby (beloved by President Abraham Lincoln) whom Locke effectively used to satirize racial prejudice and corruption during and after the Civil War. The effort to establish workingmen's schools by the Scott family led eventually to the founding of the University of Toledo and reflected the reform sentiment rooted in the community.

Jones faced a number of concrete and immediate problems when he assumed office in this city of intellectual independence. Growth had been rapid—from 50,137 in 1880 to 81,434 in 1890 to 131,882 in 1900. During each of these two decades, population increased more than 60 percent, the greatest jump in any of the 32 largest American cities. Streets needed paving; public utilities had to be expanded; more public transportation was required; housing had to be built and taxes had to be raised as thousands flocked into the city seeking jobs in the growing glass, bicycle and foundry industries.

The depression of the '90s aggravated problems of urban growth. The panic of May 1893 left a number of local businesses bankrupt. In 1897, Lucas County housed 6,000 paupers. The city's large municipal debt of $7 million aroused property holders.

The city also had the troubles associated with port cities. Petty crime—larceny, drunkenness, prostitution and liquor violation—was widespread. In 1894, the politically active Citizens Federation of Toledo organized religious groups to attack gambling, saloons, prostitution and the failure to enforce the law requiring saloons to close on Sundays.

City government was antiquated. It was based on an 1870 state law which required a two-house assembly along with fourteen boards and commissions. The system made it difficult to establish responsibility for the performance of municipal functions.

During his first term, Jones was able to carry out some of his program. He introduced a civil-service merit system in the police and fire departments, and acquired considerable celebrity in Progressive circles when he substituted canes for clubs for policemen on their beats, arguing that the police sometimes intimidated and harassed citizens and the club was a symbol of those practices.

Jones was continually concerned with the problem of unemployment and the poor. He reported that up to 50 requests for employment reached his office daily, and this concern drained his emotional energy. Jones personally assumed much of the financial burden of helping the unemployed. With the cooperation of the Toledo Humane Society, the city aided those without work by providing a bath, bed and food in return for work on the city's streets.

Brand Whitlock, a journalist and attorney who served as Jones' legal advisor, told a story to demonstrate Jones' view of the poor. At the end of the day, the two men were strolling in downtown Toledo when a stranger asked for 50 cents to obtain lodgings for the night. Jones reached into his pocket, and, finding no change, gave the man a five-dollar bill and asked him to return the change.

David Ross Locke, the favorite humorist of President Abraham Lincoln.

Locke pokes fun at the Democrats using Petroleum V. Nasby in an 1870s drawing.

*P*etroleum Vesuvius Nasby was the creation of David Ross Locke (1833–1888) who edited and owned the Toledo Blade at various times between 1865 and his death. The first of Nasby's satirical letters appeared in the Findlay (Ohio) Jeffersonian on March 21, 1861. The rest appeared in the Blade after Locke became editor. The last was dated December 26, 1887. The letters were enormously popular and helped make the Blade famous nationally. The circulation of its weekly edition reached 200,000.

Locke was a dedicated reformer who fought for the rights of blacks, women and labor. Petroleum Nasby—a dissolute, cowardly, ignorant, lazy bigot—represented everything Locke opposed. The letters were entirely political and devoted to the issues of the day. By today's standards, they are crude and heavy-handed. But when they were published, they reflected the prevalent standards of humor—including the use of ethnic and racial epithets. They are important historical documents.

Abraham Lincoln frequently read from Nasby letters to visitors and government officials. Lincoln told Charles Sumner, the famous abolitionist senator from Massachusetts, that he had written to Locke, "For the genius to write these things I would gladly give up my office." Once during the Civil War, Lincoln read Nasby aloud to Sumner for over twenty minutes while 30 people waited to see the president. Locke refused political appointments offered him by both Lincoln and Grant, but he finally managed to win the office he wanted—alderman of Toledo's third ward. He died while in office.

The letters demonstrate insight into the nature of big-city politics in the nineteenth century and may reflect Locke's knowledge of political life in Toledo. They also indicate Locke's deep hatred of racial prejudice.

Nasby became the proprietor of the Harp uv Erin saloon in New York City. The former owner had been killed during an election day argument with his work half done—he had only voted thirteen times.

Difficulties developed in the political machine when blacks were enfranchised by the Fifteenth Amendment, and a resolution was offered to take them into the party. "The meetin didn't want to pass it," Locke relayed via Nasby. "The feelin agin em wuz too deep not to be rooted out in a minut, but O'Grady was determined. O wat a minut wuz that! Wuz the niggers to be killed by us, or wuz they to be taken to our buzzums? Their fate hung tremblin in the balance. Finally it wuz put to vote, and the niggers wuz safe. By one majority the resolution was passed. . . . I took the crape off the door, bottles and picters, and immejitly illoominated in honor uv the event, and the next mornin I put up a placard on my door. 'No distinkshen at this bar on account uv color. Ekal rites!'"

On election day, one repeat-voter refused to cast his ballots because he had to stand in line behind blacks. "I soothed Teddy all I cood," Nasby said. "I told him how it wuz—the situashen we wuz in, and begged him to be pashent and endoor wat he coodent help. But he woodent. . . . Rather than have him lose his day's work I took the five votes at wunst and certified for him that he had voted ez per contract, that he mite draw his money. . . . We didn't count the votes till late at nite, after Tweed had heard from the rural desstricks. A messenger come into the room and announced that everything wuz ready now to be counted.

"'How much majority do you require uv me?'

"'Lemme see,' said the messenger running his finger down a list, 'this is the sixteenth districk uv the 6th Ward. You are set down for 312 majority. Did you pole that number uv votes?'

"'No! only 270, and of that number probably 40 wuz for Woodford.'

"'That don't matter. Count em 312 and all for Hoffman.'"

87

Pauline Steinem (above) was the first woman elected to Toledo's School Board in 1904. Her granddaughter Gloria continues the family feminist tradition; members of the Lucas County Equal Suffrage League (left) outside headquarters in 1912.

Whitlock said he never expected to see the man again. But as Whitlock and Jones continued to talk, the man appeared with the change. The mayor put it in his pocket and the man asked why he had not counted it. Jones replied, "You counted it, didn't you?" A faith in mankind—sometimes approaching naiveté—became the hallmark of the Jones administration.

Although his accomplishments were not striking, by the spring of 1899, Jones' reform philosophy had alienated many conservatives. The Republican Party denied him the mayoral nomination; and later in the year, Senator Joseph Foraker read him out of the party for his "municipal ownership nonsense and other fads."

Jones refused to accept defeat and organized an independent campaign for mayor. In addition to his loss of business support, Jones lost support from the moral reform group. Despite being a teetotaler, Jones believed that saloons served as workingmen's social clubs. Later he infuriated church leaders who asked him to drive prostitutes out of Toledo. He replied, "To where?" He suggested instead that ministers all take lost sisters into their homes and rehabilitate them. The plan received no support.

Jones campaigned in 1899 on the issues of home rule and municipal ownership of public utilities. His wide support among labor groups and ethnic voters won him an overwhelming victory as he polled 70 percent of the votes cast for the three candidates. Later in the year, he tried unsuccessfully to become governor on an independent ticket. Although he ran well behind the Republican and Democratic candidates, he accomplished the remarkable feat of carrying the counties where Toledo and Cleveland are located.

During his second term, Jones tried to establish a municipal lighting plant. He also supported the building of a plant to distribute gas during the period the city owned its own pipeline. But he was unable to push his programs of municipal ownership through the council.

The mayor appointed bright young idealists to many city offices. Under the leadership of Sylvanus P. Jermain, a park

system was born, the zoological garden was expanded into one of the country's leading zoos and the city began to construct a series of boulevards. With his belief in exercise, Jones enthusiastically supported the building of one of the first public golf courses in the nation at Ottawa Park. He began a music-in-the-park series and fought fairly successfully for the establishment of kindergartens and playground facilities.

Like many Progressives, Jones felt that much crime stemmed from poverty and called for reform of the judicial system. The poor, he said, "have no money, they have no council and for petty offenses that are not offenses at all when committed by the rich, they are fined, imprisoned, disgraced and degraded." Jones often served as a substitute police magistrate and dismissed most cases that came before him. This caused so much opposition that the state eventually passed a law forbidding mayors to perform that function.

CARRYING ON THE GOOD FIGHT

Despite lack of any mention of his campaign in local newspapers, Jones easily won a fourth term in 1903 and faced the last battle of his political career. The city's street railway company insisted on a 25-year extension of its franchise. Jones opposed the extension and demanded the lowering of streetcar fares to 3 cents. The city council passed the extension and prepared to override the mayor's veto. During a city council meeting, angry citizens shouted down traction company officials. Under this pressure, the council backed down and sustained Jones' vote. The jubilant crowd hoisted Jones in the air and carried him out of the council chambers. At another packed council session, the traction company lawyer asked Jones if the rowdy crowd indicated the kind of government Toledo had under the supposed "Golden Rule" mayor. Jones replied, "No, this is the kind of government we have under the rule of gold!" The franchise

PENS AND PINS: *Drafting students (above) and a girls' sewing class (below) at the Toledo Manual Training School around the turn of the century.*

89

90

A drum and bugle corps leads the parade down Superior Street on Labor Day 1910. Toledo's labor movement played a vital role during the Progressive era.

91

MOVING INTO THE TWENTIETH CENTURY: Samuel M. Jones, the popular four-term mayor (left); activity abounds in the Blade newsroom (top); The Ashley block (above) housed a variety of offices and businesses at 811 Jefferson Street.

was not extended during the Jones administration.

The popular mayor died in office in 1904 at the age of 57. Fifty-five thousand people viewed his body lying in state. Five thousand people attended his funeral, including men and women from all walks of life—pickpockets and prostitutes, factory workers and businessmen.

Jones' followers were committed to keeping the independent movement alive. Using the issue of the street railway, their new Independent Party elected three councilmen in 1904. In 1905 they turned to Brand Whitlock, Jones' advisor and friend, as their mayoral candidate. Whitlock wanted to be a novelist, but he felt obligated to carry out the work of the man he considered eccentric and simple, "as naive as a child," but one who had been completely dedicated to just causes. Campaigning against the boss-machine system and for municipal ownership of public utilities, Whitlock won an easy victory,

carrying all but two of the city's wards with a 5,000-vote plurality.

During his eight years in office, Whitlock carried out a substantial portion of the Progressives' municipal program. Unlike Jones, Whitlock recognized that political organization was necessary to accomplish reform, and the Independents gained control of the council. Home rule, a key demand, was achieved in 1912. A new waterworks and a new garbage plant were established. Enforcement of anti-smoke measures, a meat inspection act and further changes in the local judicial system were instituted. Unrealized when he left office was his "City Beautiful" dream of a civic center to include a new city hall, a new memorial building and other public structures.

Whitlock's major fight was against the traction company—the greatly overcapitalized Toledo Rail and Light Company. Whitlock stood firm against renewing its

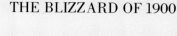

WOODEN STREETS AND WARTIME: *Thirteenth Street (top) was paved with wooden blocks around 1916; WWI soldiers march in review (above) down Summit Street. About 300 Lucas County residents lost their lives during the war effort.*

*O*n February 28 and March 1, 1900, over twenty inches of snow fell and paralyzed the city. At that time, snow removal was largely done by hand. Snow was piled high along the downtown streets and later hauled away by wagon and dumped into the Maumee River. The streets commissioner hired any able-bodied man who wanted to work to clear the downtown streets.

Fire was a constant threat to the nineteenth-century city, but the fire chief warned of the additional danger of fire when the streets were clogged with snow. "If a fire should break out in the business district, the result would be appalling," Chief Wall stated. "It would be impossible to drag our heavy engines any great distance in time to be of much service."

Long-time residents often state that the winters are not as harsh as they used to be, and the statistics compiled by the Toledo Times *in 1940 support that claim.*

Decade	Inches of snowfall
1889–1899	341
1899–1909	305
1909–1919	352
1919–1929	283
1929–1939	261

franchises. He forced its recapitalization and obtained a limited 3-cent fare. New ownership took over the company which verged on bankruptcy in 1912, and the street railway was reorganized on an efficient and sound financial basis.

This was not the municipal ownership Jones, Whitlock and the Independents had advocated, but it was a limited victory and an important one.

Whitlock refused to run again for mayor in 1914. He was appointed Minister to Belgium, where he envisioned a quiet life with time to write novels. World War I changed that plan. Whitlock headed the Belgian relief effort and won international stature as a diplomat. His *Forty Years of It* is one of the better contemporary accounts of the aims and work of the Progressive reformers who so strikingly shaped Toledo's history.

With the retirement of Whitlock from politics and the settlement of the streetcar issue, the Independent movement in Toledo politics ended. After World War I, Toledo returned to traditional urban party politics. But the Progressive interlude left legacies that continued to affect the city into the late twentieth century.

93

Brand Whitlock's The Turn of the Balance *is not widely known, but it merits comparison with the best of the realistic reformist novels that were part of the Progressive era. The work is sometimes melodramatic, occasionally oversentimentalized, and Whitlock is more interested in the characters who are poor than those who are rich. Still, it has narrative power. It also demonstrates Whitlock's insight into underworld life, prison conditions and the workings of the criminal justice system.*

Whitlock began The Turn of the Balance *in late 1903, a year and a half before his first campaign for mayor. Only with great difficulty was he able to finish the first draft in late 1905. The revisions were completed the next year, and it was finally published in March 1907 near the end of his first term as mayor.*

Brand Whitlock served as Minister to Brussels during the 1920s; he hoped European life would allow time for his first love—writing.

The Turn of the Balance *is an urban novel—city settings reflect and shape the lot of the rich and the poor. Although unidentified, the city is clearly Toledo.*

The city day was drawing to a close. Forge fires were glowing in the foundries they passed. Through the gloom within they could see the workmen, stripped like gunners to the waist, their moist, polished skins glowing in the fierce glare. . . . In some of the factories bevies of girls thronging the window, calling now and then to the workmen. . . already trooping by on the sidewalk. In the crowded streets great patient horses nodded as they easily drew the empty trucks that had borne such heavy loads all day; their drivers were smoking pipes, greeting one another, and whistling or singing; one of them in the camaraderie of toil had taken on a load of workmen, to haul them on their homeward way. The streetcars were filled with men whose faces showed the grime their hasty washing had not removed. . . .

The automobile was tearing through the tenderloin with its gaudily-painted saloons and second-hand stores sandwiched between. Old clothes fluttered above the sidewalk, and violins, revolvers, boxing-gloves and bits of jewelry, the trash and rubbish of wasted, feverish lives showed in the windows. . . . In the swinging green doors of saloons stood bartenders; and everywhere groups of men and women, laughing, joking, haggling, scuffling and quarreling. Now and then girls with their tawdry finery tripped down from upper rooms, stood a moment in the dark, narrow doorways, looked up and down the street, and then suddenly went forth. In some of the cheap theaters, the miserable tunes that never ended, day or night, were jingling from metallic pianos. They passed on into the business district. Shops were closing, the tall office buildings, each a city in itself, were pouring forth their human contents; the sidewalks were thronged—everywhere life, swarming, seething life, spawned out upon the world.

Close personal friends, Mayor Jones (right) visits the office of attorney Brand Whitlock in 1901.

RAILROADS AND MOTORCARS: A 1920s view of Madison Avenue (top) documents the emergence of the automobile in Toledo; thousands of passengers stopped at the Union Station (above) as Toledo became a major Midwest railroad center in the '20s.

The problems confronting Jones, Whitlock and the Toledo Progressives resulted in part from the rapid growth of the city in the late nineteenth century. Toledo's population continued to expand dramatically, rising from 131,822 in 1900 to 290,718 by 1930. In the twentieth century, however, the character of city growth in America changed. Suburbanization and sprawl is often associated with the automobile age in the 1920s and particularly with the period after World War II. But well before that, the classical, compact walking-city with its clearly defined limits had begun to disappear. In the 1900s, the history of Toledo—as in the early years—is not just that of a city but the history of a region turned metropolis.

Much of the new physical growth represented a form of industrial suburbanization—the construction of large manufacturing plants and necessary facilities away from the central city. The building of Edward Ford's glass company and his creation of a company town to the south of East Toledo in 1898 provided the basis for the growth of a large suburb, Rossford. As early as 1872, when the early town of Manhattan was annexed, the city also absorbed a manufacturing district to the north of East Toledo known as Ironville. In 1892 Toledo annexed the manufacturing suburb of Auburndale, about three miles northwest of downtown. Because of the three railroad lines that passed through Auburndale, numerous factories, including the famous Milburn Wagon Works, had located there after 1874.

The last major Toledo annexation before World War II involved the old town of Tremainsville in 1916. The community had the first post office in the early days of the Maumee Valley. The Willys-Overland plant, at the site of the original Pope automobile plant, stood on the western edge of Toledo, but many of its workers settled in the adjacent town. As a result of this annexation, a three-square-mile area containing 5,000 people was added to the city.

Much of the physical expansion was the result of a new and efficient form of urban transportation—electrified street railways. The streetcar system was vital to the city and intensified the confrontations of Jones and Whitlock with the local traction companies. Toledo streetcars were electrified by 1889. An interurban line linked Toledo to Maumee and Perrysburg in 1894, beginning the development of these two early Maumee Valley towns as residential suburbs of Toledo.

As settlement extended along the streetcar lines, numerous problems developed that led during the Jones-Whitlock era to a movement for systematic city planning. The subsequent rapid growth of South Toledo—which by 1923 contained a third of the city's population—presented special difficulties. South Toledo was divided from downtown by the decaying Swan Creek area lined with abandoned lumber mills and warehouses. There was great deterioration around Union Station in the section of town known as the Middlegrounds. This particularly disturbed civic leaders for the area provided

travelers with their first view of the city. Swan Creek was badly polluted. Travel from the center of Toledo to the south side required passage through a series of traffic bottlenecks. The measures necessary to change all this—bond issues, negotiations with the state and with railroad companies, new sewers, rerouting the creek bed, building a street over the old Miami and Erie Canal—required a half-century to complete.

Before the automobile came into widespread use after World War I, housing had to be built within walking distance of streetcar lines. Available residential space in Toledo was beginning to fill in. This pressure contributed to a major emphasis of the early twentieth-century planning movement—the effort to build and preserve a park system before it was too late. "In those sections of the city where population is densest," the Toledo City Plan Commission reported in 1925, "there are no public areas of any consequences except the streets. Eighty percent of all private property within the city limits is improved and new areas are now practically impossible to secure for purposes of recreation."

In the early 1900s, streetcars contributed to the growth of important secondary business districts away from the downtown—Dorr-Detroit to the south, Lagrange-Manhattan to the north, Phillips-Sylvania to the northwest. These

95

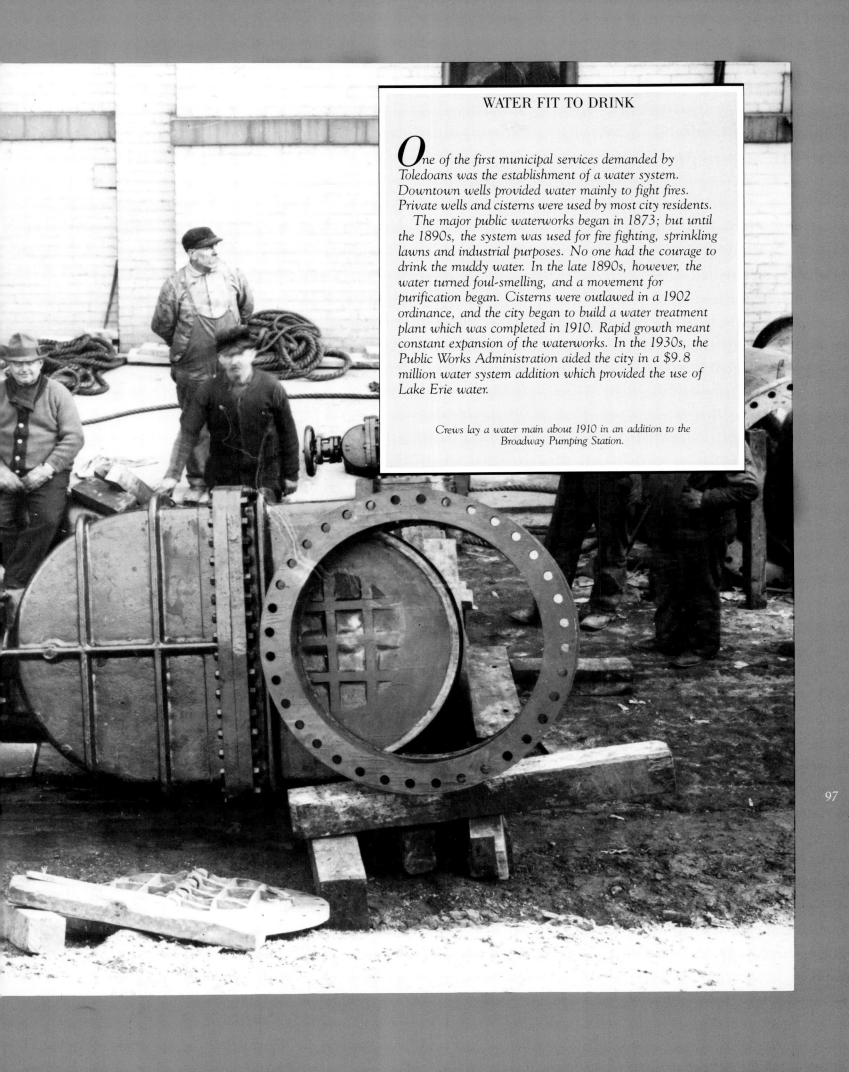

WATER FIT TO DRINK

*O*ne of the first municipal services demanded by Toledoans was the establishment of a water system. Downtown wells provided water mainly to fight fires. Private wells and cisterns were used by most city residents.

The major public waterworks began in 1873; but until the 1890s, the system was used for fire fighting, sprinkling lawns and industrial purposes. No one had the courage to drink the muddy water. In the late 1890s, however, the water turned foul-smelling, and a movement for purification began. Cisterns were outlawed in a 1902 ordinance, and the city began to build a water treatment plant which was completed in 1910. Rapid growth meant constant expansion of the waterworks. In the 1930s, the Public Works Administration aided the city in a $9.8 million water system addition which provided the use of Lake Erie water.

Crews lay a water main about 1910 in an addition to the Broadway Pumping Station.

ESCAPE FROM THE CITY

*B*efore the advent of television or major sporting events, Toledoans often relaxed on Sunday afternoons at amusement parks. Lake Erie Park and Casino, Toledo Beach, White City and Presque Isle were the most popular. Park facilities included swimming beaches, picnic areas, restaurants, game areas and dance halls. Visitors could also enjoy a vaudeville act or see a full-length theater production. Railroads often owned the amusement parks, and Toledoans were lured to the parks by inexpensive streetcar or interurban railway fares.

The parks gradually lost their popularity as Americans took to their automobiles and began to travel. The Depression of the 1930s contributed to the demise of the remaining local resorts.

AMUSEMENTS: The Toledo Beach shoreline was reached by plank walks in 1910 (above); visitors crowd the main entrance to Presque Isle Park in August 1894 (top right); The White City Park roller coaster (right upper center) was a major attraction in 1910; the dance pavilion at Toledo Beach (right lower center), 1907; the popular Lake Erie Park and Casino drew thousands of Toledoans (right bottom). Photographer Charles Mensing joins the strollers on the boardwalk as he glances back at the camera.

COMMERCIAL HUB: *The intersection of Summit, Cherry and St. Clair (top) about 1914; 20 years later, business activity had increased and autos now clogged the intersection (above).*

were located where streetcar lines intersected or where interurban terminals were located. Streetcars also permitted the development of residential areas a considerable distance from the city, such as Point Place which ran north of the city along Maumee Bay to the Michigan line. Point Place began as a resort area and the site of summer homes. The streetcar led to permanent settlement, but the area was not connected by a paved road to the city until 1933. In 1937 when it was annexed, the community had a population of over 4,600. (Unlike most twentieth-century suburbs, Point Place retained numbered street names. Toledo thus has the curious distinction of having the highest numbered street—326th—of any city in the country.)

Much closer to the city at Cherry and Summit, three city streetcar lines intersected near the interurban station where electric trains arrived from Michigan. There a colorful shopping and entertainment district developed. Visitors who came to town from the north were welcomed in the 1920s by a large electric sign showing a steamboat and a train spouting smoke and flashing the slogan, "You'll do better in Toledo." Shoppers browsed at the unusual Summit-Cherry Market where all types of products were sold by owners of independently owned stalls in an early-day combination of department store and supermarket. Gamblers haunted the back room of the Jovial Club where guards armed with machine guns checked customers. People bought horse meat at a market that sold

99

*T*oledo's streetcar business has been both colorful and controversial. In 1860, horse-drawn cars ran along Summit Street, and electric streetcars began running around 1889. By the turn of the century, competing companies were consolidated into one organization.

Progressive mayors Samuel Jones and Brand Whitlock constantly fought to establish a uniform 3-cent fare. In June 1901, the Toledo Rail and Light Company purchased the streetcar lines and interurbans as well as other gas and electric utilities. The firm became known as the "Big Con." The city forced the traction companies to reduce the value of their inflated stocks and refused to grant long-term contracts (franchises). In 1919, the city and the Community Traction Company were able to agree on a contract and the conflict ended.

Streetcars played a vital part in city suburbanization. Real estate development followed along the streetcar lines as the city spread in all directions. The Old West End, West Toledo, South Toledo and East Toledo grew rapidly as transportation made fringe neighborhoods more accessible.

A series of high-speed electric cars, known as interurbans, connected the city with Cleveland, Detroit, Monroe and many other cities throughout Ohio and southern Michigan. The interurbans often traveled at 60 miles per hour and provided an efficient link in the urban transportation system.

101

Streetcars were ordered off the city streets in 1919. Community Traction officials pose (left) with cars removed to Michigan during a dispute with the city over streetcar fares; the Adams streetcar line used horse power in the 1870s (above left); passengers wait in 1905 for the interurban (above right) at the 339 Superior Street Station.

MENSING'S TOLEDO: *Charles Mensing captured a serene view of City Park, the community's first, around 1900 (above); the dashing young photographer turns the camera on himself (below).*

RELAXING IN THE PARK

*A*s the population more than doubled between 1880 and 1900, some Toledoans with vision saw the need to create open space for recreational areas. The city's rapid urban growth limited the amount of open space available for the creation of parks.

Sylvanus P. Jermain spearheaded the drive for the city to establish an adequate park system. He organized an 1891 levy drive and raised $500,000. By July 1893, $763,000 was spent adding to Riverside Park, City Park and the Courthouse Mall area. Collins, Walbridge, Ottawa, Central Grove and Willys parks were established. Major Samuel "Golden Rule" Jones and other progressives also aided in the campaign to establish public parks and playgrounds.

The purchase of the 280-acre Ottawa Park created a controversy as citizens complained about the $100,000 price and the location a half-mile beyond the city limits. Under Jermain's leadership, one of the first public golf courses in the nation was built in Ottawa Park. By 1905, Walbridge Park was expanded, and many animals were added to the zoo.

Riverside Park was the city's second park; it was a popular spot for river ice skating in the 1900s.

SMOKE
GREENBACK

THAT'S ENTERTAINMENT!

*P*arades, carnivals and street fairs were major sources of entertainment in the nineteenth and early twentieth centuries. Fraternal, political, civic and church organizations often sponsored carnivals and street fairs to raise funds.

The circus parades down Summit Street in August 1894.

Marching bands and drill squads were popular in 1883. The Broom Drill Squad was organized for a charity performance at the Wheeler Opera House.

107

A police parade at Summit and Orange streets in June 1898, followed by an open streetcar advertising minstrels.

Toledo welcomes the 42nd encampment of the Grand Army of the Republic in late summer 1908; the GAR was a fraternal society for Civil War veterans.

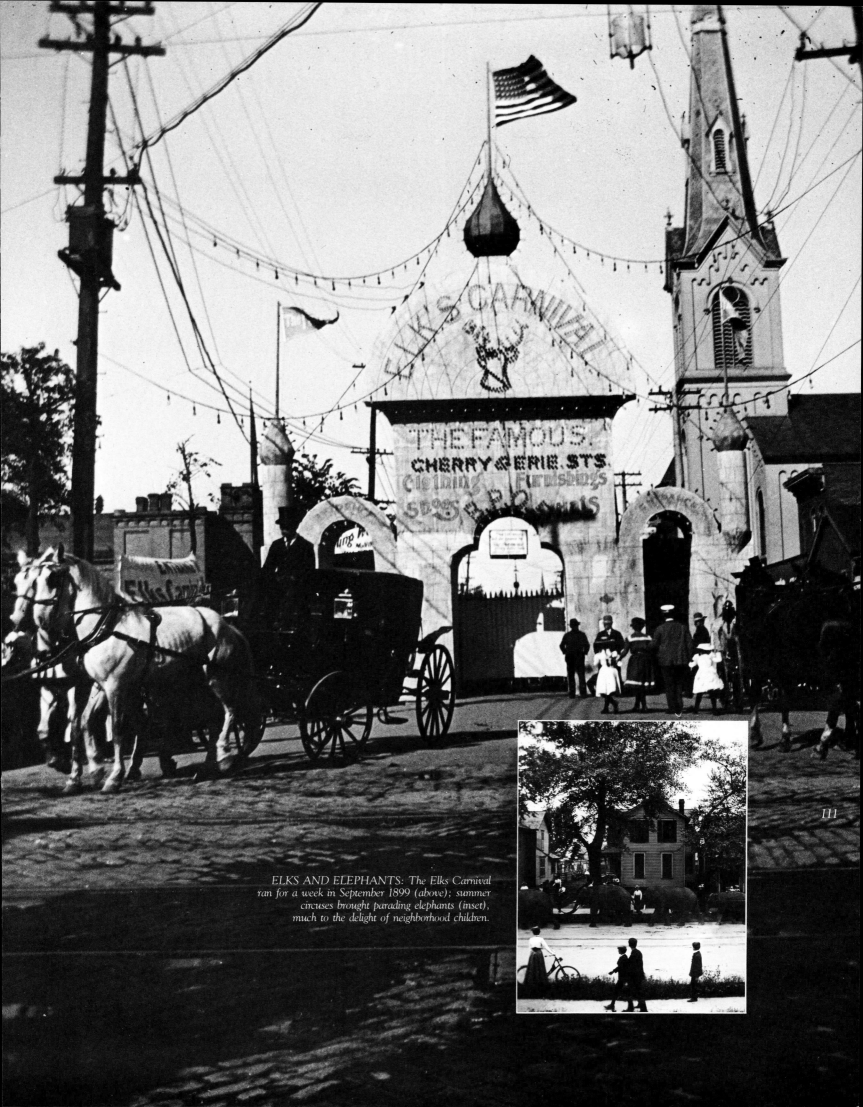

ELKS AND ELEPHANTS: The Elks Carnival
ran for a week in September 1899 (above); summer
circuses brought parading elephants (inset),
much to the delight of neighborhood children.

*T*oledo's first aviators were doers of the spectacular —good showmen who depended on the dimes they gathered from those who came to be amazed. They took the little money they earned and carried on their aviation experiments.

Their names are written in bold letters in the memory of Toledo —Roy Knabenshue, Lincoln Beachey, Jack Dallas, Tony Nassr, L. M. Rakestraw. Before airships, they went aloft in awkward dirigibles —homemade bags that looked as flimsy as they actually were. Playing the fairs in all parts of the United States, they made Toledo known as the home of the intrepid birdmen.

A. Roy Knabenshue was Toledo's most famous aviator. He made aviation history on October 25, 1904, at the St. Louis World's Fair when he flew the first successful dirigible flight in the country. Later he said the flight was an accident. He was having trouble with the engine and asked the crew to turn the engine off, but in the confusion they thought he said "let 'er go." Powered by a ten-horsepower engine, the crude dirigible landed in East St. Louis. Some people were surprised at how well the aviator steered the ship. Knabenshue later said, "I wasn't maneuvering—I was hanging on."

Knabenshue returned to Toledo and designed the airship "Toledo Number One." On June 30, 1905, he flew from the Dorr Street fairgrounds and landed on top of the ten-story Spitzer Building. He won $500 from A. L.

Spitzer for his accomplishment. The craft—58 feet long and fifteen feet in diameter —had a gas capacity of 7,000 cubic feet. Toledoans were amazed as the aviator maneuvered the aircraft among the downtown buildings, avoided wires and landed with only a few feet to spare on the Spitzer Building.

Other flights around the country followed. Knabenshue often went under the name of Professor Don Carlos so as not to embarrass his family who frowned upon such activities. His father, S. S. Knabenshue, was a Toledo newspaper editor.

An inventor and electrical engineer, Knabenshue also worked with the Wright brothers and airplane builder Glenn L. Martin.

Anthony M. Nassr, another pioneer aviator, built dirigibles and was a flying partner of Knabenshue. Nassr's interests turned to airplanes, and he became an instructor and the superintendent of the first Toledo airport.

Lincoln Beachey, a student of Knabenshue, became a stunt pilot and died in the crash of his new monoplane on March 15, 1915, as a San Francisco crowd watched. Two years before his death, he commented about the audiences at airshows, and noted, "I am convinced that the only thing that draws the crowd to see me is the morbid desire to see something happen. They call me the Master Birdman, but they pay to see me die."

*Roy Knabenshue guides his airship between the Spitzer and
Nasby buildings during his historic 1905 flight (above left); he steered his
fragile ship by walking up and down the flimsy frame (above right).*

nothing else, listened to sidewalk preachers, looked at the fine bronze statue of Toledo's Civil War hero, James B. Steedman, or took a bath at "Soaphouse Pete's" public bathhouse in the Navarre Hotel. And at the same hotel after December 1933, thirsty customers could buy a drink in the first bar in Toledo to open after the repeal of Prohibition. (This type of district began to disappear from the heart of American cities after World War II. The Cherry-Summit area fell victim to urban renewal in the mid-1960s, and much of it is now occupied by Vistula Meadows, a public housing project for the elderly.)

The early metropolitan era when many of the later ethnic neighborhoods were forming in East Toledo and elsewhere witnessed considerable diversification in community development. Less than two miles northwest of the Cherry-Summit district, along the Cherry Streetcar line, two unusual and secluded residential projects— Bronson Place and Birckhead Place—were built in the early 1900s. Both later organized as nonprofit corporations; Bronson Place incorporated in 1913 and Birckhead Place in 1922. The corporation stockholders owned the individual properties. They established the park areas that were a distinguishing feature of both projects, provided and maintained streets, lighting, sidewalks and other services. (The two places still retain the organization, and the neighborhoods have kept their corporate organization despite commercial decay along Cherry Street.)

The enclosed enclave of Bronson Place contained twenty houses built between 1899 and 1913. They were designed primarily by the famous Toledo architect, Harry Wachter, in Dutch Colonial, Colonial Revival and other period building styles. Birckhead Place, three blocks to the south, was larger with 68 houses constructed mainly between 1904 and 1930. The gates and six-foot-high iron fence enclosed a park-like area with excellent examples of most of the period architectural styles. Birckhead Place attracted a number of rising industrialists, businessmen and lawyers, many of whom had earlier lived in the Old West End.

In the early years of the automobile age after World War I, a number of residential areas were developed west and northwest of the original Toledo. As the South End filled in before the Depression, population expanded along a few major roads that later became thoroughfares such as today's Bancroft and Monroe streets. A leader in the early Toledo city planning movement, Badger C. Bowen (1872–1931) and his Wells-Bowen Company, developed several middle-class and upper-middle-class city additions—Westmoreland, Park Side, Fairmont Park, Old Orchard, De Veaux and Hampton Park. Many remain as identifiable neighborhoods. The farthest west is Old Orchard, roughly a half-mile-square area of Americanized English Tudor with some Spanish Colonial Revival houses. Old Orchard is one of the city's more attractive residential neighborhoods built in accord with the traditional American urban gridiron street pattern. Because many of the original trees remain, the area presents attractive vistas at all seasons of the year.

Just to the west of Old Orchard, the E. H. Close Company, which had been responsible for the Bronson Place enclave, began in 1916 to develop 1,280 acres of hill and valley land extending three miles along the course of the Ottawa River. Ottawa Hills became one of the most famous of the garden suburbs of the 1920s, ranking with Roland Park in Baltimore, the Country Club District in Kansas City and Shaker Heights in Cleveland. It was designed with the assistance of the landscape architecture firm of Frederick Law Olmsted Jr. who had carried on the ideas of his father, the pioneer planner and creator of the American city park movement. Ottawa Hills successfully employed a curvilinear street pattern to enhance an attractive natural setting. With its many grand estates and large landscaped residential lots, it was the epitome of the garden-style community. One local authority considers its short Parke Street—perpendicular to the creek near the southeast edge of the area—the most aesthetically appealing residential street in the metropolitan area. (Surrounded on three sides by an expanding Toledo, Ottawa Hills has remained an incorporated village, with 4,065 residents in 1980. It is one of the country's wealthiest municipalities with a startling per-capita income of $23,222 in 1981.)

GARDEN PARKS AND SKYSCRAPERS

Garden cities and garden suburbs were part of a general planning movement in the twentieth century. The movement had origins in the "Great White City" of the 1893 Chicago Columbian Exposition, the "City Beautiful" and the "City Efficient" of the Progressive era and in the urban park effort that had begun much earlier. Planning in the twentieth century, as was the case in Toledo, also represented a response to the problems created by the unrestrained growth of the sprawling metropolis. Brand Whitlock had worked with E. O. Fallis, a prominent local architect, on a plan published in 1908 for a new civic center. It included a city hall, an auditorium and other public buildings, but Whitlock had been unable to carry through the plan. His effort led, however, to the organization of a volunteer Toledo City Plan Commission in 1916 which began receiving public funds in 1921. Toledo

In the first decade of the new century, Edward Drummond Libbey provided the leadership and a good share of the money to establish the Toledo Museum of Art. It became one of the great American art museums, largely through Libbey's endowments; a 1923 drawing class works on an assignment.

113

TOLEDO LANDMARKS: Two Lucas County courthouses were visible in the winter of 1897 (left). The old one in the foreground was torn down; prominent Toledo architect David L. Stine designed the new Lucas County Courthouse (inset left) which opened on New Year's Day 1897. The Courthouse area was often used for political rallies in the early twentieth century; volunteers rush to the National Guard Armory on April 27, 1898, for induction in the Spanish-American War (top); the Toledo Public Library stood on the corner of Madison and Ontario (above) for 50 years. The Romanesque Revival structure was razed in 1940 for a parking lot.

TOLEDO TAKES CARE OF ITS OWN:
*The Soldiers Memorial Building (left inset)
was used by veterans groups for meetings and
social functions; designed by E.O. Fallis, the
Toledo State Hospital and its grounds (left)
drew national attention and was a source of
civic pride; the hospital's dining room, around
1910 (above); the ivy-covered Toledo Hospital
at Cherry and Sherman (right), around 1910.
Note the gleaming streetcar tracks and
overhead electric lines.*

THE CHANGING SKYLINE: The Spitzer Building (above left) at Madison and Huron in 1900. Note the shadow of the Nasby Building on the facade; the Pythian Castle (above right) was completed in 1890 and added architectural flavor to the business district; the Nasby Building (right) lost its tower for safety reasons in 1934.

leaders were instrumental in obtaining state legislation that permitted planning on a metropolitan basis. This resulted in the creation of the Lucas County Plan Commission in 1923. (The two were eventually joined as the Toledo-Lucas County Plan Commission in 1973.)

Through the guidance of Harland Bartholomew, a leading national city planner, the Toledo City Plan Commission presented a series of reports between 1924 and 1928. The commission's comprehensive Toledo city plan stressed the need for zoning as a means of separating the jumbled commercial, industrial and residential development. (Zoning came into use in America after 1916 and was authorized in Toledo in 1923.) The reports also stressed numerous changes in streets and transportation patterns, another bridge across the Maumee, expansion of parks, playgrounds and parkways and the development of Whitlock's civic center. Planning in Toledo, like city planning elsewhere in the period, was generally sponsored by business leaders such as Edward Libbey and Badger Bowen who were interested in making the metropolis a more rational and efficient place in which to work and do business. The Toledo reports said virtually nothing about the problems of slums and inadequate housing. That kind of planning was a product of the New Deal era.

Only portions of the Bartholomew plan were realized before the Great Depression. There was progress in improving the passage to South Toledo. Railroad grade crossings were eliminated. Streets were widened. Traffic to East Toledo across the Cherry Street Bridge had always been a problem, and one of the most spectacular engineering feats of the period occurred on Sunday, December 15, 1929, when an entire business block on Main Street was moved ten feet back from the street in a single action. There was some development of the belt of parklands that became

118

Willys, Beatty, Jermain, Ottawa, Collins, Ravine, Bay View, Navarre and Riverside parks. Important for the future of the regional park system was the establishment of the Toledo Metropolitan Park Board in 1929. Whitlock's dream of a civic center began to be realized when the first city hall was built in 1924, followed by the Federal Court and Customs Building in 1929–30.

Storer Broadcasting's WSPD mobile unit in the 1940s.

Civic centers with monumental public buildings were a central feature of the twentieth-century American city. Skyscrapers and distinctive downtown skylines were another. Although Toledo developed no original school of architecture, the city acquired a number of well-designed commercial buildings that reflected the architectural styles of the period. They serve today as monuments to its early metropolitan history. Toledo's first skyscraper was the nine-story Security Building (originally the Nasby Building) built in 1893 at Huron and Madison. It was designed by E. O. Fallis and reflected the early Chicago skyscraper style. The ten-story Spitzer Building at Madison and Huron constructed in 1896 resembled the buildings of Louis Sullivan; its clean, simple, symmetrical design produced a notable city landmark. The seventeen-story National Bank Building of 1906 at Madison and Huron was the focal point of Toledo's commercial main street and the tallest building in Ohio at the time.

The second wave of commercial building began in the 1920s. The concept of the skyline as representative of the big city took root in American culture. There were a number of distinctive structures built in Toledo. The 21-story Toledo Trust Building, initially the Second National Bank Building (1912–13), at Summit and Madison was designed in the Renaissance style of the famous architectural firm of Daniel H. Burnham of Chicago. The nine-story Lasalle and Koch Building (1917)

at Adams and Huron was an unusually attractive department store structure. The seventeen-story Commodore Perry Hotel (1925–27) at Jefferson and Superior was at the time one of the most luxurious and lavishly decorated hotels in the Midwest; in 1931 its roof became the site of facilities for Toledo's first radio station—WSPD—one of the earliest in the country.

Toledo's most famous skyscraper of this period was the 28-story Owens-Illinois Building at Madison and St. Clair. It was designed in the fashionable modernistic Art Deco style inspired by Eliel Saarinen's second-place design in the Chicago Tribune Tower competition. One of the last buildings completed during the great American cities skyscraper race in the 1920s, it was finished in 1930—the same year as New York's Empire State Building, the white elephant of the Depression decade. Toledo's great skyscraper shared the hard times. The Ohio Savings and Trust Company had built it, but the huge financial institution went under in 1931 during the wave of bank failures in the early years of the Depression, and the building quickly passed to other hands.

By the time Lasalle's was built, the department store—with its division into departments, fixed prices and use of advertising—had become a standard part of big-city merchandising. In the 1870s Frederick Eaton, a pioneer merchant, began expanding his Lion Store into a department store. Lion's acquired its name from the statues

THE BIG BOOM

*T*he local economy boomed as automobile and industrial production increased in the 1920s. Retail trade grew as the Lion and Lasalle stores expanded. There were many new downtown buildings, including the Ohio Savings Bank, the Commodore Perry Hotel and other office facilities.

Retail stores dominate the 200 block of Summit Street in 1925 (left); the Lamson Store, now One Lake Erie Center, opened on November 13, 1928 (left inset); the Tiedtke store advertised bargain days in the 1930s (above); located in the 400 block of Summit Street, the store sold everything from coffee to shoes (above inset); the intersection of Adams and Superior in 1937 (below left); a policeman directs traffic on Adams Street during the 1930s (below right).

COMPETITION: *The Scott High School team (above) won the national high school football championship in 1921, scoring 263 points to the opponent's 54; Miss Manewski, right, won the title "Miss Toledo" in a 1920s beauty contest (left) sponsored by the American Legion.*

of two lions which stood in front and provided a downtown landmark for over a hundred years. (After the downtown store closed in 1980, the lions were first moved to the Toledo Zoo and recently to a shopping center Lion Store.) The Lamson Brothers Store, which had existed as a drygoods store since 1885, became a large downtown department store, particularly after it occupied a new structure in 1928.

Tiedtke's was Toledo's most distinctive downtown store. Started in 1894 and moved to Summit Street in 1910, Tiedtke's has been called "America's first supermarket." One of its original owners had said, "Looks just like a circus." Actually, during much of its history, Tiedtke's represented a unique effort to apply big-city merchandising techniques—advertising, price-cutting, unusual displays—to the old-fashioned general grocery store. During its heyday, it became a kind of combination grocery, fish market, coffee house, cheese market and bakery employing the flamboyant methods of a Wanamaker or a Macy—pipe organ music booming through the store, mammoth cheese wheels, crazy mirrors on stairwells to entertain children. Each year, a seven-foot giant served the store's 1,000-pound, eleven-foot high anniversary cake, and yellow horse-drawn wagons lumbered through the streets delivering groceries free. The Tiedtke brothers themselves expanded into selling department store lines of merchandise. Under other owners in the postwar years, the grocery operation was all but eliminated in 1969. Tiedtke's was acquired by a national chain which went bankrupt in 1972, and the store closed abruptly. In May 1975, in one of Toledo's most spectacular fires, the abandoned Tiedtke building burned to the ground. Many residents thought the fire a symbolic end to the era of personalized merchandising in Toledo.

MUD HENS AND MOVIE PALACES

During its early metropolitan period, Toledoans shared the entertainments that became a part of big-city life during the prosperous early years of the century and the roaring '20s. In professional sports, the Toledo Mud Hens were a charter member of baseball's American Association organized in 1901. After 1909 they played in Swayne Field, recognized as perhaps the finest minor-league ball park in America. The Mud Hens won only one early pennant—in 1927, with the colorful Charles Dillon "Casey" Stengel as manager. But because of its name, the team was one of the best known minor-league clubs in America. (A long-time Toledo resident recalls growing up on the prairies of North Dakota, acquiring a Mud Hens' pennant and following the fortunes of that strange, far-distant team for years.)

Professional boxing took root in the city. In 1919 Toledo's Bay View Park was the site of one of the most famous prize fights of the twentieth century—Jack Dempsey's defeat of Jess Willard for the heavyweight championship. The Inverness Golf Club, organized in 1903, built one of the country's well-known golf courses. It was the site of two early National Open championships in 1920 and 1931. (Another held recently in 1979 became a major civic event.) In the era of "Red" Grange when college football became a national pastime, Toledoans were devoted to high school football. Scott and Waite high schools made

WILLARD-DEMPSEY FIGHT: On July 4, 1919, Toledo hosted the boxing event of the century. Heavyweight champion Jess Willard and sparring partner (top) work out before the fight; (above) Dempsey, left, shakes the hand of fight promoter Tex Rickard.

postseason trips throughout the country including the East and West coasts. Both claimed national championships in the early 1920s as a result of postseason games before they were prohibited for high schools. The annual Thanksgiving Day Waite-Scott game was one of the city's most popular sporting events.

The Blade Building, at the intersection of Superior, Beech and Huron streets, has been headquarters for the newspaper since 1927.

124

Joe E. Brown, who grew up in the "Irish Hill" area, mugs for the camera in the 1940s wearing a Fourth Ward Old Timers Club uniform.

Movie palaces were a product of the 1920s and early 1930s. Toledo's most grandiose theater, the Paramount, opened on February 6, 1929, with Richard Dix starring in "Redskin." It was accompanied by a pit band and music from the "Mighty Wurlitzer" built the year before at a cost of $28,000. (The Paramount was razed for a parking lot in 1965.) One of the city's most popular and fondly remembered places of entertainment, the Trianon Ballroom, opened on May 25, 1925, with Bernie Krueger and his Brunswick Recording Orchestra. During the 1940s the Trianon became a required stop for the big bands. (The Trianon was also razed for a parking lot in 1954.)

The planners of the 1920s were not yet designing parking lots, but traffic congestion brought on by the automobile had been one of their primary concerns. The culmination of their efforts and of Toledo's early metropolitan era came on October 27, 1931, with the dedication of a new bridge across the Maumee, officially named the Anthony Wayne Bridge but called the High Level Bridge ever since early construction days. In the Bartholomew Plan, it was to be the Warren G. Harding Memorial Bridge, but the revelations of the scandals of the Harding administration had necessitated a change. Depression had already struck the city, and bargains in the stores and free taxi and streetcar rides attracted thousands downtown for the celebration. The A&P offered three large cans of Alaska pink salmon for 25 cents and Tiedtke's sold a lunch of fricasseed rabbit for 10 cents. That evening of "Toledo Day," 40,000 people gathered in a steady rain to watch the ribbon-cutting and the long parade proceeding from East Toledo. The splendid bridge was a spectacular symbol of the new metropolis, and again, as so often in the past, the "dawn of a bright new era" was proclaimed. But the cold steady rain of October 27 was also a symbol. There would be long years of depression and war before the bright new era of Toledo arrived.

125

*N*o city was considered cultured in the nineteenth century until it had an opera house. In 1873, the Wheeler Opera House had a grand opening; twenty years later, it burned in a spectacular Saint Patrick's Day fire. During its brief life, the theater featured opera, plays and some vaudeville productions.

The turn of the century was the great era of Toledo theater as theatrical touring companies and vaudeville productions played the city. Toledo's location on the New York to Chicago railroad lines provided the opportunity to feature major attractions.

Burt's Theater on Jefferson Avenue was the home of the 10-cent melodrama. Other popular spots included People's Theater, The Auditorium, The Toledo, Keith's, Rivoli and the Empire.

A new era began in 1917 when the Valentine Theater was converted from a stage theater to a new form of entertainment—the movies. In 1928, the Vita-Temple showed the first talking picture in Toledo, "The Singing Fool," starring Al Jolson.

The golden age of the silver screen followed with the opening of the Paramount Theater on February 16, 1929. The $2-million structure was one of the finest in the Publix chain. Statuary, gilded grillwork and grand stairways accented the auditorium's lavish decor. The theater was torn down in 1965 to make way for a parking lot. The loss of the Paramount signaled the demise of downtown theaters.

The Palace Theater in 1936 (above left); a November 1942 State Theater audience (left center); the Valentine Theater was converted to a hotel in 1936 (below left); the Paramount Theater opened in 1929 with a gala celebration (below); the Vita-Temple (right) presented the first talking movie shown in Toledo; the People's Theater (right inset) was eventually to become the Capital Theater.

126

127

BRIDGING THE MAUMEE

Since the first rickety wooden Cherry Street Bridge was built over the Maumee River in 1865, the crossing has been a source of many strange incidents. Since that time, nine bridges have been built, today four are in use. Five bridges have come down, often with the help of Mother Nature.

The first Cherry Street Bridge owners collected 2 cents per person, 10 cents per horse (or two for 15 cents), 5 cents a head for horses and cattle in droves and 1 cent for sheep and hogs. Schoolchildren crossed free. Toledoans protested the unpopular tolls. Ater the bridge was damaged by ice and floods, the city purchased it in 1875 and rebuilt it, abolishing the tolls.

The third Cherry Street Bridge was completed in 1884. The steel bridge —built on concrete piers instead of wooden pilings —was supposed to last indefinitely. In 1908, the steamer Yuma broke away from its moorings during a spring flood and crashed into a span, ending the life of the third bridge. Frugal city fathers had the steel carted downriver and used it to construct the Ash-Consaul Bridge. (It also was rammed several times by freighters and finally was taken down in 1957.)

In 1913, the city appropriated $525,000 for a new steel-and-concrete Cherry Street Bridge, with a lift span to accommodate large ships. The cost of its construction in 1914 was $1.2 million, more than double the estimate.

The Fassett Street Bridge was constructed in 1895–96. The bridge was the second to cross the Maumee. Citizens were concerned about the apparent weak construction. Horse-drawn fire wagons were raced across the bridge at top speed to assure the public that the bridge was safe.

The Fassett Street Bridge crossed the Maumee flood plain from Walbridge and South avenues to the high bluffs on the east side of the river. The bridge served as an icebreaker for the other downstream bridges and its location on the narrowest part of the river added to the annual poundings from the heavy ice floes. In 1906, ice carried the center span away. On September 20, 1935, the bridge collapsed in a high wind. Luckily, no one was on it. The city and the WPA rebuilt the structure. On April 5, 1957, the lake freighter Champlain crashed into the middle of the bridge. This time the bridge remained down.

The tall, graceful High Level Bridge is the most majestic bridge crossing the Maumee. When the $3-million bridge opened on October 27, 1931, it was one of the longest suspension bridges in the world. Its 200-foot towers held up more than a half-mile of bridge roadway. Unlike the other bridges, this one has not been seriously damaged by mishaps. However, large vessels sometimes scrape the bridge with their tall masts. By 1975, at least 37 Toledoans had chosen the bridge as a place to commit suicide.

The Michael V. DiSalle Bridge was the last to open and is the longest of Toledo's bridges with a length of 3,403 feet. The cost of $13.4 million also made it the most expensive bridge to span the Maumee. Plans for a grand opening were cancelled when political factions refused to cooperate. The bridge opened without ceremony on November 22, 1963, the date President Kennedy was assassinated.

The eastern approach to the Cherry Street Bridge,
around 1905. Note the streetcar tracks and fresh
horse droppings.

129

Completion of the new Cherry Street Bridge in 1914, the old bridge in the background (right); the steamer Yuma rammed the bridge (far right) in 1908.

A 1932 broadside view of the Anthony Wayne Bridge, better known to Toledoans as the High Level Bridge.

Construction crew, around 1931, on the
High Level Bridge (far left); 1895-96
construction of the Fassett Street Bridge features a
diver (left).

131

The WPA employed hundreds of Lucas County women in 1936 making clothes for the needy.

THE DESPERATE DECADE

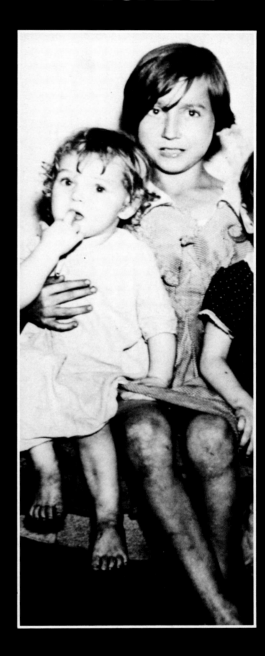

The city looks prosperous in the 1930s, but Toledo suffered greatly during this difficult decade.

The 1930s were the darkest years in the history of Toledo. They started with bank closings. Industrial production plunged, particularly in the automobile industry on which the city depended. Devastating unemployment ranged from 30 to 50 percent. Thousands required relief. Violent labor-capital struggles in the city affected the nation. Eventually, as private and local efforts to deal with these problems failed, the federal government poured millions of dollars into the city providing relief, jobs and public works. These New Deal programs changed the face of Toledo; they also radically changed the character of the city's government, economy and society.

Toledoans, like other Americans, did not believe that the collapse of the stock market on October 24, 1929, would affect the prosperity of their city. Few noticed that bank deposits fell about $6 million dollars during 1929. As banks began to experience difficulties the next year, representatives from the banking community continually expressed confidence. Early in 1931 one member said, "Toledo's seven state and two national banks weathered the critical year of 1930 and have embarked on a new year on a sound basis." But on June 17, 1931, the Security-Home Trust failed to open.

There was an immediate run on the city's other banks. Three of the largest invoked a rule requiring depositors to give 60 days' notice before withdrawing funds. Civic leaders tried to calm the public's fear. But four banks—including the Ohio Savings Bank and Trust in its splendid new skyscraper—failed to open on August 17. The closings —brought on by loans to stock market investors and

by real estate investments in another Toledo boom of the 1920s—were felt across the nation. The local banks were some of the largest in the country to fail during the panic. Toledo Trust, however, had stayed in conservative investments during the 1920s and weathered the storm. After the reorganization of financial institutions during the banking holiday of March 1933, it profited greatly from a return to stability.

The immediate effects of the financial crisis were critical. A third of the $80 million in deposits disappeared. Small firms were forced into bankruptcy. Businesses that survived had to extend vast amounts of credit to customers. Thousands lost all or part of their life savings. The city government lost over $610,000 and had more than that tied up for varying periods of time.

Unemployment accompanied the financial crisis. The phenomenal growth of the automotive industry in the 1920s had sustained Toledo's prosperity. Large corporations such as Electric Auto-Lite, Owens-Illinois and Willys-Overland employed thousands and appeared the soundest companies in the city. Drastic cutbacks in the industry caused a sudden and dramatic reaction among the more than 1,100 auto-related factories and shops. Between March and November 1929, Willys-Overland reduced its work force from 10,000 to 4,000 and put those still on the job on a partial work-week. Other auto-related industries cut back production and laid off equivalent numbers of workers. Layoffs spread to most of the factories.

Social service organizations and individuals tried to meet some of the needs of the unemployed. The Old Newsboys' Association sponsored legislation in city council that

The Ohio Savings Bank and Trust closed in August 1931, shortly after opening their new building on Madison Avenue.

135

The B&O Railroad docks were busy in November 1935 in spite of the Depression.

allowed unemployed heads of households to sell apples on the street—the traditional Depression activity that yielded the average Toledo vendor $1.84 a day in 1930. Addison Q. Thacher, a maverick Republican politican, distributed free food—collected from the unsold perishables of grocers—from a vacant building on Cherry Street. About 2,000 people came each day. In December 1929 alone, the Toledo City Mission fed 3,250 men and provided lodging for 1,179. Neighborhood organizations, such as the West End Community Welfare Club, gave small cash donations to the unemployed.

The Social Service Federation was an organization from the '20s designed to coordinate private and municipal relief. It administered local charities effectively, but the problem was enormous, and Toledoans—like most people—demanded jobs not relief. An incident at the city's street maintenance department demonstrated the unrest. The department provided jobs such as clearing snow and cleaning street gutters on a day-to-day basis. On January 24, 1930, a supervisor told a group of about a thousand waiting hopefuls that there would be no work that day. The disbelieving crowd smashed through the shop gate and stormed the office. A squad of police had to be called to disperse the rioting mob.

Unemployment strained the city's treasury. In 1929,

Toledo spent $73,000 on poor relief, over $400,000 in 1930 (with an extra $200,000 added by private charities) and by 1933, $1.7 million for the year. The city was nearly bankrupt. There were 30,000 people on relief. Uncollected taxes exceeded $6 million by June 1932, and the city owed local grocers a half-million dollars.

Only the intervention of the federal government prevented the collapse of Toledo. After May 1933, the new Federal Emergency Relief Administration began to provide funds to the city. The agency reported that Toledo was hit harder by the Depression than any city in the state. Twenty-one percent of the city's families were on relief, a rate nearly double that of the state as a whole.

A second new agency, the Civil Works Administration, operated for about six months over the winter of 1933–34 and was the first of the New Deal agencies to put people to work. The CWA employed 15,000 in Toledo and over 21,000 in Lucas County. Working 30 hours a week at 50 cents an hour, CWA employees began a number of public projects, most of them completed later. The public works programs for the city included the construction of a highway to the southwest from downtown, Canal Boulevard (later named the Anthony Wayne Trail), as well as construction at the Toledo Zoo, the Toledo Naval Armory, the Waite and DeVilbiss high school stadiums and

The grimness of the Depression years is reflected
in the faces of some of Toledo's children.

BUILDING PROJECTS: *The city owes one of its most valuable landmarks, the Jefferson Avenue YMCA building (above), to Depression building projects; most of the work on the Anthony Wayne Trail (below), completed in 1937, was done by hand to employ as many as possible.*

an artificial lake at the Boy Scout reservation in western Lucas County. The initial CWA program was continued by the FERA until January 1935, when the Works Progress Administration became the principal agency supplying direct jobs.

At its height, the WPA employed about 16,000 city residents. Under the local administration of Clarence Benedict, it completed earlier projects and launched a number of others, including street repairs, bridge and building improvements, installation of new sewer lines and expansion of facilities in the Toledo parks.

Among the agency's most notable accomplishments was the transformation of the Toledo Zoo in 1935. The WPA expended $900,000 along with $48,000 in city funds. The Toledo Zoological Society salvaged bricks from the old Milburn Wagon Works and the Wabash Roundhouse and blocks from the old Miami and Erie Canal bed. Thus, they were able to construct a reptile house, a monkey house, an aquarium, an aviary, a museum of natural history, a band shell, an open air amphitheater, a seal pool, new walls, gates, walks and bridges, heating and water mains, and a pedestrian subway under the Anthony Wayne Trail. The WPA project transformed the Toledo Zoo into the sixth largest natural history facility in the country.

The other New Deal agency of employment—the Public Works Administration—contracted public projects with private companies. The PWA authorized 28 projects in the city and spent over $5 million. Most notably, PWA funds helped complete one vocational and nine new elementary schools. This was the largest school project undertaken by the PWA in Ohio. As a result, Toledo schools acquired one of the finest physical plants in the nation.

CLEANING UP THE CITY

Most federal public works programs in cities ended with the coming of World War II. But one aspect of the federal government's efforts to reconstruct cities physically—first called slum clearance and later urban renewal—continues today. Initially, it was an effort to provide employment. But in the postwar period, it became part of the federal government's effort to restructure urban society and American society in general. After the creation of the housing division of the PWA in 1933, the new Toledo Metropolitan Housing Authority immediately identified blighted areas. A Toledo project, Brand Whitlock Homes was located in the old Lenk's Hill-Pinewood area on Nebraska Avenue and was one of the first of 29 public housing projects authorized by the federal government. Begun in 1936, the $2-million project was completed in 1938 and expanded in 1940. A second major Toledo project, the Charles Weiler Homes in East Toledo, opened in 1939.

In the postwar era, Toledo continued to be much involved in urban renewal and public housing. Incredibly, at one time 20 percent of the city land area was included in urban renewal projects. One of the country's first public housing projects exclusively for the elderly was Spieker Terrace on Fassett Street in East Toledo which was

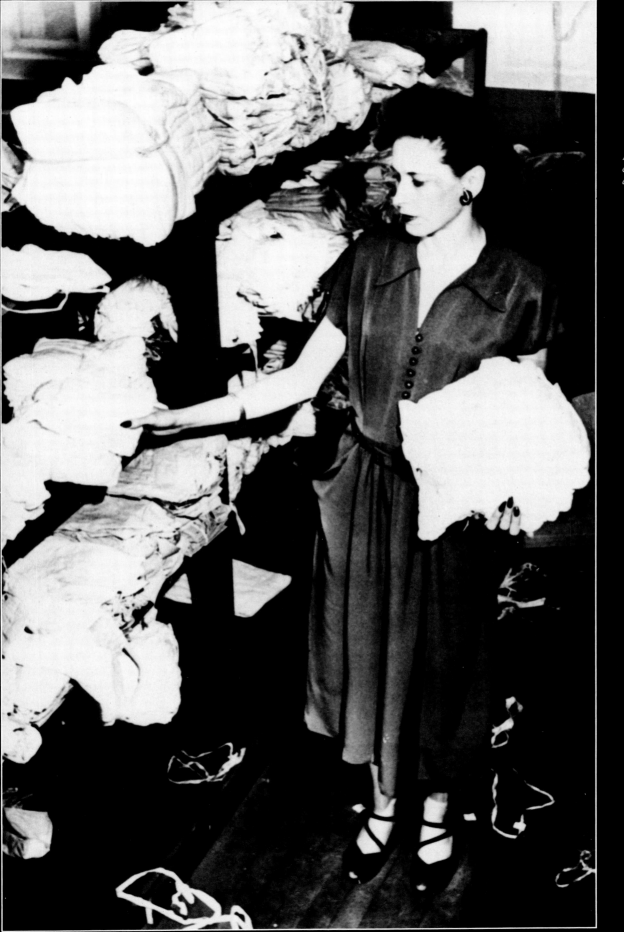

The WPA financed construction work on Broadway at the water works around 1937.

140

141

WHEELS AND MEALS: *Capital Tire and Rubber on Cherry Street (above) in 1937; Grace Smith opened a cafeteria (below) in the middle of the Depression at Madison and Erie; it closed in 1971.*

ACCOMPLISHMENTS OF THE '30s: Much of the Toledo Zoo was built as a WPA project. Many Toledoans remember rides as youngsters on the elephant, Babe (left); the soaring clock tower of University Hall (right) is a landmark on the West Toledo skyline.

completed in 1958. Vistula Meadows, finished in 1967, was among the earliest projects designed to provide public housing for both handicapped and elderly.

When the national economy began to rebound in 1937, the federal government began to cut back on its relief and employment programs. The resulting slump led to the layoff of 10,000 industrial workers in Toledo. During the first three months of 1938, the city's Division of Poor Relief processed 15,000 applications; and in that period, relief costs reached almost $1 million. Toledo met these new obligations by borrowing heavily against future tax revenues and by delaying payment to creditors.

The situation became critical in 1939. The city owed $700,000 to local wholesalers who refused to extend any more credit. On September 15, 1939, the city cut off all relief aid to the 8,562 people on its rolls. A Citizens' Emergency Fund Committee provided a quart of milk to children of those without work, but for a time many Toledoans were at the edge of starvation. An increase in WPA employment and a dramatic rise in industrial production that fall, stimulated by the outbreak of war in Europe, saved the city from disaster.

SETTLING THE WORKINGMAN'S DISPUTES

Through much of the Depression, Toledo experienced labor unrest that at times immobilized the city. The most serious episode occurred after April 13, 1934, when workers at the Electric Auto-Lite Company walked off their jobs for the second time that spring. The company brought in strikebreakers. For several days, there were violent confrontations among strikebreakers, company guards, picketers and city police.

On May 18, Auto-Lite management shut down the company, and during that week the city's unions prepared for a general strike. On May 24, President Franklin D.

Roosevelt sent a special mediator, Charles P. Taft, to Toledo. Governor George White called up the National Guard which marched into Toledo on the same day. Violence peaked at the plant. Tear-gas bombs were hurled into the crowds, and strikers threw them back at the troops. Workers stormed the plant causing $150,000 damage. The National Guard fired into the crowd, killing one man before the mob was dispersed.

As matters quieted slightly during the following days, one-third of the guardsmen were withdrawn on May 31. This gesture facilitated a settlement. Two days later, the city's unions called off their threat of a general strike, and on June 5 the plant reopened. Among other benefits, the local Electric Auto-Lite union gained company recognition and a five percent wage increase.

Between 1934 and 1935, Toledo experienced 32 strikes involving 13,181 workers. In April 1935, a strike at the Toledo Transmission Plant of the Chevrolet Motor Company immobilized the giant manufacturer. The settlement the next month provided the model for later agreements with unions in the auto industry.

Because of the continual strikes, Toledo leaders sought some method of settling industrial disputes peacefully. Edward F. McGrady, a federal negotiator, offered a proposal for a peace panel composed of industrialists, union leaders and citizens to investigate labor disputes and provide mediation. On July 15, 1935, the "Toledo Plan" for industrial peace was inaugurated with funding from the Department of Labor. During the next eight years, the board helped settle 379 disputes involving 59,425 people. The program became a model copied by other cities across the nation. After World War II, the board emerged with a new title—the Labor-Management Citizens' Committee. (It has continued to be an effective agency to the present day.)

The New Deal programs involving the cities had a number of unfortunate long-term effects. In the light of these, the positive contributions to the amenities of urban

143

High unemployment, cuts in wages and new federal laws prompted unions to organize collectively. Strikers picket the Cannon Cleaners (above and below) in September 1936; a Communist party circular advocated a general strike in support of Auto-Lite workers (right).

The Communist Party of Toledo calls a

MASS MEETING

Roi Davis Auditorium (cor. Jefferson and Michigan)

Thursday, May 31st, — 7:30 P.M. [1934]

TO DISCUSS THE

Auto-Lite Strike

THE NEED FOR A

GENERAL STRIKE

AND THE

Danger Of a Sell-Out

The finest courage ever shown by men and women has already brought victory within the reach of the Auto-Lite workers. In the fumes of tear gas and the new deadly KOCS and DM gas, over the bodies of their murdered brothers, the Mass Picket Line has held firm and has ABSOLUTELY CLOSED DOWN THE PLANT.

Up to the beginning of this week the Auto-Lite strike has been the most outstanding triumph of strike action in closing down a scab plant in 15 years of American Labor history.

The Auto-Lite workers have not been without support. The many thousands of Unemployed in Toledo have NOT scabbed, but have been mobilized by the Unemployed Council to help on the picket line. This is an example for the whole country.

The TRADE UNIONS have voted by overwhelming majority to support the struggle with a GENERAL STRIKE. This splendid resolution, if carried out, would mean an unparalleled triumph for Toledo Labor.

Sixty-Eight Trade Unions out of 103 affiliated to the C. L. U. HAVE VOTED FOR THE GENERAL STRIKE.

But no General Strike.

Why?

Just at the time when an immediate General Strike could bring an overwhelming victory, we have "postponement" of the General Strike and, instead of the expressed desire of the trade unionists being carried out, we have a whole series of maneuvers and offers of "ARBITRATION" which can only mean surrender of the victory already within our grasp. The "offers" of the millionaire capitalist Chas. P. Taft are only offers to break the strike and to turn over all questions of Wages, Conditions, etc., to an "Arbitration" board—which means to Miniger and his friends.

"Arbitration" and "Postponement" of the General Strike are swindles intended only to snatch a victory—already won up to this time—out of the hands of the workers.

What are the Labor Officials doing behind the doors of the Commodore Perry Hotel? The Bosses KNOW EVERYTHING THAT IS BEING SAID AND DONE BEHIND THOSE DOORS! WHY CAN'T THE WORKERS KNOW?

The workers in every Shop and Local Union must take action themselves. Call the General Strike NOW. Elect rank and file committees in every Local Union and Shop. A General Strike Committee should be elected from the shops, with a decisive majority of workers on it that will energetically carry out the wishes of the workers. The local strike committee should immediately formulate DEMANDS FOR EACH SHOP AND TRADE in addition to supporting the demands of the Auto-Lite workers and for withdrawal of the National Guard. The General Strike must involve all workers and their organizations. Only the unity of employed and unemployed—of white and Negro workers—will carry thru this great battle to victory.

The Main Speech will be made by a member of the Central Committee of the Communist Party.

ROBERT MINOR

Other speakers will include:

John Williamson—State Organizer of the Communist Party.

I. O. Ford—Communist Candidate for Governor of Ohio.

Jim Wilson—Toledo Negro Leader.

K. Eggart—Local Communist Organizer.

Dorothy Cheyfitz—Young Communist League.

Re-establish the Mass Picket Line Thursday Morning!

Immediate General Strike Must Be Called.

National Guard Must Be Withdrawn!

Direct Negotiations—with the Open Knowledge of the Workers.

No Arbitration!

Settlement Only After National Guard Is Withdrawn!

Sheriff Krieger Must Be Removed!

Win the Wage Increase!

COMMUNIST PARTY OF TOLEDO **137½ North Erie Street**

Tear gas canisters explode at the bitter Auto-Lite strike in May 1934; the strike was settled after the National Guard was withdrawn (inset).

147

Toledo acquired its best example of Art Deco design with the WPA-built public library (left) in 1939; one-of-a-kind glass murals decorate the lobby (right) and children's department.

life are often forgotten. One of the last New Deal projects in Toledo, the Public Library constructed between 1939 and 1940, supplies a striking case in point. The building provides one of the best examples of modernistic Art Deco design found in Ohio. Toledo architect Alfred A. Hayes designed the building with an extensive use of glass, reflecting the key industry of the city. The famous glass murals made by the Libbey-Owens-Ford Company are located in the central court and in the children's room. They are glass mosaics inlaid in large slabs of vitrolite, a colored glass. This priceless art treasure, so appropriately symbolic of the city, could not be duplicated today.

GANGSTER'S INTERLUDE

During the era of Prohibition from 1920 to 1933, American gangsters, like sporting heroes, became national celebrities. Newspapers sensationalized the gang wars and other crimes of the big cities. On February 7, 1921, Joe Urbaytis and his gang of five men robbed the Toledo post office of $1.6 million. It was one of the early spectacular crimes of the roaring '20s. But Toledo's most infamous episode of gangland violence occurred in the early years of the Depression.

Toledo's proximity to Detroit, Chicago and Canada made it an ideal location for rumrunners. Bootlegging, gambling, speakeasies and prostitution flourished openly.

Thomas "Yonnie" Licavoli, an enterprising gangster with organizational ability, was a member of one of the two main gangs in Detroit. He visited Toledo several times in the 1920s, possibly trying to extend the gang's influence. In 1927, at the height of his bootlegging career, Licavoli was arrested for running whiskey between Detroit and Canada. After serving a two-and-a-half-year prison sentence, he moved to Toledo, bringing with him his brother, Pete, and his cousin, Jimmy. Other gang members came with Licavoli, and two Toledoans, Jacob "Firetop" Sulkin and Joseph English, were recruited.

The Licavoli gang harassed and bombed breweries in its campaign to dominate the illegal beer business in Toledo. "Chalky Red" Yaranowsky operated a small distillery and brewery which the Licavoli gang decided to take over. When Yaranowsky refused to surrender control of his business, his brewery was blown up and his home riddled with bullets.

In the latter part of 1931, the Licavoli organization decided to take over the numbers racket in Toledo. On October 6, gamblers Abe Lubitsky, Norman Blatt, Hyman Adams and one unidentified man drove down Franklin Avenue and stopped at a light. A black sedan approached and sprayed bullets into the car. Lubitsky was found dead at the wheel. Other gamblers met a similar fate, but Toledo police made no arrests. As a result of this terrorism, a Licavoli lieutenant was able to install bookkeepers in the local numbers organization and funnel a substantial share of the take to the gang.

The Licavoli gang also decided that dry cleaners needed mob protection. Christopher Engel refused to be intimidated, and one evening in October 1932, his dry-cleaning establishment on West Bancroft Street near Upton Avenue exploded.

Jackie Kennedy, an extravagant spender with considerable charm, stood in the way of the Licavoli gang's control of the liquor business in Toledo. Kennedy operated the Studio Club, a popular St. Clair Street night spot. He defied the Licavoli gang by underselling beer and refusing to pay tribute.

Licavoli opened his own nightclub called the Golden Rose on Edgewater Drive. However, business slumped after Toledo police, led by Captain George Timiney, began coming regularly to the place.

Fearing for his life, Kennedy hired bodyguards and began practicing with a machine gun. On the night of November 30, 1932, Kennedy and his girl friend, Louise Bell, went to the Paramount Theater. Returning to the club, they were met by a hail of bullets at the corner of Superior and Jackson streets. Miss Bell died a few hours later.

*T*he Roaring '20s and the Depression years of the 1930s brought changes in attitudes toward law and law enforcement. Prohibition took effect locally in 1920. For many Americans, the "drys" were the enemy, and the criminal who defied the law received recognition, especially in the sensational news stories of the yellow press. In this environment, the well-groomed and personable Joe Urbaytis gained notoriety for a robbery and subsequent escape from jail. Bootleggers Yonnie Licavoli and Jackie Kennedy also gained local fame.

In the early morning hours of February 17, 1921, Joe Urbaytis and his gang of five set a crime record for mail holdups by robbing the main post office of an estimated $1.6 million. The gang had planned the robbery for the previous evening, but they failed to start the high-powered Marmon car they were trying to steal. Instead, they settled for a Studebaker, but it was too late to complete the robbery that evening. This failure to obtain a getaway car made the robbery look well planned. By a stroke of luck, the government sent $30,000 in new currency and $900,000 in liberty bonds to the post office on the mail truck the following day.

The robbery went off without a hitch. Ten mail sacks were grabbed as the mail truck pulled into the main post office at Madison Avenue and Thirteenth Street after which the gang split up. Four days later, Joe Urbaytis was captured on a train heading for Chicago.

On Labor Day 1921, Joe Urbaytis and two colleagues escaped from the Lucas County Jail. Joe and Frank Urbaytis were captured on May 5, 1924, after a shootout with Columbus detectives. Although critically wounded, Urbaytis recovered and was sentenced to 274 years in prison. He again attempted to escape and was sent to Alcatraz where he became a model prisoner. He was freed on February 13, 1943.

Urbaytis came home and became a partner in the Bon-Aire Supper Club where he was murdered on November 5, 1946. Even as he lay dying, he refused to name the murderer.

During the 1920s and early 1930s, Toledo —along with the rest of the nation —observed Prohibition. Speakeasies emerged and local stills began to produce alcoholic beverages for thirsty citizens. Rival factions fought for the control of the bootlegging business. After several gang-style murders, the town was in a uproar. Thirteen members of the Licavoli gang were convicted of conspiracy to commit murder in the death of Toledo bootlegger, Jackie Kennedy.

Gang leader Joseph Urbaytis (above) and his gang of five set a crime record in 1921 with a post office robbery; Urbaytis and George L. Rogers (right) are featured in 1921 wanted posters.

Joseph Urbaytis,
aliases: Joseph Urbaitis, Joseph Urbytis.
BERTILLON: 79.2; 82.0; 96.8; 18.5; 16.0; 65; 26.5; 11.6; 9.2; 48.5.
FINGER PRINT CLASSIFICATION:
25 0 II
19 1
I Vert. cic. of 2.5 on 1st Jt. left little fgr.
1 Irreg. cic. on 3rd pha. left index fgr.
Age 21; height 5 feet, 10½ inches; weight 154; complexion fair; slender build; dark chestnut hair.

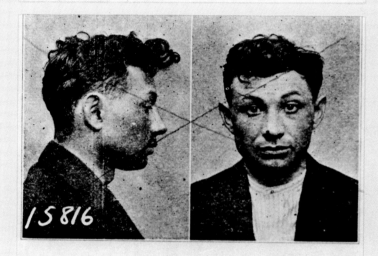

George L. Rogers,
aliases: George Lewis, George Harris, Joe Morris, Mike Cuttacaper, "Spaniard."
BERTILLON: 69.3; 80.0; —.–; 18.9; 15.7; 6.4; 25.8; 11.4; 9.2; 47.0.
FINGER PRINT CLASSIFICATION:
9 Roo   o
31 I
I end first fgr. rt. hand mashed.
Age 32; height 5 feet, 6¾ inches; weight 140; complexion dark; eyes maroon.

149

MURDER TRIAL: Jacob "Firetop" Sulkin (above) was one of thirteen members of the Licavoli gang convicted in 1934 for the murder of Jackie Kennedy; gang leader Lonnie Licavoli (far left); Frazier Reams, the prosecuting attorney (left), headed the investigation.

The local press made Jackie Kennedy into a hero. The public demanded the arrest of the Licavoli gang. They had already elected as prosecuting attorney a bright young lawyer named Frazier Reams, who had vowed to clean up the city. On December 8, 1932, Licavoli and several of his gang were indicted on violations of the federal Prohibition laws. Licavoli was found guilty on May 10, 1933, but the Prohibition laws were repealed that year, and he never had to serve the sentence.

On July 7, 1933, Kennedy strolled along Edgewater Drive with Toledo beauty queen, Audrey Rauls. A slow-moving maroon sedan pulled up behind the couple and two men jumped out. One man grabbed Audrey Rauls and flung her to the side of the road while the other fired at the back of Kennedy's head. Fourteen bullets sent Kennedy sprawling to the street. It was the most sensational gangster murder in the city's history and marked the beginning of the downfall of the Licavoli gang.

Frazier Reams worked diligently on the investigation, but few clues emerged. The break in the case came when two guns—which the killers had apparently tried to throw into the lake—were found near the Point Place shoreline. One gun was traced to a Monroe Street pawnshop and later the pawnbroker admitted selling the gun to "Firetop" Sulkin, a member of the Licavoli gang. Sulkin was indicted for first-degree murder; Licavoli and twelve other members of the gang were charged with first-degree murder and conspiracy. It was one of the first times the two crimes were successfully linked in a criminal prosecution and the month-long trial received extensive national publicity. Yonnie Licavoli and the rest of the gang were convicted and given varying sentences. Licavoli spent 37 years in prison. Toledo's reign of racketeering terror had come to an end.

Kennedy's car was shot up in November 1932.

Jackie Kennedy lost his life in a battle over control of local bootlegging in the 1930s.

CHAPTER SIX

Toledoans remember streetcars, ice-cream sodas and 25-cent matinees along a very busy St. Clair Street in 1943.

PROSPERITY AND TROUBLES

153

The economy of Toledo, with all its varied manufacturing enterprises, was particularly well-suited to the needs of war. As the United States began to arm European powers and itself in 1940, recovery from the Depression was rapid. By April 1941, the number of people on WPA rolls had dropped to 4,000. As Americans built armies and went to war after Pearl Harbor, Toledo experienced a continual shortage of labor. Women moved into Toledo's factories for the first time—and in large numbers. The Lucas County Selective Service Board operated from October 1940 until March 30, 1947, when Uyless Williams raced to Board Number 8 and registered five minutes before the board closed its doors. During that time, it had sent 42,200 men to war. Unemployment seemed a thing of the past.

Between Pearl Harbor and June 1, 1945, Toledo factories produced over $3 billion in war equipment and supplies. Willys-Overland was one of the larger producers of war material in the country. It turned out over 300,000 of its famous Jeeps and a variety of other products, including four million high-explosive shells, over a billion small-caliber bullets and 3,000 wing sections for the Navy's Corsair fighter planes. Electric Auto-Lite produced gyro stabilizers, Libbey-Owens-Ford built nose assemblies for almost every type of aircraft, DeVilbiss made smoke generators to protect troops and Toledo Scale constructed wind tunnels. Parts of that ultimate weapon of war, the atomic bomb, came from Baker Brothers and Electric Auto-Lite.

The corporate headquarters building (below) for the Willys-Overland Company in the 1940s; Toledo's greatest contribution to the WWII effort was the jeep (right). About 300,000 of them rolled off the assembly line during the war years.

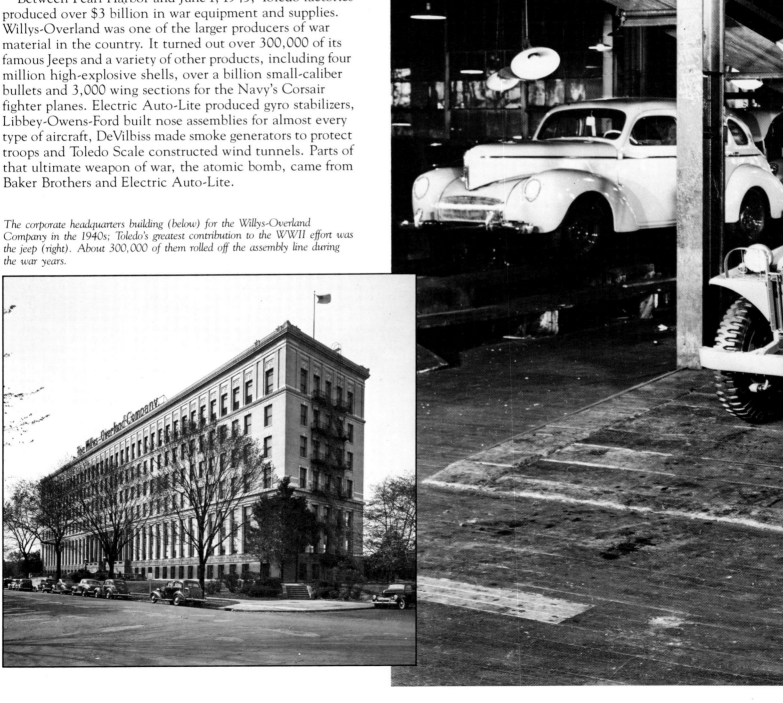

TOLEDO TOMORROW

On July 29 and August 9, 1945, the atom bomb brought the war to an unexpectedly quick end. Americans experienced a period of euphoria and optimism about the future. Depression forgotten, Toledo was again a place of faith in the "future great city of the world." It had already produced one of the first and, by all odds, the most exuberant visions of the brave new urban order. On July 4, 1945, a spectacular exhibit called "Toledo Tomorrow" opened in the auditorium of the Toledo Zoo's Natural History Museum. On display was a scale model 61 feet in diameter—reported at the time to have cost $150,000 and many years later raised to $250,000—of how the city should look in 1995. The exhibit would have warmed the heart and fired the pen of Jesup Scott.

As with so many grandiose Toledo plans of the nineteenth and twentieth centuries, "Toledo Tomorrow" was the work of the *Toledo Blade.* The year before, the paper's publisher, Paul R. Block Jr., had commissioned the

Women flocked to the factories as the men went off to war. Ladies riveted aircraft parts for the Willys-Overland Company in 1943.

famous New York designer Norman Bel Geddes to prepare the model. Bel Geddes was born in nearby Adrian, Michigan, but from time to time, he claimed to be from Toledo. He had become famous for his streamlined style of design in the 1930s. Early in the decade, he had prepared such a plan for the expansion of the Toledo Scale factory. His "Toledo Tomorrow"—constructed with the assistance of the aviation expert Major Alexander de Seversky and the architect Geoffrey Lawford—reflected the futuristic city of technology that had been a main emphasis of the two world's fairs of the 1930s and especially of Bel Geddes' popular "Futurama" at the New York World's Fair of 1939.

"Toledo Tomorrow" showed a city of superhighways, industrial parks, blocks of high-rise modernistic buildings, open green spaces and self-contained residential communities built along curving streets. Its main feature, within walking distance of downtown, was a grand Union Terminal—a large airport that contained underground railroad and bus facilities.

As part of the general interest in America's postwar future, "Toledo Tomorrow" attracted widespread national and some foreign attention. *Life,* the popular pictorial magazine, presented an extensive photographic essay on "Future Toledo...A Prophetic Look at the Wonderful City They Could Have in Fifty Years." Eleanor Roosevelt in her national column predicted that the "kind of foresight shown in 'Toledo Tomorrow'" would inspire other cities. But as the realities of the problems of urban growth after the war intruded, the plan was forgotten, and even the model disappeared somewhere between 1955 and 1966. Toledo got a new Union Station in 1956, but it was only a traditional railroad facility. By the time it was finished, passenger traffic on railroads had begun to disappear, and the station was deserted much of the time.

Many years later, Block asserted that he had intended the plan as a "stunt," an effort to provide "a shot in the arm" to postwar civic efforts. It perhaps served that purpose. The Toledo-Lucas County Plan Commission (which combined the city and county agencies in 1947) and other civic groups—especially the Chamber of Commerce—moved to carry out uncompleted provisions of the prewar Bartholomew Plan. As early as 1945, a reporter surveying planning efforts around the country found Toledo to be the "most planning conscious city in Ohio, perhaps in the nation...but it has a long way to go toward any of its dreams."

In the next two decades, the Toledo planning movement produced a number of positive accomplishments that improved the economic welfare and quality of life in Toledo. Toledo was the first city in Ohio (and the second in the country) to pass a payroll income tax. Only Philadelphia among cities above 50,000 had passed such a measure in the prewar period. The new tax permitted expanded services in the years of rapid growth after the war, including three new fire stations, the purchase of parklands and the beginning of an airport.

In 1955, the Toledo-Lucas County Port Authority was established to take advantage of the opportunities created by the building of the St. Lawrence Seaway, one of Jesup Scott's nineteenth-century dreams. One of two large new cranes named "Big Lucas" became a lesser city symbol.

A Kroger truck loaded with rationed sugar (above) must have caught a few eyes as it stopped in the 2000 block of Adams Street in 1942; V-J Day on August 15, 1945, at the intersection of Jefferson Avenue and Ontario (below).

WAR PRODUCTION BOOMS: *Toledo was a major coal shipper in the 1940s (top); Owens-Illinois quality control inspectors (center) around 1940; Spicer Manufacturing (forerunner of Dana Corporation) machinist watches production in 1944 (above).*

Other improvements permitted the port to handle the very largest cargoes. By the late 1970s, Toledo had the fourth largest total port tonnage on the lakes, only behind Chicago, Duluth and Detroit. It had also become the largest foreign export-import port on the lakes.

Industrial parks began in 1964 with the conversion of the Rossford Army Depot by the Willis Day Warehousing Company. The parks were another innovation that encouraged expansion of production and employment. The next year, eight plants located in Fort Industry Industrial Park in the northern part of Toledo. By 1968 there were seven such industrial parks with more than 100 companies employing over 6,000 people.

The planning effort that most substantially improved the quality of life was the extension of the metropolitan park system started during the WPA era. Swan Creek Metropark was developed between 1963 and 1968 in the southwest section of the city. A special levy passed by the county in 1974 permitted the opening of Wildwood Preserve to the north of Ottawa Hills.

The most distinctive innovation was the adoption in 1957 of a charter amendment that allowed new areas being annexed to retain their own school districts. In the next years, the city annexed much of the area northward and westward to the Michigan state line and southward to the city of Maumee. This annexation policy tended to prevent Toledo's being ringed by independent (and sometimes hostile) suburban municipalities which used city facilities but did not pay their share of the costs—a problem which occurred in many midwestern and northeastern cities.

From 1957 to 1979, the land area of Toledo grew from 43 to over 85 square miles. It became the second largest city in Ohio in land area. Between 1960 and 1970, Toledo added 85,020 residents through annexation. Only Memphis and Tulsa surpassed this kind of gain in population. Toledo's annexations greatly expanded the city's tax base through the income tax on residents in the new areas and through property taxes on extensive decentralized commercial and industrial developments.

These changes contributed to Toledo's economic welfare during the long period of prosperity that followed the war. By 1974 only Akron among the six largest Ohio cities had a higher per-capita income than Toledo. Among twelve nationally representative large manufacturing cities surveyed in 1967 and 1972, only Detroit had a higher average of weekly earnings from manufacturing. As a result of significant general diversification in manufacturing, Toledo was less dependent on the automobile industry in the 1970s than in earlier decades. In addition, the city's economy had shifted slightly away from manufacturing to commercial and service activities. Among large Ohio cities, only Columbus—the seat of state government—was less dependent on manufacturing.

The climax of this period of growth and the culmination of the early postwar planning movement was the reconstruction of about 12.5 acres of downtown bounded by Madison and Jefferson avenues, St. Clair Street and the Maumee. This urban renewal project called Riverview I cleared the area of over twenty buildings including such landmarks as the old Federal Building. A spectacular 30-story skyscraper, the Owens-Corning Fiberglas Tower, was completed in 1969, and several other buildings— Toledo Edison, Ohio Citizens, a new Federal Building and the Holiday Inn—were constructed in the area. Levis Square Park provided an attractive open space in the district for downtown workers.

Evening view of the 700 block of Madison Avenue around 1945; the last streetcar heads down Summit Street on December 31, 1949 (inset).

159

SUPPLYING THE ENERGY: The Acme Power Plant (above) in the 1940s; the 308-foot catalytic cracking tower at Sun Oil (inset), completed in 1950, was one of the tallest industrial structures in the world.

THE SUBURB GROWS OUT AND UP

By 1970 as Riverview I neared completion, Toledo had already entered a time of troubles that was to continue into the 1980s.

Toledo had begun to experience the flight of people from city to suburb, the decline in downtown business and inner city decay. All had roots in the early planning movement. During the prewar period, Toledo was one of the first Ohio cities to project expressways. It completed its system of 34 miles in 1972. The city had experienced extreme congestion in the 1950s, and the expressways greatly facilitated movement on the New York-Chicago auto and traffic corridor. But expressways removed a great deal of property from city tax rolls. Their construction required the acquisition of 4,500 parcels of real estate containing about 4,000 buildings; the process involved the equivalent of relocating a city of 25,000.

Long before the expressways were completed, they had greatly intensified suburbanization. During the period, the suburbs that grew around Toledo reflected a wide-ranging diversity. Maumee grew from 5,548 in 1950 to 15,747 by 1970. Perrysburg—less directly affected by expressways

—grew from 3,989 to 7,693. Like the Old West End in the nineteenth century or Ottawa Hills between the world wars, these two old river towns (particularly Perrysburg) became the fashionable places for the rich to live. New mansions and large estates began to line both sides of the river. Despite rapid growth, both communities successfully preserved and restored old Greek Revival homes and buildings. (Because of this strong commitment to their history, Maumee and Perrysburg today recapture some of the spirit of flush times in the early Maumee Valley.)

The old rural town of Sylvania was originally about ten miles northwest of Toledo. Founded in 1835, it became the nucleus of a substantial city within the Toledo metropolis. The city of Sylvania grew from 2,199 in 1950 to 15,527 in 1980; by then it and the surrounding urbanized Sylvania Township had reached a population of 33,061. Because of its size, the Sylvania area demonstrated some of the range of wealth and poverty of the city itself, including a slum-like section called Dogpatch. On a lesser scale, Sylvania confronted problems in schools and services comparable to those of Toledo in the 1970s.

Oregon, incorporated as a city in 1959, sprawled eastward from East Toledo across the completely flat land of the old Black Swamp. Between 1960 and 1980, its population

GLASS AND GRAIN: Mid-States grain elevators (left) loading cargo for the markets of the world; Glass Capital skyline at twilight (bottom left); new world headquarters for Owen-Illinois at SeaGate Center (below top); soaring glass facade of the Toledo Edison Building (below bottom).

161

GLASS CRAFTSMEN: A master craftsman
(left) for the Libbey Glass Division of the
Owens-Illinois Corporation shapes molten glass,
around 1950; a Libbey glass worker (above)
polishes a world-famous product.

increased from 13,319 to 18,675. With its gridiron reaching outward and its miles of substantial but similar houses, Oregon seemed most clearly to fulfill the traditional concept of the homogeneous, middle-class residential suburb. By 1970 some more distant places from the metropolis had begun to grow rapidly. The town of Waterville was about four miles upriver from the southern edge of Maumee. Between 1960 and 1970, Waterville had grown from 1,856 to 2,940—a 58 percent increase. By 1980 its population stood at 3,885. ·

Only Toledo's annexations kept its population from declining between 1960 and 1970 when it registered a census gain from 318,003 to 383,818. The area of the city existing in 1960 actually decreased in population by 26,639 or 8.4 percent. During the next decade, Toledo lost population, along with all cities of over 100,000 in the Northeast and all but seven of the 38 cities of that size in the North Central census districts. As the city's population shrank from 383,818 to 344,182, extensive areas of unoccupied and decaying housing were left in portions of the inner city.

Although financial and corporate activities still concentrated in the new towers of downtown, the retailing and recreational activities of the central business district were radically decentralized in this era of suburbanization. Toledo's central symbol of the 1970s became the large roofed-over shopping center. (In Toledo as elsewhere, it is always called a "mall," probably a deliberate misusage by early developers attempting to invoke favorable images from other urban times. "Let's go to the mall and hang out"

became a rallying cry of youth, and "hanging out" became a recreational activity of the old as well. In the process, many Toledoans forgot what a mall really was.)

The first of these enclosed malls—Woodville—opened outside East Toledo in 1969. At the time, it was the largest shopping center in Ohio. In 1971, the second—Franklin Park—opened in the northwest part of the city on the site of an early airport. The same year, the last important structure, the Edison Building, was completed in the downtown Riverview I project. At the time, Franklin Park contained three large department stores—including one dating back to the nineteenth century in downtown Toledo, Lamson Brothers—and 75 smaller shops. By 1980, the automobile had created more than 40 shopping centers throughout the area. The Colony was the first, built in 1940 on Central Avenue near Monroe. It had itself begun to look like a downtown commercial block with several stores boarded over by the '80s.

As shopping centers grew, business downtown declined drastically. Retail sales fell nearly 35 percent from 1958 to 1972. In 1958, downtown sales represented over 40 percent of the metropolitan sales; by 1972 the percentage had fallen to ten. Only Cleveland, among fifteen comparable large cities, approached Toledo's downtown percentage of losses in sales of general merchandise. Although many of the new commercial facilities were within the city and hence a part of the tax base, the necessity of expanding services—particularly streets, sewerage and drainage—taxed city resources and especially intensified the flooding that had

Toledoans braved the cold for the 1954 dedication of the Toledo Express Airport.

always been one of Toledo's problems. During this time, restaurants, motion pictures, department stores and dozens of small shops closed or left for the shopping centers and the ribbons of commercial development along major streets toward Oregon, Sylvania, new areas of southwest Toledo and the southwest suburbs.

Toledo even obtained a suburban civic center, privately built by the Masonic Lodge in the rapidly growing southwest section generally called the Heatherdowns area. Opened in 1969, the Masonic Temple provided a Great Hall for meetings and an excellent Civic Auditorium which became the site for performances of touring theater companies and other entertainers.

The fall of 1971—the year of the Edison Building and Franklin Park—provided two events which mark the passing of downtown Toledo and downtown America as it had existed from the late 1800s. Rose La Rose, one of the most famous striptease performers of the 1940s and early '50s, had bought the Town Hall Theater in 1958. She had attempted to keep the dying urban art form of burlesque alive in the city. But the Town Hall was swept under by the Vistula Meadows renewal project in 1963, and after successfully fighting a city ordinance banning burlesque, La Rose moved south to the Esquire Theater. Sometime in October, the last traditional live burlesque performance in the city took place there. Rose La Rose, who had become a local celebrity and a patron of civic projects, died the next summer at the age of 53.

On November 4, 1971, Smith's Cafeteria, which for 35

years at Grace E. Smith's second restaurant site had been one of the most popular eating places in the city, served its last meal downtown. A version of the restaurant, located in a shopping center and part of a chain, lasted a few years longer.

TIME OF TROUBLE

Metropolitan growth and suburbanization in Toledo reflected developments in cities throughout America after the war. Toledo shared its problems with other cities—radical and racial unrest in the late 1960s, recessions and depressions in the next decade, inflation, crises in the automobile industry and the rise of the cities of the Sun Belt. But Toledo's experience in its time of troubles was distinctive. As in the Great Depression, national attention focused on the city.

It began with the black uprisings of the late 1960s. Toledo had a relatively small but growing black population. In 1970 the city was less than fourteen percent black—the smallest percentage of any large city in Ohio and less than half the percentage of Cleveland or Cincinnati. The black population of Toledo, however, was concentrated in one section with some census tracts nearly 97 percent black, and its black community confronted the same problems that set off rioting in the nation's major black ghettos.

In July 1967, there were two days of violence. Arson,

163

BEAUTY OF LINE: Civic Mall sculpture (near right) offers a new vista from every angle; Rosary Cathedral, an awesome Old-World sculpture in stone (far right); the classic grace of the Toledo Museum of Art (below).

164

165

ER LOOK: The sweep of an
(page) at the Ohio Building;
se from above) glass panels
*Lake Erie Center; graceful
25 Jefferson; intricate frieze
the Courthouse; Playdium
eater features ornate detail.*

STREETS COME AND GO: Construction on Interstate 75 near Bancroft Street in 1969;
Erie Street (below), in 1948, between Orange and Cherry streets, was removed during
downtown urban renewal—much needed by the 1940s.

SERVING THE SHOPPERS: *Colony Shopping Center (top right) at Central and Monroe was the city's first; the 400 block of Adams Street (bottom right) was closed to traffic in the summer of 1959 to encourage shoppers; Northtown Mall construction (above) in 1979.*

looting and brick-throwing in the Dorr-Detroit and Franklin-Bancroft areas caused over a half-million dollars in property damage and resulted in 179 arrests. In September, during another summer of violence in the cities, a black riot along Dorr Street resulted in 22 injuries and 50 arrests. Compared to other cities such as Newark, Detroit and Milwaukee, these were mild episodes in those years of violence.

In the spring of 1970, many black radicals came from other cities as part of a national black movement to change education in America. They joined students and faculty to close the University of Toledo. During this emergency, the university met their list of demands for special black educational programs. The last battle in Toledo during this period of racial unrest occurred on September 17, 1970. A policeman was killed as he sat in a patrol car, and a gunfight between police and Black Panthers outside the Panthers' Dorr Street headquarters followed.

In the 1970s, Toledo—a city with perhaps the strongest union tradition in America—became the site of bitter labor struggles as it had in the '30s. This time it involved public employees. In 1968 the American Federation of Teachers won the right to represent teachers in the Toledo public schools. Serious financial difficulties developed after the recession of 1974, and in December 1976 the Toledo public

schools became the first large city system to close down because of lack of funds. The shutdown lasted about a month.

When wage negotiations with the Toledo AFT chapter broke down in the spring of 1978, the teachers union launched an illegal strike on April 10 that lasted 22 days. The national television networks focused on Toledo as union militants and their supporters harassed and physically attacked teachers attempting to stay on the job and vandalized their automobiles and homes. The city police—heavily committed to the militant municipal labor movement—did little to protect teachers and their property. Only a secretive and guarded transportation system organized by some school administrators not in sympathy with the militant union effort kept the schools open until the strike was settled—without penalty to strikers or their union.

The municipal unions wielded great power in the city administration during the long years of domination by the Democratic Party. Beginning in the late 1960s, they won a series of lucrative wage contracts. As inflation accelerated in the 1970s, the unrestricted cost-of-living clauses included in these contracts put heavy pressure on available city funds.

When negotiations over new contracts with several city

167

OUTDOOR DIVERSION: *Toledoans go to the zoo (top); spend a pensive moment at the German Festival (center); visit the Farmers Market.*

THE CHILDREN: *Greek Festival dancers (top); riding the Waterfront Railway (center); you've got to stop and smell the tulips (bottom).*

TWO IS COMPANY: *time out for a stroll (top); a tête-à-tête in the park (center); Greek souvlaki chefs (bottom) cook it up right.*

Toledo's black community confronted the same problems in the late 1960s that set off rioting in the nation's other large cities.

municipal unions—including those of firemen and police—broke down in June 1979, they launched a two-day general strike unprecedented in the history of American cities. Again Toledo presented frightening images to the nation and demonstrated the fragility of the web of urban society in twentieth-century America. Scores of locked police vehicles were abandoned at the Safety Building with flashers turning in a day-and-night kaleidoscope of red. Citizens were forced to try to extinguish fires with garden hoses as their houses burned.

Toledo experienced its night of urban terror on July 2, probably the blackest day in its history. Only a few fire and police officers and administrators remained on the job. Gangs of vandals roamed the streets setting fires and throwing rocks and bricks. Fifteen buildings burned in just a single block. A landmark—part of the former Plaza Hotel under construction as an apartment building—was bombed and destroyed by union members opposed to work practices at the site. Settlements with three city unions the next day and a stringent injunction ordering firemen and policemen back to work restored order. The extent of the damage caused by the illegal strike was never fully assessed nor reported.

Settlements did not alleviate the problems. Unemployment rose steadily, reaching over twelve percent in 1982. Financial constraints necessitated widespread layoffs of city employees. The voters' rejection of an increase in the city income tax in June 1981 contributed to a drastic curtailment of many services.

Despite the worsening economy, after the 1979 crises there seemed to be a revival of civic spirit—a rallying in time of trouble. Later negotiations with both municipal and teachers unions proceeded much more amicably and reasonably than in the past. Although local disillusionment with the public schools was widespread, thousands of citizens seemed to be saying let the bitter bygones of the strike be bygones. They organized to obtain an essential increase of the schools' operating levy. After one major failure, it passed in 1980 at a time when the city's economy was rapidly deteriorating.

At a time when the economy had worsened even more, Toledo voters, with the support of most organizations in the city, approved in June 1982 a substantial addition to the city income tax.

Over the 1980 Labor Day holiday Toledofest opened. A surprisingly well done and successful festival of arts, it brought thousands to downtown. Those who came saw a downtown and its immediate neighborhoods once again undergoing dramatic reconstruction.

LAUNCHING A NEW ERA

On a pleasant, sunny spring day in May 1979, over 10,000 people watched the ground-breaking for a new world headquarters of Owens-Illinois at a site called SeaGate Center. The organizers invoked the spirit of early promotional days on the Maumee and established a new world's record for the number of groundbreakers. Arthur Young & Co. counted 5,714 people who manned the ceremonial shovels, and the line to participate lasted from 11:40 a.m. to well after 2 p.m.

ARCHITECTURAL TREASURES: An interesting angle on the Boody House restaurant (top left); night view of the Masonic Auditorium (bottom left); the lower lobby scale (top) and clock (above) at Fort Industry Square renovation; halving the circle on a wing at the Medical College of Ohio at Toledo (full page right); another facet of Toledo's glass industry is the Owens-Corning Fiberglas Tower (inset left) and the beautiful glass-paned skylight at Franklin Park Mall (inset center); towering vertical detail on the Stranahan Building (inset right).

170

Childhood singing star Teresa Brewer began her singing career in the 1940s on local radio shows.

The Toledo Symphony Orchestra bass section digs in during a concert.

About 8,000 free hot dogs were eaten, and 6,192 soft drinks were sold. It was another grand and glorious celebration in Toledo's history.

The new building was the result of a master plan issued for the city in 1977. Unlike other plans of the century, this one was carried out quickly. The 32-story O-I headquarters—the city's tallest building—was completed in 1981. Toledo Trust moved into its new headquarters building near the SeaGate complex later in the year. A 22-story city-state office building on Erie Street was under construction. Promenade Park running southward from SeaGate was renovated and expanded. Streets had been widened in the area and traffic rerouted. A boulevard and a new public transit loop were a part of the project. The huge SeaGate renewal had shifted the entire center of downtown northward and had stimulated at least twelve major downtown building renovations.

Just to the north of SeaGate, the early fashionable Vistula neighborhood was being restored with the assistance of federal renewal funds.

To the south of SeaGate at the original site of Toledo, the restored Fort Industry Square—with offices, shops and a restaurant that took its name from the city's most famous early hotel—represented an effort to preserve some of Toledo's history at the place where it all began.

Dignitaries who participated in the O-I groundbreaking, as on all such occasions in the past, predicted that the magnificent project would launch a golden era in the city's history. Toledo was still Jesup W. Scott's future great city of the world. The mayor of the city predicted that Toledo would again be a city of neighborhoods that looked to downtown. Those aware of the history of a vital and dynamic American city hoped that the prophecy was true.

THE SPIRIT OF TOLEDO

At any season or time, the network of communication in America provides images of Toledo. The year 1981 was no exception. A New York advertising executive said that his clients would follow him anywhere—except to Toledo. A national columnist who wondered whether people could migrate from the North to jobs in Sun Belt cities wrote that there might even be people who liked living in Toledo. A national magazine that pioneered the sexual revolution satirized the Moral Majority movement of the period and placed the site of its Prayboy Club in Toledo. The villains of a motion picture about women's wrestling were a rough-and-tough team of two black women named the Toledo Tigers. A typical joke made the rounds: What do Toledoans do on Memorial Day? Lay a six-pack on the tomb of the unknown bowler.

Toledoans—unlike the sensitive spokesmen of Cleveland, Detroit or Terre Haute, Indiana—take all this in stride. It has been going on so long that it has almost become a fond part of the city's tradition. Even when satirists of Toledo perform in the city, they play to full and warmly enthusiastic houses.

As with all caricatures, there is accuracy in the view that Toledo is a tough, gritty, immigrant, manufacturing, down-to-earth town. Toledoans do work in factories and are proud of it. At almost any hour of the day, a visitor can (and should if he wants to sense Toledo) find a tavern to drink a shot of factory country's most popular blended whiskey and a glass of beer. He can see a man thrown through a barroom window as patrons only casually glance

The Federal Building, a landmark since 1888, is torn down in 1964 to make way for Levis Square.

173

A young clown prepares a new face for Toledo Festival.

174

ALPA RICHARDSON

*T*he old schoolhouse might have perished if it had not been for Alpa Richardson. She had taught several generations of Toledo's most influential families. When she retired, she remained active in the Maumee Valley Historical Society and maneuvered the restoration of the schoolbuilding which now stands behind Wolcott House. There, until her death in 1981 at the age of 93, she spent four days a week greeting visitors—with only a log fire and her dog Muffin for warmth and companionship. Her charming stories delighted all those who listened.

Dedicated in May 1982, Dimitri Hadzi's Propylaea *sculpture at SeaGate Center communicates the sense of optimism about the city of Toledo.*

up from their drinks, wander into the haunts of motorcycle gangs or join the call for the blood of the referee and opponents when the local professional hockey team plays. In sections of the city, an individual risks as high a chance of mugging as anywhere and, in others, faces certain assault for denouncing unions or telling Polish jokes. He has to know how to play euchre and can end up his declining years in a mom-and-pop bowling league.

However, the outside views of all American cities —Chicago, San Francisco, Houston, Gary, Indiana or Toledo—are slightly skewed. There is more than first meets the eye. Toledoans work in factories and stores, but they also run large corporations and inherit the wealth of the city's great industries. A person can doze with those of substance in evening dress in the splendor of a magnificent country club listening to America's best known conservative deliver an erudite after-dinner speech. He can watch a yachting regatta, eat the most lavish of cuisines and drink the best of wines in the mansions of the rich or examine one of the finest private libraries of American history in the Midwest. He can drink early morning Bloody Marys on the velvety lawns of the far southwest suburbs watching marathon runners make their tortured way past miles of luxurious estates at the height of late summer's

beauty. He can attend the symphony or the opera and the fashionable ball that supports them both, or see the elite emerge every few years as Toledo sponsors a national golf tournament. He can note the jewels that betoken great wealth as women play contract bridge on an afternoon in a setting that evokes the most grand and glorious days of Toledo wealth in the twentieth century.

As a result of past and present efforts of the Toledo aristocracy, a traveler does not enter the land of the Philistines when he crosses Toledo's borders. This may be the falsest of all the derogatory images of the city. Toledo has one of the country's best art museums, and two critics claim it is one of eight in the country that should not be missed. It presented one of the most significant exhibits of American art held during the bicentennial year. The city supports an excellent regional symphony. Toledo shares the benefits of a large and diverse university. Although the University of Toledo remains true to the Scott family tradition of providing utilitarian training to the children of workers, a determined citizen can see an obscure German impressionistic film, listen to a scholar talk about the more arcane aspects of twentieth-century imagist poetry or look at an imaginative exhibit of the designs and plans from his own city's past. The city has an excellent system of public libraries that are well-used and provide scholarly as well as practical information.

Toledoans often take advantage of the cultural facilities of nearby larger cities. Toledo is a minor-league town in sports partly because Toledoans can reach the major-league facilities of Detroit more easily than many in the Detroit metropolis. Early on fall Sunday mornings, caravans of Toledo revelers head northward to one of the new shrines of modern America—the football stadium.

Although midwestern cities are often called intolerant and narrow-minded, Toledo is not. All life-styles and fashions in sin and vice flourish, as they probably always have in the city. Ladies of the night may move from one section of downtown to another, but they are generally there anytime but Christmas. Anyone who wants to can find a bookmaker who will take bets in any amount. Gay bars of both persuasions, go-go joints, call girls in hotels, singles bars—anything in style Toledo usually acquires. In the 1970s the pornography business—shops and theaters—went out to the suburbs and into the shopping centers, along with everything else. Nobody seemed to mind a massage parlor next to a family restaurant. The spirit of openness that early visitors to the city encountered and found refreshing is still there.

In short, Toledo shares the diversity of big-city life in America today. But what is distinctive about it? It is impossible to say. No one can experience a city, for dwellers move only in its orbits. (Some lifetime West Siders take pride in never having made the crossing to East Toledo.) We react only to some of its symbols, and ultimately there is only one person's Toledo.

But insights are possible. First are the notable civic assets seen by the tourist—museum, zoo, metroparks, the Old West End. But there is more. On a clear day from the top of the High Level Bridge, the skyline evokes the power and glory of corporate America. There are ships and huge carriers of coal and ore, factories and sprawling grain and oil terminals. The port ties Toledo to the American farm and to the markets of the world. On the east side of the river, patterns of house and factory mingle. In East Toledo on a winter night, a huge refinery presents vivid, precisionist images of industrial America. Birmingham is still a cohesive turn-of-the-century ethnic neighborhood. Oregon, with its mile upon mile, row upon row of warmly lit houses, embodies the suburban dream.

ACROSS THE RIVER

The radials from the heart of the city indicate Toledo's diversity. Northeastward along river and bay to Point Place, suburban life is tied to the water. Northward along Cherry Street, splendid old areas have deteriorated. Northwestward to Sylvania, a ten-mile commercial strip is part of the merchants' city. Straight westward is black Toledo, and the attractively preserved old neighborhood of Westmoreland. From the university hills, new vistas sprawl out—cluttered sites of commerce, plants, shops, railroads, diverse housing and Toledo's academe. Southwestward are the varied neighborhoods of South Toledo, the luxury of Maumee and Perrysburg and their evocation of times past. The Farmers' Market is busy on Saturday morning, and so is the American Motors paint plant at afternoon shift change. Manufacturing goes on in the industrial parks and the spirit of the city is bustling at any mall before Christmas. On a cool morning in late May, before the heat-of-summer mists obscure the clarity of greens, the jewel-like suburb of Ottawa Hills strikingly represents the realization of the great American dream of wealth.

There is more to understand about Toledo. Most Toledoans live in single-family houses. The city is tied to the automobile, but it is surprisingly easy to get around. It does not take long to reach vast areas of farms and countryside. Toledo is a corporate and manufacturing city; but in a sense, it is also a very large farm town. There are extensive areas of ugly commercial activity and dismal commercial decay. Although housing is drab in parts of the city, it is not badly deteriorated. Space to live—the countryside, river and lake, all kinds of commercial and cultural facilities—are within easy reach. There are no slums or tenements. Perhaps Toledo *is* the "livable city" its spokesmen claim.

Other things begin to fall into place. Toledo is a metropolis with great concentrated wealth but with much less real poverty than in larger cities. It is a city of neighborhoods where great diversity and ethnic enclaves still persist. It is heavily suburbanized, but much of the suburbanization is in the city itself. Toledo encompasses and dominates its metropolitan area unlike a St. Louis or Detroit.

There are no real generalizations to be made about a prevailing style of life in a big city. Bag ladies, downtown drunks, swinging corporate executives and bohemians in garrets all live in Toledo. But there are also churches everywhere and scores of playgrounds with children of all ages organized for baseball, soccer and football. Toledo seems to be tied to the family. Toledo mothers still believe

Manager Carl Ermer explains game strategy to Mud Hens baseball players (top); Dick Miller comes up with the ball (above) against rival Bowling Green State University. In 1979 the TU team won the MAC conference basketball championship.

"a single man in possession of a good fortune must be in want of a wife;" grass widows still believe the perfect mate can be found, and children, to whom parents dedicate their lives, may move to far-flung parts of the metropolis but never leave home. Perhaps in addition to being a "factory town," a "livable city" and a "city of neighborhoods," Toledo is also a "city of families."

TOLEDO'S MANSIONS: The charm and solidity of another era is still manifest in Toledo's gracious old homes. The Old West End contains some of the best examples of High Victorian residential architecture in America. The Stranahan-Rothschild House (top); the Barber House (above); the Libbey House (below); the Tillinghast House (below right); and the Leeper-Geddes House (above right).

POWER AND SAIL: *Lake Erie powerboats (above); a still life of masts at North Cape Marina (right inset); a shadow against a full sail projects confidence (left inset). Wildlife frequent the Maumee environment and often leave a graphic image (left).*

THE BLIZZARD OF '78: A motorist digs out of the worst snowstorm in Toledo's history—the blizzard of 1978 (right); snow piled high in front of the Blade Building (above).

In the fall and winter of 1981, signboards yielded the most important insight of all—elusive and uncertain as it might be. In large letters, the signboards read simply, "Ohio's Newest City," a message that puzzled anyone with a sense of history. It was intended to emphasize the physical reconstruction of so much of downtown and surrounding areas. Five years earlier, the same signboards had misquoted Jesup W. Scott to proclaim "Toledo the Future Great City of the Midwest." Perhaps Toledo is still Scott's city, still the city of dreams and promoters. But the Toledo promoter is not a booster in the tradition of George F. Babbitt of Zenith City. He has been a force for continual change—much of it for the better—and has shaped a central quality of the city. Above all else, Toledo seems an up-and-doing place. Mourn not past glories! Rebuild—the great future lies ahead, let's go out to eat, buy something, times are tough, but tomorrow will be better.

People weary of those who continually boost and never knock. But Toledo leaders with their slogans and campaigns reflect the existence of a genuine spirit of civic pride in the community. Newsboys risk life and limb in the middle of thoroughfares in winter's cold still selling their newspapers for one of the city's oldest charities. Toledo is Jesup Scott's city, but it is also Brand Whitlock's city. His civic ideal persists. Despite the urban problems of our time and depression again stalking the city of glass and the auto, Toledo seems committed to the belief that a better city and a better community for all can be created in late twentieth-century urban America.

182

A short drive transports Toledoans to an idyllic countryside setting.

City for all seasons, snow blankets Wildwood Metropark.

PARTNERS IN TOLEDO'S PROGRESS

The corporate community has made dynamic contributions to the growth, development and quality of life in Toledo. The city's leading businesses have lent their support and financial commitment to the publishing of *Toledo: Gateway to the Great Lakes*. Their corporate histories follow:

BancOhio Corporation
Bauer, Stark and Lashbrook, Inc.
The A. Bentley & Sons Company
Bostwick-Braun Company
Champion Spark Plug Company
The Collaborative Inc.
The Sam Davis Company, Inc.
Davis Junior College of Business
Doehler-Jarvis Castings
Dura Corporation
Flower Hospital-Crestview Center
General Mills, Inc.
The Huntington National Bank
Kuhlman Corp.
The Lane Drug Company
The Mather Company
The Mellocraft Company
Ohio Citizens Bank
Owens-Illinois, Inc.
Parkview Hospital
Plaskon Products, Inc.
The Prestolite Company,
    An Allied Corporation Company
Riverside Hospital
Rudolph/Libbe/Inc.
St. Luke's Hospital
St. Vincent Hospital and Medical Center
Schindler Haughton Elevator Corporation
Seaway Food Town, Inc.
Seeger Metals and Plastics, Inc.
Sisters of Mercy
The Standard Oil Company
Storer Broadcasting Company
Sun Refining and Marketing Co.,
    Toledo Refinery
Surface Division Midland-Ross
    Corporation
The Sylvania Savings Bank Co.
Teledyne CAE
Toledo Area Chamber of Commerce
The Toledo Blade
The Toledo Edison Company
The Toledo Hospital
The Toledo Museum of Art
The Toledo Trust Company
The University of Toledo
Willis Day Management Inc.
WSPD Radio
WTOL-TV

185

Maumee Valley Historical Society

The roots of the Maumee Valley Historical Society date back more than 110 years to the Maumee Valley Pioneer Association founded in 1864. The pioneer scout Peter Navarre was its first president until his death in 1873. The association served the counties of northwestern Ohio and principally encouraged remaining pioneers to write their remembrances of the early settlement of the Maumee Valley. During this time, General John E. Hunt, who resided in Maumee from 1816 until 1853 and served as a state senator, wrote his memoirs of pioneer life in the valley. The manuscript disappeared, but was found in the 1960s and published by the Maumee Valley Historical Society in 1978 as the *John Hunt Memoirs*.

Among the accomplishments of the original society was the successful appeal to Congress to purchase the site of Fort Meigs as a memorial to the men who fought there during the War of 1812.

In 1818 a new organization emerged— the Historical Society of Northwestern Ohio. The new society stated in its constitution the following purposes: to maintain a library, to encourage the publication of local history volumes and to preserve and collect museum objects and manuscripts documenting Maumee Valley History.

The society diligently pursued its literary goals, and in 1928 sufficient funds were available to permit the publishing of the first issue of the *Northwest Ohio Quarterly*. During the first two decades the society's library grew. The collection of books, manuscripts, maps and photographs are now housed in the Local History and Genealogy Department of the Toledo-Lucas County Public Library where the materials receive professional attention.

In the late 1940s a small annual appropriation by the Lucas County Commissioners allowed the society to hire a director and editor. Dr. Randolph C. Downes, professor of history at the University of Toledo, served the society continuously until his death in 1975. Dr. Downes not only edited the *Northwest Ohio Quarterly*, but embarked on research which led to the publication of four classic works of Lucas County history: *The Conquest, Canal Days, Lake Port* and *Industrial Beginnings*. He published a young reader's history of the Maumee Valley and was instrumental in the establishment of *Ohio Cues*, the only statewide historical publication for young readers. Dr. Downes also wrote a three-volume *History of Lake Shore Ohio* and became an expert on local Indian history. During the 1950s the Society promoted local history through radio and television broadcasts given by Dr. Downes.

The Historical Society of Northwestern Ohio and the Maumee Historical Society pooled their resources and combined in 1963 to become the Maumee Valley Historical Society and fought to preserve the Hull-Wolcott House. The grass-roots campaign led to the establishment of a local history museum, first opened to the public on a regular basis in 1965.

The museum complex grew substantially during the decade of the 1970s. A log cabin was added in 1961; the depot and the "1840 House" (Percy Frederick home) in 1971; the Flanigan home (salt box architecture) in 1977; and a privy in 1981. The above buildings were substantially restored during the 1970s.

The Landmarks Committee of the Maumee Valley Historical Society, organized in 1968, became a driving force within the society in the 1970s as it fought to save historic buildings, sponsored the first architectural surveys of historic buildings in the state of Ohio and published the award-winning volume, *Look Again* (1974).

The 1980s brought shrinking budgets and increased demands for resources of the society. To meet these demands, the society has turned to innovative activities such as the publication of this volume to keep the programs of the society vibrant, forward-moving and a contribution to the community.

In 1957 Rill Hull, the last member of the Wolcott family, died and left her house and property to St. Paul's Episcopal Church. The City of Maumee purchased the property for a possible future water treatment plant.

A series of events led to the house and land being made available to the historical society. The Historical Society of Northwest Ohio had funds and political backing. The Maumee Historical Society had the desire and enthusiasm to develop the Hull-Wolcott house as a museum. Rill Hull had been a member of the Maumee group and a staunch promoter of all things historical.

Judge Lehr Fess of Toledo proposed a merger of the two historical groups. After many torrid meetings a compromise was reached and the Maumee Valley Historical Society was born in 1963. The top priority of the new organization was to create a historical museum from the old Wolcott House. By 1965 the house was substantially restored and opened for visitors on regular basis.

A tradition of security and progress

BancOhio National Bank in the Toledo area has a long and successful tradition of providing quality financial services to residents and businesses. The bank's roots can be traced to a number of the area's earliest financial institutions, including the Exchange Bank of Perrysburg, the Peoples Savings Bank Company of Delta and the Napoleon State Bank.

In 1871, the Exchange Bank of Perrysburg opened its doors with E.D. Peck as president, H.A. Hamilton as vice president, F. R. Miller as cashier and N.L. Hanson as teller. Hanson, a Dartmouth College graduate, had left his position as principal of the State Street Schools in Columbus, Ohio, to accept a position as teller for the bank.

When Peck died in 1879, the Exchange Bank was liquidated, and Hanson went on to form what is now the oldest bank in Wood County, the Citizens Bank. In 1892 it was reorganized and chartered as a state bank and was incorporated as the Citizens Banking Company, with a stock capital of $50,000.

Hanson served as cashier and as a director of the new bank. Jacob Davis was the first president and J.O. Troup was vice president.

In 1906, the Peoples Savings Bank Company of nearby Delta was chartered, followed in 1909 by the Napoleon State Bank (later known as the Community Bank).

In 1925, Citizens Banking Company constructed a new office on Louisiana Avenue, two doors from the site of the original building. This office served the financial needs of Citizens' customers until a branch office opened in the Country Charm Shopping Center. In the late 1970s, the Country Charm location was enlarged and became the bank's main office.

Continuing an expansion program that began in the 1930s, BancOhio Corporation, the state's first bank holding company, in 1970 added to its banking family the Community Bank of Napoleon. In 1971, the two offices of the Citizens Banking Company joined BancOhio, as did Peoples Savings Bank Company in 1973. Fifteen other banks joined BancOhio during the 1970s, bringing the total number of separate banks to 41.

On February 10, 1979, a third office of BancOhio/Citizens Banking Company was opened in Haskins.

In 1979, the Ohio Legislature enacted a law permitting banks to branch into

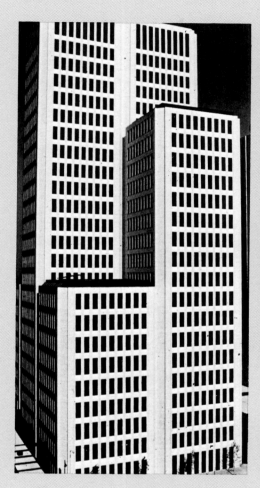

Citizens Banking Company's original Perrysburg, Ohio building, built in 1871 (above). BancOhio National Plaza, headquarters for BancOhio National Bank in Columbus, Ohio (left).

contiguous counties, and BancOhio Corporation merged 40 of its banks into BancOhio National Bank (BNB). The Citizens Banking Company became the Toledo Area of what was then the 31st largest bank in the United States, with assets of more than $4.2 billion. BancOhio's affiliate bank in Delta became BNB's Fulton County Area and the BancOhio/Community Bank of Napoleon became BNB's Henry County Area.

In 1979, Ohio State Bank, located in Columbus and Franklin counties, was the only BancOhio bank not merged. It remains a separate bank in order to continue the multi-bank holding company's franchise with both a state and a national charter.

Today, BancOhio National Bank has assets of $5.5 billion, with more than 245 offices serving customers in 45 of Ohio's 88 counties. Its customer service is extended by more than 130 AnytimeBank automated teller machines located throughout the state. In late 1981, the AnytimeBank network was expanded

when BancOhio announced plans to share its statewide network with other financial institutions. By 1986, BancOhio expects to have 50 participating companies, with more than 300 machines in operation.

BancOhio currently operates offices in Delta, Haskins, Lyons, Napoleon, Perrysburg and Swanton. The bank's commitment to corporate customers in the Toledo Area includes a loan development office in downtown Toledo's newly renovated Fort Industry Square. This office will provide a full range of corporate services, including lending, leasing, trust, accounts receivable and agribusiness. Commercial customers will also benefit from BancOhio's lending capacity to an individual customer of more than $30 million.

BancOhio Corporation is owned by more than 14,000 shareholders who live in every one of Ohio's 88 counties and in every part of the United States, as well as several other nations. But its roots remain in Toledo.

187

Ohio's oldest firm has been altering Toledo's skyline for 90 years

In 1892, as population and commerce exploded and a thriving Toledo struggled with urban growth, two young men combined talent, ambition and assets to form a partnership for the practice of architecture. Today, that firm continues the reputation for reliability and service to clients established 90 years ago as it designs, builds and rebuilds for industry, institutions, merchants and private individuals in locations beyond the Maumee Valley, Ohio, and even the United States.

George Strafford Mills and Harry Wilcox Wachter started business with a $100 capital investment and a small office in the Nasby Building. After six years, the partnership formally dissolved, and Mills incorporated the organization known for responsible professionalism, if not a single identifiable style. He selected specialists carefully and used them advantageously to construct an office able to work as an integrated team. The strategy of offering the combined services of architect, draftsman, engineer and construction supervisor strengthened the firm's flexibility and increased its effect on Toledo's skyline.

Equally impressive is the impact of the association on the community through the leadership, vision and visibility of its partners as citizens. Mills served many professional, social and civic organizations, but he is particularly remembered as an influential member of the 1909 delegation to Indianapolis which convinced John N. Willys to purchase the closed Pope-Toledo Automobile Company. The locating of the Willys Overland Company in Toledo is germane to the city's industrial history—and to the fortunes of the Mills establishment. Between 1910 and 1920, the firm designed 167 buildings and plant extensions in addition to local residences for Willys and many other officers of the company.

On May 1, 1912, the firm reorganized to include partners George V. Rhines, Lawrence S. Bellman (both former students of Mills at the Manual Training School) and Charles M. Nordhoff. Rhines, an industrious engineer, learned French and German to master the then-new concrete technology; he later developed a widely used concrete building process known as "flat slab" construction. Bellman brought an extraordinary eye for detail and was the partner contact for many large residences. Nordhoff's abilities

The Boody House (inset). Toledo's first modern "skyscraper" is still considered one of its finest buildings. Buildings designed all over the world started with the world headquarters of Willys Overland, Inc. (below).

at observation and analyzation added to his natural talent as a designer.

The partnership flourished until the 1930s. During the Depression, the staff was reduced to only the partners, one stenographer and an artist; yet the name Mills, Rhines, Bellman and Nordhoff remained a community constant.

Mills died in 1939. Other deaths, retirements and new associations were reflected in the 1944 name change to Bellman, Gillett and Richards. John Gillett, an engineering graduate, began with the company in 1913 and worked with Rhines on buildings for the War Department. He advanced to partnership, as did John N. Richards, who entered the office as a designer in 1932. Richards, retired since 1976, is known as the "Dean of Toledo Architects." He served a distinguished two terms as national president of the American Institute of Architects, advocating that architecture and architects must be a force deeply involved in the shaping of the American scene. Richards' prodigious contributions to his art, to public service and to the spirit of Toledo, especially downtown revitalization, are incalculable.

Over the years, the individuality and expertise of partners John Chester B. Lee, Reeve Kelsey Biggers, George H. Erard, Michael B. O'Shea, Raymond A. Etzel, Robert M. Lutz, Orville H. Bauer and Robert C. Moorhead added to the firm's prestige. Thomas Ewing King's skill with perspective won him eminence in the 1920s as an artist and delineator.

From its early mansions in the Old West End and along the river in Perrysburg, to the downtown Ohio Building, to the University of Toledo campus, to Ohio Turnpike service centers, the firm has operated continuously under the organization concept set in motion by George Mills at the turn of the century. Now known as Bauer, Stark and Lashbrook, the corporation includes the services of graphic artists, landscape architects and interior designers to meet new needs and challenges of clients.

Designer Charles Stark and engineer Dean Lashbrook head a 50-person staff which enjoys a distinction for producing acoustically fine auditoriums, creative design for well-engineered buildings and for committing to adaptive reuse and preservation of Toledo's impressive architecture, many structures of which originated in the office of Mills, Rhines, Bellman and Nordhoff.

Building Toledo for more than a century

Anderton Bentley came to Lucas County, Ohio, from Yorkshire, England, in 1871 seeking the opportunities which the thriving distribution center for agricultural and forestry products offered to an energetic young master carpenter. His skill earned him 22 cents an hour helping to build the Boody House in Toledo and the Lonz Winery on Middle Bass Island. By the early 1880s, he was firmly established. He rebuilt Hall Block, then Toledo's most prestigious office building, which had burned in 1882. The successful execution of this contract led to contracts for the Gardner and Spitzer Buildings, St. Paul's Methodist Church and the first plant at Rossford, Ohio, for the Edward Ford Glass Company.

By 1907, when the partnership of Anderton and his two sons, James and Tom, was incorporated, they were ready to undertake construction of the Nicholas Building (First National Bank Building), the Secor Hotel (125 Jefferson Building) and had introduced a new construction material and technique to Toledo— reinforced structural concrete.

Anderton had for years done much work for the Toledo Railways and Electric Company. By 1915, the Toledo Edison Company, which had recently been formed from the sale of the railway company, decided to build the Acme Station to meet the growing demand for electric power for lighting. Bentley was awarded the contract. When John Willys started the Overland in Toledo he came to the Bentley Company for his building work, as Edward Ford had done twenty years before. When Orville Wright needed a new house in Dayton, Bentley did the work.

With the entry of the United States into World War I, Bentley received a series of national defense orders to build facilities in Ohio, Illinois and Florida. In 1917, James was named director of a Navy Department project to construct concrete-hulled ships. Several of these ships were floated and were in commission for a number of years.

After the war, the company was engaged in plant expansions for the Edward Ford Glass Company at Rossford, the Overland, Mather Spring, Spicer Manufacturing Company, National Supply Company and many others as the U.S. economy rode the high tide of industrial expansion. It also built the Ohio Bank Building (the O-I Building), the Park Lane Hotel, the Second of Christian Science Church, the Richardson Building

Putting up the steel (above left) in 1905 for the Nicholas Building (First National Bank of Toledo). A. Bentley & Sons (above right) at work on the Libbey-Owens-Ford Building in Toledo in 1959.

(Board of Trade Building), the Lasalle & Koch Store, the Bayview Park Sewage Treatment Plant, Toledo Hospital and the 1930 addition to the Toledo Museum of Art.

The Great Depression of the 1930s saw the collapse of construction. Like all industry, the company retrenched drastically, and during the mid-30s, the local Works Progress Administration office leased Bentley's office building.

In 1934, Ohio Pipe Trades Service Company (now Ohio Pipe Trades, Inc.) was formed as a Bentley subsidiary in the electrical and mechanical contracting field.

With war again threatening in Europe, the American economy began its recovery from the Depression. During the late 1930s, the company built an expansion to the Acme Station for the Toledo Edison Company, plants for Libbey-Owens-Ford Glass Company in Toledo and Ottawa, Illinois, and in 1941, with the outbreak of war, the Rossford Ordinance Depot (now Willis Day Industrial Park).

The World War II period was one of great construction activity to support the

war effort. Bentley built plants for Spicer Manufacturing Company, Electric Auto Lite, Toledo Scale, Willys-Overland and L-O-F Glass Company.

During the 1940s, Bentley served such customers as the Dana Corporation, E.I. duPont, Electric Auto Lite, L-O-F, the State of Ohio Department of Highways, the Ohio Turnpike Commission, St. Vincent Hospital, Toledo Edison Company, the University of Toledo, the City of Toledo and Owens-Illinois, Inc.

The major construction projects executed during the 1955 to 1975 period included work for General Motors Corporation, Standard Oil, Dana Corporation, Electric Auto Lite and Owens-Illinois, Inc. Also completed were three units at the Bay Shore station for Toledo Edison, glass furnaces and float facilities throughout twenty years of growth and construction for L-O-F, shopping center construction for Macy's Toledo Lasalle & Koch store and Sears & Roebuck Company, the Davis-Besse nuclear power station for Toledo Edison and the Owens-Corning Fiberglas corporation headquarters in Toledo.

189

Leaders in hardware distribution
with a proud past and a bright future

On July 2, 1855, W. and C.B. Roff and Company, a family-owned business, placed an ad in the *Daily Toledo Blade* which read "Wholesale and Retail Dealers in American, English and German hardware, announce their first day of business." The "sign of the anvil" was established at 130 Summit Street.

Oscar Alonzo Bostwick joined the firm in 1862 as the company's first traveling salesman. When he bought into the firm in 1865, the name was changed to Roff and Company.

The very next year, Carl Braun came aboard, and two years later his cousin George joined the company. The Brauns purchased an interest from W. Roff, who retired, followed shortly by C.B. Roff. From then on, the firm was known as The Bostwick-Braun Company.

During the company's early years, the phenomenal growth of business forced several moves to larger quarters. Between 1850 and 1855, the city gained over 4,500 people—a 121 percent increase. Bostwick-Braun's growth closely paralleled that of Toledo as the tremendous development of business and industry created a big demand for hardware.

Finally, Bostwick-Braun purchased the entire block surrounded by Summit, Monroe, Perry and the west bank of the Maumee River.

In 1908, an eight-story structure, designed and constructed specifically for wholesale hardware purposes, was completed. It contained six acres of floor capacity equal to 3,660 railroad cars.

From 1913 until 1939, Mr. Henry L. Thompson led the continuing progress of Bostwick-Braun. He was the financial genius behind Toledo Trust Company and a powerful figure in Toledo's history of industry, business and finance. Because of his leadership, Bostwick-Braun was able to weather World War I and the Depression of the 1930s.

In 1936, after 81 years in the retail and wholesale business, Bostwick-Braun closed its retail business to concentrate strictly on wholesaling. The objective of the firm was to predict the needs of the retailer and industrial buyer, order the necessary items directly from the manufacturer and make them available for quick delivery.

One of the aims of the company was to lead the industry in the introduction of new items which showed promise for retail sales. The company realized that patronage of hardware dealers depended on providing them with the newest and best merchandise available. Bostwick-Braun was constantly searching for more effective methods of aiding its dealers in merchandising profitability.

Since 1961, Bostwick-Braun has been franchising PRO hardware stores in parts of eleven Midwestern states.

In addition to hardware sales, Bostwick-Braun has an industrial sales department with a large and varied stock serving industrial plants and building and electrical contractors, saving them the expense of large inventory investments. The firm boasts over 2,500 sources of supply from every state in the union and worldwide.

In 1963, growth in another direction became a necessity. In May of that year, Bostwick-Braun bought J.T. Wing Company, an industrial supplier in Detroit. A move in 1972 located the Wing division in Livonia, Michigan, providing industrial customers in that area with a close base of operations.

In 1964, more than 45,000 items in stock were numbered, counted and loaded into a complex electronic data processing system. Many of Bostwick-Braun-pioneered computer applications are now in common use in the hardware industry.

Bostwick-Braun was extremely proud when, in 1980, it formed an ESOP (Employee Stock Ownership Plan) and became the first hardware wholesaler in the country to be owned 100 percent by its employees through an ESOP, giving them the assurance that the company will continue into the future. Forty-three members of its workforce numbering 320 have served the company for over 25 years.

It is a tribute to the most recent past presidents, H.L. Thompson Jr. and D.M. Humphries Jr. that Bostwick-Braun continues to expand. Today, under the direction of Richard E. Smith, Toledo's third oldest business is one of the nation's leading hardware distributors. As Smith puts it, "We're proud to be a part of 'Ohio's Newest City' and our employee-owners are excited about the bright future that lies ahead for the city of Toledo and The Bostwick-Braun Company."

A 1924 Bostwick-Braun delivery vehicle (left). The Bostwick-Braun Company, c. 1920 (below).

190

THE BOSTWICK-BRAUN COMPANY
TOLEDO, OHIO
ESTABLISHED 1855   INCORPORATED 1865

——JOBBERS OF HARDWARE——

Mechanics' and Machinists' Tools; Mill, Railroad and Factory Supplies, Bar Steel, Sheets and Metals, Blacksmiths' Supplies, Roofing Material, Tinners' Tools, Gas Pipe and Fittings, Nails, Wire, Fencing, etc., Bolts, Screws, Belting, Packing, Tackle Blocks, Rope and Cordage, Wagon Hardware, Agricultural Tools, Electrical Supplies, Radios and Radio Supplies, Builders' Hardware, House Furnishings, Cutlery and Sporting Goods, Guns, Ammunition, Fishing Tackle, Hammocks, Skates, Children's Vehicles, Bicycles and Sundries, Automobile Accessories and Garage Supplies.

A diversified company producing more than its name implies

Champion Spark Plug Company, founded just after the turn of the century in a Boston suburb, grew up with the automobile, helped mechanize the farmer, soared with the early aviators and ignited some of man's first attempts at the moon. Its history is the history of man propelling himself.

In the early 1900s, personal transportation can only be described as chaotic—there were steam cars, electric cars, gasoline cars, frightened horses and indignant, skeptical people.

It was into this melee that the Stranahan brothers stepped. F.D. Stranahan was already in business when his brother, R.A. Stranahan, joined him shortly after graduating from Harvard. At that time, most automotive parts and accessories were imported from Europe.

The Stranahans faced a particularly annoying problem—spark plugs were both their highest volume part, yet their lowest in quality. By 1909, R.A. had designed a better plug—the Champion X—and no other single achievement in the company's history stands any greater.

About a year later, he set out to sell his new product to the automobile companies springing up around Detroit and Toledo.

John Willys, manufacturer of the then-popular Overland automobile, agreed to purchase the plug, but with the provision that the manufacturing facility be moved closer.

In 1910, the move was completed, establishing Champion on the second floor of a downtown Toledo laundry building.

In rapid succession, nearly every car maker then in existence became a Champion customer. Chief among them was Ford. The relationship between these two companies remained in force for nearly 50 years, with Champion acting as sole spark plug supplier.

In 1912, Champion outgrew the laundry building and moved to its present location on Upton Avenue in Toledo. The company's growth during this period was fantastic.

By the mid-thirties the company had become a well-oiled machine, clear in its purpose and consistent. R.A. Stranahan was president, F.D. Stranahan was vice president and treasurer, and the second generation had entered the picture. R.A. Stranahan Jr., who was to succeed his father as president and board chairman, had begun his career as a laborer in the production department. He followed the same arduous route taken by his father—a thorough grounding in each phase of the business, which led ultimately to his appointment to the executive committee in 1947.

In the meantime, company sales had outgrown the boundaries of the United States, and a network of international manufacturing facilities was initiated. Champion's research and engineering had anticipated the needs of a yet-undeclared war with superior aviation and automotive plugs, and its production equipment transcended anything in existence.

Champion now has available more than 400 types of spark plugs, covering every conceivable form of engine-driven transportation and work. Champion is also the world's largest manufacturer of turbine igniters, such as those that power the Boeing 747, and a more sophisticated version that helped launch the second-stage, oxygen-hydrogen space engine in the Saturn C-1.

In 1958, the company built at its Toledo headquarters the most modern and complete spark plug research and engineering center in the world, followed in 1963 by the Automotive Technical Services building, which houses elaborate training, testing and service facilities. In 1967, a $12.5 million modernization and expansion program of the Toledo manufacturing facilities was completed.

Also in 1967, the company acquired the DeVilbiss Company, which manufactures spray guns and systems and a quality line of air compressors. A great number and variety of products manufactured by industry throughout the world have a protective or decorative finish that has been spray-applied, most likely using DeVilbiss products. The company also manufactures robots for spray painting or welding uses.

DeVilbiss is also a leading manufacturer of medical equipment used primarily in the treatment of respiratory diseases in that branch of medicine known as inhalation therapy.

In 1964, Champion purchased the Baron Drawn Steel Corporation of Toledo. A principal processor of bar and coil steel for the company's domestic spark plug manufacturing plants, it also sells steel to a large number of outside customers.

In 1977, Champion purchased Arman, S.p.A., of Turin, Italy, and in 1978 it acquired the Anderson Company of Gary, Indiana, both manufacturers of windshield wiper products.

Champion is an independent manufacturer. Unlike its competitors, it has no captive market and must depend solely upon product superiority for its existence. This independence, however, is not a liability—it was accepted long ago as an invitation to excellence.

In addition to spark plugs, Champion manufactures windshield wiper products, coating application items, health-care equipment and cold drawn steel.

Teamwork produces better environments

When a group of accomplished architects, engineers, landscape architects and planners decided in 1973 to combine their talents in an independent organization, they chose to name their new business The Collaborative Inc. The word "collaborate" aptly expresses the concept of the group's functional philosophy—the concept of team effort and "teamwork."

Departing from traditional procedures, which are static and sequential, the founders of The Collaborative were committed to a more dynamic approach to project development. The owner, architect, landscape architect, planner, engineer and contractor work together as a team from the outset. The knowledge, ideas and talents of the team members converge in a single group commitment to the execution of the project. The Collaborative soon became recognized as a group that "makes things happen" by turning obstacles into opportunities. Continuous refinement of this integrated team effort has led to the firm's outstanding reputation for award-winning project designs, as well as cost containment and reduced project-completion time.

Another of the underlying principles on which The Collaborative was founded is that, while the primary responsibility is to the client, there is also an obligation to the community as a whole and, where applicable, to the existing natural environment. Private, public and natural concerns about the utilizations of land and other assets must be coordinated and solutions worked out so that all are mutually benefited. The Collaborative's expertise in this area has been applied to many Toledo projects.

Health facilities, shopping malls, recreation facilities, institutional buildings, commercial and corporate headquarters, social services facilities and private residences are among the projects executed by The Collaborative in the Toledo area. The group has been actively involved in revitalization of the downtown area—from preservation of the historic in the restoration of Fort Industry Square, to creation of the city's striking, multi-story, curvilinear parking facility, connected to SeaGate Center by underground concourses.

Other Collaborative projects include the University of Toledo's Parks Tower, a high-rise student dormitory; the addition to the Law Library; Centennial Mall, the Campus core; and revitalization of Toledo's major Catholic landmark, Queen of the Most Holy Rosary Cathedral.

The Collaborative joined in the early planning stages of the revitalization of the Warren-Sherman area, a 300-acre economically depressed, inner-city Toledo neighborhood. This was a multifaceted effort in which the firm assisted the economic development team, and was then commissioned to develop an overall master plan—housing, industrial and commercial development, designation of open spaces, recreation areas, and vehicular and pedestrian traffic patterns. The Collaborative designed many of the Warren-Sherman structures, such as the Business and Technology Center for Control Data Corporation; the "Super Block" industrial park; Owens-Illinois, Inc.'s Warren-Sherman plant; the Bancroft-Franklin Shopping Center; and a rehabilitated apartment building which is also a solar prototype.

In a study funded by a grant from the National Endowment for the Arts, The Collaborative was commissioned to develop proposals for renovating a number of Toledo's older structures to serve as prototypes for urban revitalization programs. Eventually, four prototypes were selected and studied, and two have attracted developers and have been renovated. One, a 60-year-old building located at 900 Adams Street, has received a design award in the extended use category from the Architect's Society of Ohio and won national recognition as a standard for recycling.

On a national scale, the firm is recognized as a leading designer of resorts, country clubs and convention/conference facilities. Among The Collaborative's designs are the popular Innisbrook Resort in Tarpon Springs, Florida; Saddlebrook Resort, north of Tampa, Florida; and Tamarron Resort in Durango, Colorado, for which the firm received a National Merit Award from the American Society of Landscape Architects.

The Collaborative continues to win national recognition, yet remains totally committed to playing a major role in the realization of Toledo's long-range goal—to develop and maintain a community that is functional, economically viable, interesting and esthetically attractive.

Sunforest Medical Building, Toledo, Ohio (below). Centennial Mall, the University of Toledo (bottom).

Business college traces a family's history

In 1881 a young Canadian, Matthew H. Davis, left his chair in the mathematics department and his position as director of the business department at Albert College, Belleville, Ontario, to accept the management of Toledo Business College.

The small school of 35 students, which had been established in 1858, rapidly grew to 350 students. Many were coming to the big city for the first time. The young men might clean stables for their room and board of $3 per week, while the young women lived with relatives or earned their subsistence by helping with household tasks and children. Even students living only ten miles from Toledo usually lived in town, going home one weekend each month. Most Davis graduates worked hard, saved their money and became leaders in the community.

Both Davis and his wife, Rachel, became well known through their activities, especially in religious and educational circles.

During the 23 years Davis directed the school, four less successful schools were absorbed, and the name was changed to Davis Business College. The curriculum was gradually changed from Latin, German, Greek, calculus and epistolary writing to banking, mercantile trades, shorthand and typing. (When typewriting was introduced to the curriculum, it was the first such course in Toledo.)

Prior to the 1930s, it was difficult to find teachers with college degrees in vocational fields, and Davis was one of the first schools chosen by the state of Ohio to train business teachers. These teachers had received their baccalaureate degrees before attending Davis.

After Davis' death in 1904, his son, Thurber P. Davis, left the University of Michigan to take over the management of the Davis Business College. Only 20 years old and an outstanding student and baseball player, he had looked forward to playing professional ball after graduation and teaching at Davis in the winter. This was not to be—for the next 44 years, until May 1, 1948, he managed the school. The college's prestige continued to grow, and he was honored in his vocation, his church and the Masons, receiving the honorary 33rd degree. He was also active in Rotary, and pursued his athletic interests in bowling, golf and handball. The contacts made through his many activities aided the school in the placement of its graduates in the outstanding businesses in Toledo.

When Thurber P. became ill, his daughter, Ruth L. Davis, a business administration graduate of the University of Arizona with one and a half years of graduate work, became the third generation of the Davis family to head the school. Soon after she assumed active management in May 1948, the school was incorporated.

Since then, changes have been rapid in business colleges. Educational requirements have increased for teachers, libraries have been added, career goals have been expanded and equipment requirements have changed. In 1953 Davis Business College was among the first to be accredited by the Accrediting Commission for Colleges and Schools. In 1964 it met commission requirements for a junior college of business.

Ruth Davis, as her father and grandfather before her, has been active in the community. She has served as president of the International Association of Personnel Women; Zonta International, Toledo Chapter; the Administrative Management Society and the Ohio Business School Association, as well as board member of the American Society for Training and Development, Mid-American Bank and the Ohio Council of Schools. Because of these contacts, Davis' placement of its students has remained outstanding.

Feeling that Davis Junior College has a debt to the community in its continuance, Ruth Davis now shares its ownership with John Lambert, a man devoted to the high educational standards of the school and the welfare of its students.

From its horse-and-buggy-days beginning to today's classroom computers, Davis has kept pace.

Graduation exercise 1893, held in Memorial Hall at Adams and Ontario streets (above). Bookkeeping and banking were taught at Fifteenth and Adams in 1902 (below).

193

Three generations dedicated to quality service

The sign which Sam Davis posted over his first business enterprise in 1904—a coal, flour, feed, baled hay and straw store at 1943-45 Canton Avenue—bore the challenging slogan "A trial order from you will prove me worthy of your future business." In the late 1920s, when Sam Davis was at the height of his career, his motto had become "Service is the seed of success."

According to legend, at age 13 Toledo-born Sam Davis walked the railroad tracks picking up fallen coal from passing freight cars, then sold his findings door-to-door from a bushel basket. He was soon able to afford a push cart, then rode a donkey, then made his deliveries with a horse-drawn cart. By 1939, with a vast fleet of trucks, moving vans and extensive real estate holdings, The Sam Davis Company had become Toledo's largest coal dealer, mover, warehouse facility and the owner and operator of more commercial, industrial and apartment rental properties than anyone else in the city. Through a little-known firm, Mutual Heating and Lighting Company, it supplied heat to some 30 downtown buildings.

The firm built, owned and operated the former Fort Meigs Hotel at Jefferson and St. Clair, now the site of the Fiberglas Tower. As an investor and developer, Sam Davis' firm had acquired or constructed and managed buildings that housed many of Toledo's major industries.

Service was indeed the seed of Sam Davis' success. Service meant giving new industry a chance to grow, improving living conditions for his apartment tenants, constructing buildings of architectural merit and furnishing and decorating them in good taste—a family-honored tradition adhered to by his son and grandson.

Sam Davis put his philosophy into practice in a variety of ways. In the early 1920s, he acquired the Toledo Factories Building, one of the first steel-reinforced concrete industrial structures built in America. Construction began in 1911 under the sponsorship of the Chamber of Commerce, with the assistance of John Willys. The Factories Building opened on January 1, 1913, as an "incubator of infant industries," among which were City Auto Stamping and Doehler Die Casting Company.

Sam Davis built additions to the two-city-block complex and offered small industries as little as three and four hundred square feet of space at low rentals to help them grow and become established. He even provided some adjacent vacant land for the original Toledo Tennis Club. The Toledo Factories Company merged with Sam Davis' other holdings in 1928. In 1980 the property was sold by Guy Davis to Control Data Corporation, which has since restored and reestablished the complex as an incubator of small business, now known as the Control Data Business and Technology Center.

When Sam Davis opened the 220-room Fort Meigs Hotel on July 9, 1925, it was heralded in a special sixteen-page supplement to the *Toledo Times* for the beauty and quality of its Italian Renaissance architecture, its original oil paintings, rare Chinese porcelains, marble floors, oriental carpets, bronze railings and mirrored walls of unusual beauty, as well as its use of the most advanced, best available construction techniques, materials and systems.

Sam Davis and his company operated with flair and a keen sense of style and graciousness. When he opened his corporate headquarters, coal yard and warehouse facilities on March 28, 1927, at 1510 Elm Street, it could easily have been mistaken by the 15,000 guests who attended the party Sam threw for a private bank or art gallery. Its entrance facade was of cut stone, with double bronze doors flanked by ornamental bronze lamps. The interior was finished with black marble counter tops, black walnut-paneled walls, bronze chandeliers

The Woods Building, 1981.

Sam Davis' first Canton Avenue coal, flour and feed store, in 1904 (left). Elegant interior (above) of the Park Lane Hotel, Christmas 1956.

from England, oriental carpets, oil paintings and sculptures.

The Ann Manor, 2200 Scottwood Avenue, built in 1929 under the direction of Roi Davis, was and remains today one of Toledo's most lavish, comfortable and well-maintained residential apartment buildings—an Old West End landmark and stabilizing influence. It was designed by architect Sidney Aftel and finished with concepts well beyond its time.

Roi Davis was also responsible for the acquisition and total renovation of the Park Lane Hotel which the firm operated from 1947 to 1970 as one of the most outstanding and distinguished small luxury hotels in America. A showplace, the Park Lane's lobby, cocktail lounge and public rooms were of Georgian Colonial graciousness and provided the intimate setting for many of Toledo's most prominent weddings, receptions, after-concert parties and social events. Each of Park Lane's guest rooms and suites were individually decorated. No two were alike. Many prominent Toledoans, including Mr. and Mrs. John Rohr, Mr. and Mrs. Jerome Kobacker and General Lauris Norstad, made Park Lane their home in large, gracious apartments. Mr. and Mrs. Edgar Kaiser maintained an apartment at Park Lane during the period that Kaiser Motors owned the Jeep Corporation. The hotel was host to corporate guests of such firms as the Dana Corporation, Macy's, Owens-Illinois and Abby Etna Machine Company; to the Toledo Orchestra's guest

conductors and soloists and to visiting celebrities from all over the world. The world premiere of the movie *El Greco* was celebrated at the Park Lane. It was the meeting place for many of Toledo's service clubs, headquarters for The Toledo Ski Club and The Toledo Women's Club and a favorite place at which to celebrate St. Patrick's Day and Bastille Day. Its TGIF parties became a legend.

Park Lane's guests and residents were served with the utmost efficiency, dignity and courtesy, perhaps best typified by its distinguished doorman and head bellman, Fred Taylor, and its vice president and manager, Clarence A. Day. Personalized, gracious service continued to be the seed of its success.

Following World War II, under Roi Davis' stewardship, the firm sold the coal, moving, storage and warehousing business, and real estate investment and management and the Park Lane Hotel became its principal endeavors.

Following his father's death in 1977, Guy Davis, with his brother Roi Davis Jr. and cousin Ronald A. Harris, launched an aggressive corporate expansion and revitalization program, investing only in real estate of the highest quality. Committed to Toledo and its downtown revitalization, Guy Davis completely renovated the former Welever Building, adjacent to Questor Corporation's world headquarters, and renamed it in honor of Clarence A. Day on the occasion of his retirement as executive vice president.

Davis' acquisitions have included the Woods Office Building in Sunforest Court, numerous properties in Toledo and shopping centers in Colorado and California.

As a founding member of and contributor to the Toledo Zoological Society, Sam Davis also began a family-honored tradition of public service. His philanthropy to the city included bandstands and comfort stations in Willys and Ottawa parks, as well as funds with which to support public band concerts. He donated seventeen acres of land at Steams Road, north of Trilby, and established the Topha Lodge Health Camp for Toledo's undernourished children. He was an early and ardent supporter of The Toledo Symphony Orchestra and an active participant and contributor to religious and charitable organizations of all denominations.

Roi Davis served the Toledo Zoological Society as a board member and treasurer, and was largely responsible, with his friend Martin A. Janis, for bringing Shakespeare in the Park performances to the Zoo's amphitheater during the 1950s. He established the annual Park Lane Hotel Award at the School of Art at Bowling Green State University, and was a member of the President's Council of the Toledo Museum of Art. The present-day Darlington House was planned and built with his assistance, as was Pelham Manor under the building committee chairmanship of his son, Guy.

195

Largest custom die caster in the world headquartered in Toledo

The year was 1898. The young German immigrant Herman Doehler was working in a New York printing plant when one of its linotype machines broke down. He was asked to assist in repairs of the complicated machine, and became fascinated with the way it pumped molten metal into a mold to form the type.

Seven years of experimentation and hard work followed before he managed to apply that principle to the manufacture of metal parts for industrial use. In 1905, he succeeded in producing a working die casting machine and was granted a patent for his first hand-operated machine. That was the beginning—not only of Doehler's small die casting company, but of the entire die casting industry.

In 1913, in a far-sighted maneuver, Doehler moved his fledgling company to Toledo to be near the infant automotive industry. Through the years, he continued to improve his processes and machinery, employing expert engineers and metallurgists to pioneer new techniques, and casting in lightweight alloys such as aluminum.

Today, Herman Doehler's first die casting machine is on display in the Smithsonian Institution. And his company, now Doehler-Jarvis Castings, has become a world leader in component making technologies and processes for the automotive marketplace.

Perhaps the real key to the company is Doehler's basic pioneering spirit. It is always looking for new and better ways to assist industry. This customer service philosophy has taken the company from traditional die casting operations into the creation of custom components for its customers by performing machining, assembling and finishing operations as well. The company's plants cover more than two million square feet and, in addition to die casting, include extensive permanent mold capabilities.

Die casting, of course, remains the largest part of Doehler-Jarvis's business, with machines ranging in size from 600 tons to those capable of achieving over 3,000 tons locking force—the largest in the entire industry. Components produced range from small decorative and structural parts to the largest aluminum and zinc castings ever made.

Doehler-Jarvis's machining operations include everything from trimming, milling and grinding to reaming, tapping and drilling. Sophisticated computerized numerical control systems, backed by ex-

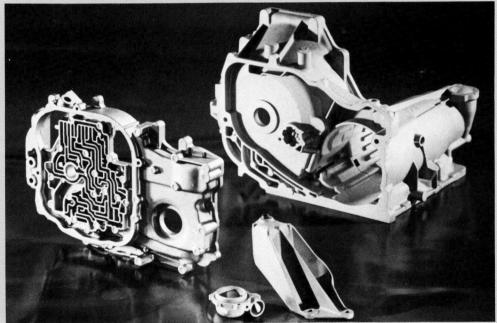

H.H. Doehler's original die casting machine (top left) now located in the Smithsonian Institution. Interior factory scenes vintage early 1900s (top right). Castings produced by Doehler-Jarvis for front wheel drive vehicles (above).

tensive engineering and tool making experience, allow Doehler-Jarvis to solve the most complex machining problems in the most cost-effective ways.

Behind these capabilities are sophisticated research and development and engineering and quality assurance operations that not only help Doehler-Jarvis customers develop their components, but constantly engage the company in finding ways to produce present components more efficiently.

Doehler-Jarvis has aligned itself with the automotive industry as one of its major suppliers. Its casting ability and extensive related services are dedicated to making the American automobile the finest in the world.

The company's success in implementing this philosophy has helped it become the largest custom die caster in the world today. In fact, there isn't even a close second. This has been the Doehler-Jarvis advertising slogan for some time, and one the Toledo-based company intends to lay claim to for a long, long time to come.

The excitement of a convertible

Long before the world had dreamed of powered convertibles and soft summer evenings slipping by overhead, a fledgling industry was beginning to grow. It was in 1913 that Milburn Wagon Works opened on Monroe Street in Toledo. It was one of many companies that would bring Toledo a reputation as a leading supplier of parts and equipment for the automotive industry.

After fire destroyed the Milburn factory in 1919, it became the Dura Mechanical Hardware Company and was located on Albion Street for three years. Dura then moved to 1336 West Bancroft Street, with plants on Fernwood and Grand avenues. These operations were combined at 4500 N. Detroit Avenue, where a new facility had been built at Matzinger Road and Deadman's Crossing. It was during this period that Dura became known as one of the pioneer American companies in the development and manufacture of interior auto fittings and window regulators.

In 1929, Dura was recognized as one of Toledo's major employers with more than 1,200 employees. Auto window regulators and decorative hardware were manufactured for Willys-Overland, Ford, Franklin, Essex, Elcar, Gardner, Hudson, Hupmobile, Jordan, Kissel, Locomobile, Marmon, Moon, Nash, Peerless, Packard, Graham-Paige, Reo, Stutz, Studebaker, Star and Velie cars.

Dura Company of Toledo was merged in 1936 with the Michigan Corporation of Detroit Harvester founded by H. Lynn Pierson, and became a division of that company.

Just prior to the war, a new option in cars was offered—a powered top. No longer would it be necessary to yank and pull a top up. No longer would it be necessary to sit on the top to get it down. Dura began production of a hydraulic electric unit which would raise or lower the top at a flick of a switch.

During World War II, the company manufactured products for the nation's defense. Several million 20 mm shell casings were produced for the small canons mounted in the propeller hub of Army pursuit planes. In addition, metal belts links used in the operation of machine guns were produced in great volume.

Returning GIs wanted any car, but the car of their dreams was the ragtop. Convertibles were analogous with good times and good living. The ticker tape parades for heroes in convertibles had become part of the American way of life. After the war, the popularity of powered convertibles continued to grow.

The company's importance as an automotive supplier expanded with the 1946 acquisition of Motor State Products Company of Ypsilanti, Michigan. Motor State was the premier manufacturer of convertible top mechanisms.

In 1957, Ford had a different idea. The Detroit-based company introduced the Skyliner, a steel-roofed convertible model. This roof was divided into two steel sections that folded together and then moved back into the trunk. The trunk lid, hinged at the bumper, opened to receive the collapsed roof. Dura was an integral part of this program.

In 1958, Dura Division diversified and began manufacturing its self-actuating contour bed for homes and hospitals called Select-A-Rest.

In 1959, Detroit Harvester formally changed its name to Dura Corporation. Dura is a Latin word and in medical terms means the hard protective covering of the brain. The word durable has long been associated with the idea of well-made products which are capable of performing under the harshest conditions.

In March 1964, Dura acquired a plant in Adrian, Michigan, to provide additional facilities for the automotive group. In 1966, Dura Corporation was acquired by Walter Kidde & Company, Inc. and became a subsidiary of that firm. Although the years that followed saw convertible sales drop to nothing, Dura Division continued to expand its other product lines. It now manufactures window regulators, door hinges, hood hardware, suspension components and shifters. The company is now the world's largest independent producer of electric window regulators.

Ragtop fever broke out in the early '80s; Chrysler, Ford and General Motors had the cure—convertibles. Again Dura Corporation responded to the demands of the American public. The new era of convertibles has begun, and Dura is proud to be once again a provider of dreams.

197

Aerial view of Dura Corporation's Toledo plant in 1982 (above). Presentation of the Army-Navy "E" award on August 13, 1943 (below).

Full spectrum health care center unique in Northwest Ohio and nation

When Stevens Warren Flower, Civil War veteran, noted business leader and "a man of true Christian virtue," bequeathed property and funds to build a hospital near his family home in Toledo during the early 1900s, little did he know that the hospital would grow, prosper and become a multifaceted regional medical center.

Flower, who died in 1908, was described by a colleague: "Men trusted him because of their profound faith in his integrity. They followed him because he possessed the qualities of leadership; they loved him because he was a humble follower of Jesus, and those who knew him best loved him most."

Inspired by his generosity, the Methodist church began a campaign to match his $20,000 bequest, and in 1910, the first Flower Hospital building opened. It was dedicated as a memorial to Cindarella Carey Brown, daughter of the Honorable John Carey, one of the most notable of the early settlers of Northwest Ohio, a U.S. Congressman in the 1850s and founder of the town of Carey.

At the opening of that first hospital building, a church official said, "No matter what creed or dogma we hold to, we can all unite in the work of caring for the sick and the poor."

From its very beginnings, Flower Hospital began to grow to meet community needs. A second building was attached in 1913 and a school of nursing was inaugurated. When another unit opened in 1926, *The Blade* observed, "Flower Hospital steps into the forefront position, becoming one of the largest and most modern denominational hospitals in the Middle West."

The hospital grew through the 1930s and 1940s, and in the mid-1950s, trustees announced a plan to establish a "cradle to grave" health care center in Toledo, with Flower Hospital as the central component. In 1957, more than 80 acres of land were purchased in suburban Sylvania, and the announcement was made that the historic Harroun Farm would become the site of the new Crestview Center complex.

In 1960 the first building of that complex opened—Crestview Club Apartments, providing luxury private living for retirees. In 1966, Lake Park Hospital was dedicated, adding yet another level of medical care for the elderly and persons in need of specialized rehabilitative services.

Flower Hospital in 1913 (above), three years after its founding. The 80-acre Flower Hospital (below)—Crestview Center complex in 1982. (From left, 5300 Medical Building, Flower Hospital and Lake Park Hospital).

At the same time during the 1950s and 1960s, the Flower Hospital facilities at Cherry and Collingwood were growing to provide added medical services. New emergency facilities (with the first drive-up emergency entrance in the United States) were added, maternity was expanded and an educational services building and School of Nursing dormitory were built.

In 1972 construction began on the new Flower Hospital at the Harroun Road site, a nine-story ultramodern building which was dedicated in March 1975. One important feature of that facility was the McKesson Memorial, honoring Dr. Elmer I. McKesson, pioneer anesthesiologist, and his son. The memorial was established with a $3 million bequest from Dr. McKesson's widow, Martha.

Since the opening of the new Flower Hospital, expansion and growth have continued—the nationally acclaimed Oncology Center and the Chemical Dependency Center for alcoholism treatment were dedicated in 1979. The 5300 Medical Building and a large parking garage were completed in 1981. In 1982 an ambitious ten-year plan calling for doubling the size of Flower Hospital was announced. This plan includes construction of a new Lake Park Hospital tower, additional apartment towers and extended/intermediate care facilities at Crestview, doubling the size of the medical building and parking garage, addition of a support services building between Flower and Lake Park and a new Wellness Center and motel.

This new expansion is yet another step in meeting the health care needs of the community at all levels—acute care, rehabilitation, intermediate and extended care and retirement living.

Twenty-nine years of growth

In 1953 General Mills was having severe growing pains, and was definitely in need of a new production facility. A search was started for the ideal site—a strategically located city with a good labor force, growth potential of its own and with excellent transportation facilities. Toledo met all of those qualifications, and the decision to move was followed by the acquisition of the 180,000-square-foot Lee and Cady Grocery Warehouse on Laskey Road.

At that time General Mills had three other package foods plants, annual sales of $483 million and net earnings of $11.5 million. Today, General Mills, which operates in the five business areas of consumer foods, restaurants, toys, fashion and specialty retailing, has annual sales of almost $5 billion with earnings of nearly $200 million. That's a staggering 1,035 percent increase in sales and 1,739 percent growth in earnings. The Toledo plant is very proud to be a part of this extraordinary progress.

The growth of the Toledo Package Foods Plant has also been phenomenal. In its first year there were 75 employees who produced a limited line of Betty Crocker products—angel food cake, layer cake and brownie mixes. Today, it is producing thirteen different dessert mix items and eight cereals, including Cheerios, the leading children's cereal in the United States. The number of employees has grown to 760 with an annual payroll exceeding $18 million.

General Mills is proud of that decision 29 years ago to locate its fourth package foods plant in Toledo. The plant now produces over twelve million cases of products annually and is the largest of the six General Mills package foods facilities. The Toledo plant's daily production translates into nearly nine million servings of cereal and over 417,000 packages of dessert mixes.

When Bruce Atwater, chairman and chief executive officer of General Mills, addressed the employees at the plant's 25th anniversary in 1978, he called the Toledo facility "one of the finest plants General Mills has" and cited the excellent labor-management relationship which has existed since the very beginning.

The size of the plant has expanded fivefold since its beginning in 1953. Four major expansions have increased the plant's square footage from 180,000 to 650,000.

The first expansion came in 1955, just two years after General Mills acquired the site, when equipment for the production of breakfast cereal was added. In 1964 the warehouse was enlarged. A $3 million expansion of the cereal facility in 1974 made the Toledo plant the company's number one producer of puffed cereal, in addition to being the largest maker of Cheerios. Another expansion took place in 1977; costing $9 million, it was focused on additional warehousing and plant-wide modernization.

In January 1981 a new truck facility enabled the Toledo plant to supply finished products via truck to its ten distribution points and to customers in a nine-state service territory. This new facility reached a milestone in January 1982 with the handling of the 10,000th finished-product truck.

A $25 million expansion is currently under way in the cereal plant, adding a fourth puffed cereal system. It has a target completion date of spring 1984.

It's been 29 prosperous years and General Mills is still growing. The company is happy to be a contributing part of Toledo's corporate community and looks forward to celebrating another 29 years of growth and prosperity in the Maumee Valley.

General Mills' Toledo plant, 1982 (above). General Mills' Toledo plant, 1953 (below).

199

Its roots are deep in a city it is proud to call "home"

The forerunner of The Huntington National Bank was chartered on December 31, 1917, as The Morris Plan Bank of Toledo. From its inception, its leaders were men of stature from the foremost families and businesses of the area. Among the founders and members of the first board of directors were Thomas A. DeVilbiss (who also founded the De-Vilbiss Company, renowned makers of atomizers), Harold S. Reynolds and C.O. Miniger. Its first president was Gordon M. Mather of the well-known family which headed Toledo's Mather Spring Company.

In 1946, the bank, by then renamed the Lucas County Savings Bank, moved to a new location. When the doors of the bank opened, everything was new—pictures, furniture, carpeting. The concept of carpeting in a bank was so unusual and innovative that *Time* Magazine sent a reporter and photographer to record the event.

The new location was the E.H. Close Building, named for one of Toledo's early real estate developers. The bank occupied the first floor, while on the second floor was one of the finest restaurants in the area. One of the early associates of the bank recalls that when the bank expanded to the second floor, she found that her desk was located on the spot where she had enjoyed roast beef dinners as a child!

"The Morris Plan" for which the bank was originally named denoted a system devised by Arthur Morris which permitted banks to enter the field of personal loans, a field previously the prerogative of small loan companies. The Plan offered substantial interest savings to the borrowing public and served as the basis for personal loan banking as it is now.

In addition to making personal loans and accepting savings deposits, the bank introduced an innovative personal checking account called "Pay-By-Check" in which the bank sold fifteen checks for one dollar, required no minimum deposits and made no other service charges. It was the first such account in the area and was widely imitated.

From its founding, the bank's name changed several times. When activities expanded into commercial and real estate banking, The Morris Plan Bank became The Lucas County Savings Bank. A short time later, the word "Savings" was dropped, and in 1963, following a merger with the State Bank of Toledo, it became

Robert H. Carlile, president of the Toledo area Huntington National Bank, stands by the traditional arch of the Ohio Building, headquarters for the bank's commercial and leasing functions in Northwest Ohio.

known as The Lucas County State Bank. In 1970, the nine Toledo offices became affiliated with the Columbus-based Huntington National Bank. The name again changed—to The Huntington Bank of Toledo.

A glance at the history of The Huntington reveals that it originated in Columbus in 1866 as a single bank, The P.W. Huntington Company. From there, it is a story of growth. By the end of 1981, its assets had increased to more than $3 billion, with 123 branches providing service to 61 communities in 21 Ohio counties.

In 1966, Huntington Bancshares was founded and operated as a multibank holding company until December 31, 1979, when its affiliated banks (including The Huntington Bank of Toledo) merged into one statewide bank, The Huntington National Bank. Thus, from its modest and quiet beginning in Toledo, The Huntington has grown into a major banking institution with a broad spectrum of new bank services.

In October 1981, the commercial loan and leasing functions moved to the newly-renovated Ohio Building (formerly the home of Toledo Edison) for more efficient operation. In the same month, a major renovation of its banking lobby at 515 Madison Avenue was underway.

Today, The Huntington offers Toledoans extensions of the banking "firsts" which stand out in the history of The Huntington and, in many cases, in all of banking. Among these historic "firsts" are flexible interest rates on installment loans; variable rate home mortgage loans with fixed payments; "plain English" banking forms; and simple interest calculations on personal, automobile, home improvement and small business loans.

The Huntington National Bank in Toledo has deep roots in the area; its story is the history of not one great bank, but two—each progressive and innovative—now merged into a single entity to carry forward the best of banking traditions and services.

Eighty-one years old and still helping Toledo grow

The history of the Kuhlman Corporation—Toledo's largest and oldest supplier of building materials—goes right to the foundations of the city's growth. Kuhlman-mixed concrete makes up not only the foundations, but many elements of area structures, including streets, expressways and bridges.

Landmarks in and around downtown Toledo built with Kuhlman products include Scott and Waite high schools, the former Commodore Perry Hotel, the Anthony Wayne Bridge, the Ohio Citizens Bank Building (former Owens-Illinois Building), the Toledo Edison Building, First Federal Plaza and the new City-State Office Building and SeaGate Parking Garage.

Industrial facilities featuring Kuhlman products include the Sun Oil and Standard Oil refineries and Toledo Edison's Bayshore Power Plant. The Bowling Green State University Football Stadium, numerous University of Toledo buildings and Southwyck Mall are among other users.

Nearly a century ago, Adam R. Kuhlman was a bricklayer and molder who became a mason/contractor. He joined with Richard Kind to form the building supply firm of Kuhlman-Kind Co. In 1901, it merged with three other firms to become Toledo Builders Supply Co., predecessor of today's Kuhlman Corporation.

The first supply yards were near Cherry and Champlain streets and 22 Main Street on the east bank of the Maumee River. Later yards opened at 420 Water Street, 153 South St. Clair Street and in what were then outlying areas—Sylvania Avenue and Bennett Road and Dorr Street near Westwood Avenue.

Adam Kuhlman was vice president of the fledgling company and became president in 1916. He broke away and formed Kuhlman Builders Supply and Brick Co., which bought out Toledo Builders Supply in 1925. Kuhlman also was a community leader who became president of the Toledo Chamber of Commerce, among other civic roles.

The addition of the word "brick" in the company's name resulted from its 1919 acquisition of the Ohio Brick Co. on Consaul Street. The brick-making operation was dropped in the 1940s when the site ran out of clay. However, the company remains a specialist in brick and is the area's largest brick supplier.

In 1928, the company was the first in Northwest Ohio and one of the first in Ohio to enter the ready-mix concrete business. When the Depression hit, the fleet of five mixers helped keep the company afloat, giving it an edge in the few construction projects that took place.

Today, the company is best known for its concrete, which accounts for about 50 percent of its business. It maintains a fleet of approximately 70 modern concrete mixers, each of which holds at least five times the capacity of one of those early mixers.

In 1933, when Adam Kuhlman died, the company was passed on to his sons, Charles and Edwin. Charles was elected president. Business declined again during World War II as equipment became unavailable but picked up after the war; the company prospered as the building industry boomed.

Charles Kuhlman died in 1956, and Clyde Stevenson was elected president. The firm made several acquisitions, including Koder Concrete and Supply, Inc., Carl Zenz and Associates Co., Knapp Ready Mix, Inc., and The Grienwahn Co. The last two purchases extended Kuhlman's operations into southeastern Michigan, the Bowling Green market was entered in 1964 through the purchase of Wood County Transit. In 1967, the company bought White Bros. Sand Co. and entered the commercial dredging business.

Upon Stevenson's death in 1967, M.S. Bartholomew, son-in-law of Charles Kuhlman and current president, took over the firm's helm. Under Bartholomew's direction, the company—now known as the Kuhlman Corporation—is expanding into other areas. One is the development, beginning in the late 1960s, of the 100-acre Charles E. Kuhlman Industrial Park along the Maumee River, now the site of the company's Yard #1, the new Cargill Grain Elevator and part of The Andersons' grain-handling complex.

In 1967, Kuhlman was awarded the concrete contract for Detroit Edison's Monroe, Michigan, generating plant—the world's largest fossil fuel power plant. Two years later, the company was awarded the contract for the Enrico Fermi II Nuclear Power Plant, and in 1972 it was awarded the contract for the Greenwood Energy Center Unit #1, all major Detroit Edison projects.

The company's latest venture is the bulk storage of materials, with potash, a fertilizer component, the main commodity to date. Great Lakes freighters dock and unload materials directly from cargo compartments onto the hard-stand riverfront pad.

As it has for the last 81 years, the Kuhlman Corporation continues to span new horizons.

One of Toledo's first ready-mix concrete mixers

Sixty years of professional service and commitment to the community

The first Lane Drug Store came into existence in 1922. It was located at the corner of Erie and Adams, across from the courthouse. The store's ads read, "We meet or beat all advertised prices. Nothing in our store is sold at full price. Every item is sold at cut rate every day."

In the '20s, people flocked downtown to do their shopping. The new store was well liked. Lane's had home delivery, and it carried a larger variety of over-the-counter drugs than the smaller stores in the area. Tonics were big sellers. They filled the bill for customers with rheumatism, arthritis or what have you. They also contained a high percentage of alcohol, and many felt that the tonics were good for what ails you. The pharmacists worked at the rear of the store filling the prescription drugs—they compounded ointments and liquids, and even made their own suppositories. They filled 35 to 50 prescriptions a day and worked 60 to 70 hours per week, as did the other store personnel.

The clerks waited on customers from behind the counters. Since the store was small, the stock was arranged on shelves the height and length of the walls. If an item was not readily available, a clerk would climb a movable ladder attached to a railing which hung from the ceiling to obtain the necessary merchandise. They weighed the merchandise, scooped candy from large bins, wrapped the items which were sold in sheets of brown paper and tied the packages with string which hung from big rolls on the ceiling. People stood in long lines to be waited on, and patience was a virtue.

Prices during the pre-Depression years would be a shopper's paradise in the '80s. One could purchase three packages of cigarettes for 35 cents, three boxes of soap for 50 cents, face powder for 29 cents and, frequently, any $2.00 item for $1.15. Store personnel made price changes on the merchandise by wetting a piece of tape with cotton and printing the change with indelible pencil.

During the next few years, five more stores were added. The second store was strategically located on Summit Street, directly across from the Tiedtke Department Store renowned for its famous deli. Two more downtown stores were opened, one on Starr Avenue, and, in 1938, the first air-conditioned "super store" on Sylvania Avenue, featuring a self-serve grocery and soda fountain. That same year, the stores were sold to K-W Drug Company of Cleveland, who was to be Lane's parent firm for many years.

In 1956, the Sidney Amster family in Cleveland, who owned Lane's at the time, sold the chain to the A.C. Israel Commodity Company in New York. Company operation, however, was retained by the Amster family until 1970. That year, Adrian Israel brought on board Sheldon W. Fantle, former executive vice president of Schuman Drug Company in Canton, Ohio, to serve as president and chief executive officer of the Lane Drug Company, and headquarters were moved from Cleveland to Toledo.

In 1971, it was announced that the New York-based Lane Drug Corporation, with stores in Ohio, Pennsylvania, West Virginia, Alabama and Georgia, would embark upon a major expansion and make Toledo its home. Fantle was elected president and chief operating officer of the parent company. In 1973, the office and warehouse were moved to the new distribution center on Waggoner Boulevard, said to be one of the most modern facilities in the United States.

The next few years brought about a number of changes. The Lane Drug Corporation made many acquisitions and consolidated its operations. The most significant change was its merger in 1976 with Peoples Drug Stores, Inc., of Washington, D.C., a chain of 250 stores. Fantle referred to the merger as, "The minnow swallowing the whale," since the much smaller Lane's had purchased the larger Peoples.

As for the corner drug store, it's now a part of the fourth largest drug chain in the country, and growing.

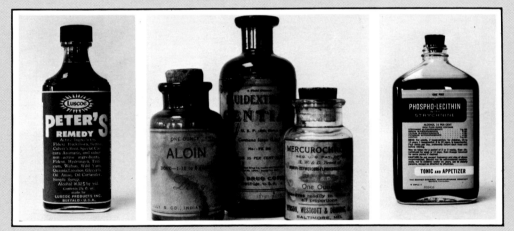

Part of a collection of early remedies on exhibit in the reception area of Lane Drug headquarters in Toledo (above). The 1953 grand opening of the eleventh Lane's Drugs outlet at Broadway and South in Toledo (below).

From automotive leaf springs to concrete silos

The original Mather Spring Co., c. 1911.

When Gordon MacDonald Mather returned from a European honeymoon, his mind was exploding with ideas for the adaption of alloy steels to be used in the manufacture of leaf springs—a development already being used in French manufacturing plants.

Mather settled in Toledo, Ohio, and founded the Mather Spring Company in 1911. Eager to exploit his newly gained knowledge, he engaged in research with American steel companies to replace the heavy, stiff carbon steel springs with lighter, stronger and more flexible alloys.

The Mather Spring Company received its first order from Henry Ford to supply leaf springs for the first mass-produced Ford cars. Mather springs were made of chrome vanadium steel—an outgrowth of Mather's research.

Mather was a recognized leader in suspension technology. As a result, many innovations in product design and manufacturing methods are attributable to him.

Financial investments intrigued the senior Mather and prompted him to establish the Morris Plan Bank, in which he held a controlling interest. He was extremely proud that this bank was the only one in the Toledo area which did not close or operate on a restricted basis during the banking crisis of 1932.

Mather Spring's reputation was further enhanced when Walter Chrysler, who was brought to Toledo by John Willys, turned to Mather for engineering assistance in the development of springs for the Overland and Willys Knight cars.

Mather, wanting to diversify and expand during the 1930s, built a new plant to manufacture automobile bumpers on a 22-acre tract on the Dixie Highway. This venture, called the Gordon Manufacturing Company, was considered the largest of its kind in operation in the United States at that time.

By 1938, growth of the automobile, truck and trailer industries had spread to the East Coast. Consequently, additional spring production facilities were required and the Mather Spring Company built a new plant in Linden, New Jersey.

During World War II, the Mather plants were devoted to forging and heat treating metal products for the Armed Forces. Mather's metallurgical knowledge helped produce battle-tested armor plate, variable-pitch propeller hubs, tank-piercing artillery shells and other defense products. So original were Mather techniques, the government used them as master plans for other manufacturers.

Keeping abreast of new technology set the stage for the construction of a second Toledo plant in 1946. Set up as a special division of the Mather Spring Company, the plant manufactured torsion bar springs, an innovation developed in Europe. The first customers were Twin Coach Company and Freuhauf Trailer Company.

In 1949, Gordon M. Mather retired from active participation in the company.

Gordon MacDonald Mather.

Henry T., one of his eight children, became president, and under his guidance, Mather Spring emerged as the largest independent producer of leaf springs in the world.

Henry T. Mather realized that growth and diversification were essential for survival. In 1959, he started the company on a series of diversification moves by acquiring a firm involved in the production and sale of thermoplastics. This led the company into another field of endeavor in 1962, when approximately eight acres of land was purchased in Milan, Michigan, for the construction of a pilot plant to fabricate products made from Teflon® Today, this division—Mather Fluorotec—is a recognized leader in the engineering and production of radial lip seals and a wide range of other sealing type products made from Teflon®

With a significant decline in the sale of torsion bars, in 1960 the technology present in this facility was converted to the production and sale of stabilizer bars to the automotive industry and currently is a major supplier of these parts.

Since the company was no longer a single-product enterprise, the word "spring" was dropped from its name in 1965.

In 1977, as part of its continued commitment to growth and diversification, the Mather Company purchased the Ruttmann Companies in Upper Sandusky, Ohio—a nationwide specialist in the construction of poured-in-place reinforced concrete silos for the bulk storage industry.

Current management, under the direction of Ernest J. Zammit, who was elected president in 1975, will continue to develop and expand the company's technologies, processes and products to fill the need for high-quality products and services wherever the need may be.

203

"Quality assured products" for half a century

Sometimes known as a janitorial supplies distributor, other times as a sanitary products distributor, but more exactly as a manufacturer and distributor of chemical maintenance products, Mellocraft was founded in the mid-1930s.

Donald Peatee Sr. started the business in his family's basement. Shortly thereafter he was joined by his brother, Harley, and a family enterprise was born.

The operation then produced four products mixed in old fifty-five gallon drums, which were packaged and sold door-to-door. Today, the company stocks about 4,000 basic items, sold nationwide.

Included in the initial line of products was a floor finish called "Mello-Wax," a derivation of the company name, "Mellocraft." It is now the well-known label for all of its manufactured products which include cleaners, disinfectants and deodorants, floor finishes, fertilizers, insecticides and weed killers and a broad selection of household and industrial soaps.

From its beginning in the family basement, the fast-growing Toledo operation faced increasing demands for more room. In sequence, moves were required to 909 Monroe Street, 120 Ontario Street, 407 Washington Street and finally to 1320 Locust Street—the former Lakeside Biscuit building and now the site of the present Toledo branch of Mellocraft.

In the fall of 1980, fire destroyed an entire Locust Street building housing the administrative offices and one-third of available warehouse space. In order to recover from the disaster, a new headquarters office and production facility was built on a ten-acre site just south of Toledo in Walbridge. Completed early in 1982, the latest expansion provided both a modern production capability and room for further expansion.

But why a headquarters in Toledo for a local Toledo company?

Immediately after World War II, Mellocraft began a steady expansion of its markets, sales force and operations. Operating branches have since been established in Cincinnati, Cleveland, Defiance, Findlay and Toledo, Ohio as well as in Detroit, Grand Rapids and Jackson, Michigan.

Defiance and Findlay were built from within. All other branches were developed either partially or totally through acquisition. Toledo acquired the Van Ness Supply Company in 1945 and the Berman Chemical Company in 1956. Later acquisitions enabled establishment of branches in Holland/Grand Rapids, Michigan, in 1972; Jackson, Michigan, in 1973; Detroit, Michigan, in 1974 and 1979; Cleveland, Ohio, in 1974 and Cincinnati, Ohio, in 1981.

Simultaneously, the original two-man sales force multiplied and remultiplied. Sixty direct sales persons now operate from the separated branch operations, serving customers not only in Michigan and Ohio but also extending to surrounding areas in Indiana, Kentucky, Pennsylvania and West Virginia.

Leapfrogging over those markets, a new national sales division as well as Berman Chemical have been responsible for the distribution of Mellocraft-manufactured products throughout the balance of the 48 contiguous states plus Hawaii and Canada.

The surge of acquisitions in the '70s was coincidental with changes in ownership. In July 1969, Mellocraft ceased to be a family business. It was acquired by Curtis-Noll Corporation of Cleveland, Ohio, a public company.

Curtis-Noll became a wholly owned subsidiary of Congoleum Corporation in 1977.

In 1979, Commercial Distribution Associates, Division of Hammermill Paper Company, Erie, Pennsylvania, acquired Mellocraft from Congoleum. They sought Mellocraft as part of their strategic planning for diversification of their own distribution capabilities and added fifteen branch operations of the various C.D.A. companies to Mellocraft's distribution potential in Delaware, Michigan, Missouri, Pennsylvania, Texas and Washington, D.C.

Despite this continuing expansion and growth, Mellocraft is dedicated to its Toledo customers; few are even aware of its chain of branches and spread of distribution into many other markets. Superior service from the company's 84 local employees has been undiminished. Today, as always, they maintain a tradition of pride, not only in providing "Quality Assured Products" but also quality assured service.

Mellocraft is proud of its Toledo origin and its close ties to its home community. It has been the company's lifetime satisfaction to hear "everyone knows Mellocraft." The company will continue to reciprocate with loyal service to every Toledo customer.

New headquarters and production facility for Mellocraft on 10-acre site in Walbridge, Ohio were completed in 1982 (below). Mellocraft products are distributed throughout 49 states and Canada (inset).

An aggressive leader in the community

Ohio Citizens Bank opened on March 28, 1932, as The Ohio Citizens Trust Company. Among the bank's founders were the prominent Toledoans Willard I. Webb Sr. and Willard I. Webb Jr. who, a year later, joined the bank as vice president and director. Webb Jr. was elected president in 1940; under his leadership, the bank's total resources rose from $16 million to approximately $130 million by the end of 1963. In 1964, he was elected chairman of the board and chief executive officer. His son, Willard I. Webb III, was named president. In 1970, Webb III was appointed chief executive officer and two years later was elected chairman of the board. Russell R. Berman, who had assumed a variety of responsibilities during his twenty years with the bank, was appointed president and chief administrative officer in 1973.

Ohio Citizens opened its first banking office at 335 Superior Street. Its trust department was located in the Ohio Building at 405 Madison Avenue which became the bank's headquarters for the next 37 years. In 1969, Ohio Citizens moved its headquarters to the Owens-Corning Fiberglas Tower, and in 1981, purchased the 27-story Owens-Illinois Building at 405 Madison Avenue. The return to this facility, renamed the Ohio Citizens Bank Building, began in March 1982 and was completed later that year.

The lobby of the main office location in the Ohio Building at 405 Madison Avenue (below) was the bank's headquarters from 1934 until 1969. The 27-story structure (right), now known as the Ohio Citizens Bank Building, serves as headquarters for the bank's executive offices and operating departments. A glassed-in atrium and connecting 500 car parking garage is planned for completion in 1983.

Mergers have played a major role in the bank's history and growth. Ohio Citizens merged with The Spitzer-Rorick Trust and Savings Bank in April 1959, bringing the bank's total deposits to over $100 million. In 1966, the Whitehouse State Savings Bank merged with Ohio Citizens, resulting in consolidated resources of $170 million. The Peoples State Bank of Wauseon merged with Ohio Citizens in 1979, contributing $34 million in assets and a capable staff serving Wauseon and the Fulton County area.

In 1980, the shareholders of Ohio Citizens Bank approved the formation of a bank holding company, Ohio Citizens Bancorp, Inc., to facilitate long-range merger and acquisition plans. In 1981, the new holding company acquired The Farmers and Merchants Deposit Company of Swanton, Ohio, and the following year merger agreements between Ohio Citizens Bank and The Farmers and Merchants Deposit Company were completed. In 1982, Ohio Citizens Bancorp announced a pending merger with National City Corporation, a Cleveland-based bank holding company. National City Corporation stated that after the merger the identity of Ohio Citizens as a separate banking institution will be preserved and its management staff retained.

Ohio Citizens Bank opened its first branch office in 1949 and has increased the total number of full-service offices in northwest Ohio to 25, including those in Whitehouse, Wauseon and Swanton. OC24 Automated Teller Machines, providing 24-hour banking convenience, are now operational in most full-service offices as well as in area hospitals and two off-premise supermarket locations.

Ohio Citizens position as an aggressive organization is reflected in its introduction of many new products and services. The bank established the first drive-in banking facility in the downtown Toledo area and opened the first bank in the city of Oregon. It was the first in Toledo to offer BankAmericard service, an open time deposit account called Golden Passbook, and the first to put teller terminals on-line to the computer system. Ohio Citizens was also the first Toledo financial institution to sell and service mortgage loans for the Federal National Mortgage Association and was the first in the world to install a mini-bank in a supermarket.

Ohio Citizens, throughout its history, has supported a wide variety of community projects to enhance the quality of life for residents of Northwest Ohio and Southeast Michigan. These projects include neighborhood development and rehabilitation programs, government projects and numerous cultural activities. The bank's continued interest in education is reflected in its support of educational institutions and programs such as the Student Investment Fund and the annual Scholarship Awards program of The University of Toledo. Employee participation in major community fund-raising campaigns such as the March of Dimes and United Way has been extensive throughout the past 50 years and has continued to be encouraged by management.

The dedication and vitality reflected in the bank's founders have been increasingly evident throughout Ohio Citizens 50-year history. With assets in excess of $645 million at year-end 1981, the bank remains steadfast in its commitment to serve the financial needs of the community and maintain the confidence of its shareholders, employees, customers and the community it serves.

205

A total packaging company with roots deep in glassmaking industry

Owens-Illinois, Inc. has roots deeply embedded in America's first industry—glassmaking.

What today is the largest corporation based in Toledo was started just after the turn of the century by inventive genius Michael J. Owens and successful businessman Edward Drummond Libbey.

Mike Owens grew up in Wheeling, West Virginia, a tough river town throbbing with industrial growth. At age ten, the boy—barefoot, with freckles big as dimes—walked up to the gate of a glasshouse and asked the boss for a job.

"I'm Mike Owens. I'm 10 years old—I've finished my education and I need a job," he said.

The boss, looking for some way to let the lad down easy, replied, "Kid, you don't have shoes. You can't work in a glass house without shoes."

Young Mike accepted this obstacle and took off. That afternoon, he scrounged the alleys of Wheeling and the next morning showed up at the plant gate wearing a pair of mismatched shoes that were much too big.

The boss was impressed with the boy's initiative, and Mike got his first job. By the time he was fifteen, he was a full-fledged glassblower, turning out 200 bottles a day by hand (a fraction of a minute's production on today's sophisticated bottle-making machinery).

Libbey, a graduate of Boston University, was born of well-to-do parents in Chelsea, Massachusetts. In 1880, his father purchased the New England Glass Company. This established glass company was started near Boston in 1818 and made fine table glassware, bottles and other products.

Edward entered his father's glass business as a partner and began on the lowest rung of the ladder learning every detail of the business. After his father's death in 1883, Edward became sole proprietor and continued the successful production methods then in use. In 1888, he took the bold step of moving the business to Toledo and incorporated it as the Libbey Glass Company.

Although Libbey came from a family with a long history of glassmaking experience, his financial position was decidedly shaky. Expenses were high, and many of Libbey's New England workmen grew homesick and returned East. As a result, quality suffered. Borrowing to the hilt to upgrade manufacturing facilities, Libbey finally put his operation on a profitable footing.

It was at this point that Mike Owens came to Toledo. Now in his early 20s, Mike decided to leave Wheeling and seek a job at the new Libbey glass plant. Libbey was happy to hire an experienced glassblower and made him superintendent of production. This began an association that would revolutionize the glass industry.

Libbey and Owens became interested in the development of automatic machinery for manufacturing glassware, and to this end, the Toledo Glass Company was organized in 1894 with Libbey as president.

With Libbey's encouragement and financial support, Owens began experimenting with a machine to blow glass. In 1903, the Owens bottle-blowing machine was perfected, making possible the production of uniform glass bottles. This was the single most significant development in glassmaking since the invention of the blowpipe more than 2,000 years before.

Despite the financial panic which swept the country that year, Libbey and Owens had faith in the future of their revolutionary machine. They reorganized Toledo Glass to form the Owens Bottle Machine Company, a firm primarily engaged in manufacturing Owens' machines and licensing them to other glass manufacturers around the world.

But Mike Owens realized that a business based on licensing alone would end when its patents expired. So in 1907, at his insistence, the Owens Bottle Machine Company also entered the bottle manufacturing field. The firm's name was later changed to the Owens Bottle Company.

As successful as his bottle machine proved to be, Owens was not content to rest easy. He became interested in a flat glass process originated by another inventor, Irving W. Colburn. Owens perfected this process and, with Libbey, founded the Libbey-Owens Sheet Glass Company. In 1930 this company merged with Edward Ford Plate Glass Company to form the Libbey-Owens-Ford Glass Company. (The name was changed to Libbey-Owens-Ford Company in 1968, reflecting L-O-F's expanding activities outside the flat glass business.)

Owens Bottle merged with the Illinois

Owens-Illinois led the revitalization effort in downtown Toledo by constructing a 32-story, glass-enclosed office tower. The building (below), located along the Maumee River, was completed in 1981. Michael J. Owens (right), the Owens of Owens-Illinois, Inc., stands in front of his automatic glass bottle-making machine which revolutionized the glass industry. Owens' invention was the first major development in glassmaking since the glass blowpipe was first used more than 2,000 years ago. Owens' machine—he is shown with a 1910 version of the one he invented in 1903—was perhaps the most complex machine mankind had seen at the time it started turning out bottles early in this century.

Glass Company (founded in Alton, Illinois, in 1873) to become Owens-Illinois in 1929, six years after Owens' death.

In 1935, ten years after Libbey's death, the Libbey Glass Company was acquired by Owens-Illinois, uniting two of the companies formed by these dynamic men—Edward Libbey and Mike Owens.

Owens-Illinois and Corning Glass Works of Corning, New York, formed Owens-Corning Fiberglas Corporation in 1938 to make fiber glass products. Glass fibers, or spun glass, had been known to glassmakers for centuries, but it wasn't until the twentieth century that production technology and profitable applications were developed. Owens-Corning also has its headquarters in Toledo.

The management of Owens-Illinois believed that diversification was an essential part of growth and began a continuous search for ways to make new and better things.

Today, the company is one of the world's leading manufacturers of packaging materials made primarily of glass, paper, plastic and metal. Its sales are about $4 billion annually.

In 1982, the company's domestic and international operations were organized into five worldwide product groups— Glass Container, Forest Products, Health Care, Plastic Products & Closure and Consumer Products.

These product groups include eight domestic divisions operating more than 100 manufacturing plants and four international divisions with affiliates and associates operating 100 facilities in 22 countries outside the United States.

This structure aligns O-I's existing product line into groups with distinct markets, proprietary technology, common production capabilities and raw material needs.

Overseas, the company manufactures all the products it makes domestically as well as some others.

Owens-Illinois is a world leader in machine-made glass tableware. Libbey Glass is America's best-known glass tableware, and O-I affiliates in Belgium, Brazil, Columbia, England and Japan also produce the company's fine tableware.

In glass and plastic scientific, pharmaceutical and laboratory products, O-I's Kimble brand name is well-known and respected around the world, as are glass

tubing products made by Buender Glas in Germany and tubing made by Kimble Italiana in Italy, both O-I affiliates. O-I also produces flat glass in Germany, Venezuela and Colombia and is a major producer of glass television tubes.

O-I has nearly 30 plastic container manufacturing plants and a 50 percent interest in a major plastic resin supplier—National Petro Chemicals Corporation. In addition, the company is a major manufacturer of metal and plastic caps, lids and other closures and fitments.

Owens-Illinois and its affiliates and licensees make about 40 billion glass bottles and jars annually. O-I plants and harvests trees on more than 1.1 million acres of owned or controlled timberland; converts the wood to linerboard and corrugating medium in four large and several smaller paper mills; and, with affiliates, operates 27 plants around the globe making corrugated shipping containers.

Founded on the wings of the revolution of glass, Owens-Illinois has soared to the forefront of American industry—not only as the world's largest manufacturer of glass bottles, but as a total packaging company.

Toledo's only osteopathic hospital was established by physicians

During World War II, several wives of Toledo area osteopathic physicians formed the Red Cross Knitting Group in 1941 to contribute their services to the war effort. Unbeknownst to these ladies at the time, this became the backbone supporting Parkview Hospital, the most comprehensive osteopathic health care institution in northwest Ohio.

Less than two years later, on a Sunday afternoon in April 1943, several osteopathic physicians and their wives met at the Hillcrest Hotel in downtown Toledo to discuss plans for an osteopathic community hospital. It was then that the physicians said to the women, "Put away your knitting. Convert your Red Cross knitting group into an auxiliary for the proposed hospital and get busy. We need money."

And so they did. Founded by seven doctors of osteopathy—Ralph D. Ladd, Harold J. Long, Wesley L. Billings, V.W. Brinkerhoff, William E. Reese, Myron J. Textor and Paul E. Black—construction of Parkview Hospital began on March 15, 1945, at 1920 Parkwood Avenue in the historic Old West End, the former homestead of the late Judge John H. Doyle. Funding came from personal donations of the founding fathers and fundraising events of the Auxiliary.

On June 26, 1946, Parkview Hospital swung open its doors for the first time. A 26-bed facility with six bassinets, Parkview had sixteen doctors of osteopathy on its medical staff and 40 employees. Dr. Ralph Ladd was president of the board of trustees when the hospital opened, and Dr. V.W. Brinkerhoff was the chief of staff. William S. Konold served as Parkview's first administrator and held this position for eighteen years.

Dedicated to the growth of their profession, the medical staff developed intern and residency programs in 1947 which were approved by the American Osteopathic Association (A.O.A.). This allowed medical student graduates of accredited osteopathic colleges to gain clinical experience at Parkview before establishing their own practices.

As the awareness of osteopathy grew, so did Parkview. Outpatient services were established within the first year. Having served more than 17,000 patients in its first four years, staff physicians and board members reached into their own pockets to raise funds for the first of several expansion programs. Completed in 1953, the new addition more than doubled the

Parkview Hospital's 26-bed health care facility was founded by seven Toledo osteopathic physicians in 1946.

number of beds, bringing it to 56, and also provided additional space for radiology, laboratory and surgery. Within four years, the board of trustees voted to expand again, adding nineteen more beds. And, in 1962, another expansion project increased patient capacity to 91.

Then, under the direction of Bernhardt A. Zeiher, who became executive director in 1964, ground was broken in 1969 for a $3 million expansion-modernization program. This three-story addition, which included a six-bed intensive care unit, opened two years later to complete the present 130-bed Parkview Hospital.

The 1970s was a decade of growth for the hospital. In 1973, Parkview officials purchased the adjacent Travel Lodge Motel on Collingwood Avenue. This 88-unit motel was connected to the main hospital and was remodeled for business and physicians' offices, as well as apartments for interns and residents. The hospital also acquired nearby land for additional parking and the adjacent Professional building for more physicians' offices and auxiliary activity rooms.

Parkview then undertook another major construction project. A roof-raising ceremony was held in October 1980 to commence construction of two additional floors to the three-story complex erected

in 1971. While this $12.2 million program did not increase the number of patient beds, it did provide for new patient rooms and nursing units. Old patient care areas were remodeled to house expanded ancillary departments.

Today, this 130-bed osteopathic hospital serves as a leading educator for future D.O.'s and other medical professionals. Along with its A.O.A. approved intern/resident programs, Parkview is affiliated with the Ohio University College of Osteopathic Medicine and offers clinical externships to its medical students and those at other osteopathic universities throughout the country. Parkview also sponsors educational programs for various health care professionals through affiliations with Northwestern Ohio Practical Nurses Training Center, Owens Technical College, University of Toledo and other area universities. Expanding its educator's role to include the community, Parkview offers many free public education classes.

Parkview Hospital recognizes its responsibility and continues to grow to meet the osteopathic health care needs of Toledo and surrounding areas. Yet, throughout its progressive history, Parkview has maintained its fine reputation for personal, individual patient care.

Fifty years in making thermosetting molding compounds

The Plaskon® story is an intriguing example of technological innovation in material and design undertaken to satisfy a specific market need. The market need was motivated by a very important consumer group—the housewife—whose demands at the marketplace culminated over 50 years ago in the invention of a new material for a specific design. The success of this development led into many other applications serving a variety of markets.

In the 1920s, housings for retail grocery and meat scales were made of cast iron. In order to fuse white porcelain enamel on the castings, an extremely thick and, consequently, very heavy iron casting was necessary. As a result, these scales were a back-breaking load for a salesman, and shipping costs were very high.

Lightweight black plastics were available, but, as a test, several black porcelain enamel housings were made and placed on trial in retail stores. Housewives refused to buy from these scales, since they immediately considered them unsanitary. A scale had always been white, and the housewives expected them to continue to be white.

Therefore, the Toledo Scale Company established a fellowship at the Mellon Institute to develop a white, lightfast, plastic material. In 1930, the results of the fellowship bore fruit with the development of a colorless urea-formaldehyde molding material that could be pigmented to any shade.

Having developed a new plastic material, Toledo Scale was faced with the problem of what to do with it. They did not want to manufacture it themselves, nor did they want to sell the process and patents. Consequently, the company set up a subsidiary concern on Sylvan Avenue in Toledo, and installed the necessary machinery for the production of "Plaskon Molding Compound."

From the beginning, the Plaskon compound found a ready market in many applications, such as buttons, bottle caps, lighting and household electrical fixtures. For many years, sales of the product more than doubled each succeeding year.

In 1936, Plaskon Company, Inc., and Unyte Corporation, another manufacturer of urea-formaldehyde molding materials, merged into a new Delaware Corporation, which adopted the name Plaskon Company, Inc. with general offices in Toledo, Ohio.

In June 1940, Libbey-Owens-Ford Glass Company, Toledo, Ohio, acquired 70 percent of the common stock of the Plaskon Company, Inc. from the Toledo Scale Company. In 1943, L-O-F acquired the balance of the outstanding common stock. The need for additional facilities prompted L-O-F to purchase the present Glendale site in 1942 and construct a new and modern plant with reserve capacity built in. However, forecasts proved conservative, and in 1958 the plant was doubled in size and capacity.

In 1953, L-O-F sold the Plaskon Division operation to the Allied Chemical and Dye Corporation.

Expansion in the field of specialty molding compounds continued with the purchase in 1964 of Mesa Products, a compounder of diallyl phthalate (DAP) molding materials. Mesa plants were located in Los Angeles, California; Des Plaines, Illinois; and Whippany, New Jersey. The latter two operations and manufacturing facilities were consolidated at the Toledo Glendale Avenue site in 1969 and were further consolidated at the Los Angeles plant in 1976.

Manufacture of epoxy molding compounds commenced in 1971 to provide encapsulation material for applications in semi-conductor and sophisticated electronic devices. Plaskon Electronic Materials, Inc., a wholly owned subsidiary of Plaskon Products, Inc., was established in 1980 to manufacture epoxy molding compounds which are distributed worldwide from Toledo.

In 1979, Plaskon Products, Inc., a wholly owned subsidiary of Hillside Industries Inc., acquired the Toledo and the Los Angeles operations from Allied Chemical. The corporate offices for the new company are located in Toledo, at a 50-acre site on Glendale Avenue, where a broad product line of PLASKON® thermosetting (heat setting) molding compounds are produced and shipped worldwide.

Today, the Toledo Glendale facility is the world's largest producer of urea-formaldehyde molding compounds that are compounded in thousands of colors for household wiring devices, circuit breakers and container closures.

Having gone full circle, with many name changes as it was passed from one to another of America's major corporations, Plaskon has emerged as a mature champion with headquarters again in Toledo.

Plaskon's Sylvan Avenue plant established 1931 (above). Plaskon's Glendale Avenue plant (below).

209

Firm's engineering innovations produce many firsts for automotive industry

Prestolite, one of the oldest names on the American industrial scene, is a name first associated with automobiles so far back that its advent is no longer chronicled in modern histories. However, today's Prestolite Company is a direct outgrowth of the former Electric Autolite Company, which was founded in Toledo in 1911.

Prestolite and its predecessor, Electric Autolite, began 71 years ago when its founder C.O. Miniger purchased the rights to a generator for powering early auto lamps. Within a year, the company placed on the market the first acceptable single starting motor. Gradually, through development and acquisition, the firm was manufacturing automotive electrical products, batteries, spark plugs, wire and cable and a vast number of components. Such companies as Studebaker, Packard and Indiana Buggy Company were among its first customers.

In 1927 the company acquired Prest-O-Lite and used it as a trade name for a battery line. With the sale of the Autolite trade name to Ford in 1961, the Prestolite name was adopted for its automotive and allied products and was later applied to the company itself.

In 1934 Electric Autolite merged with Moto-Meter Gauge and Equipment Company and a new operation began with greater emphasis in original equipment business along with the replacement trade.

Electric-Autolite acquired other companies as they were needed to produce an ever-expanding line. Divisions of such famous names as American Bosch, Magento Company and the Gray & Davis Company and U.S.L. Battery Company are now part of the Prestolite family.

In 1963 Electric Autolite and Mergenthaler Linotype Company merged to form Eltra Corporation. A diversified manufacturing company, Eltra's sales in 1978 grew to more than $1 billion. In 1979 Allied Corporation purchased Eltra and its many divisions. Today, the Prestolite Electronics, Motor and Wire divisions are part of the Allied Electronic Components Company and Prestolite Battery is part of the Allied Information Systems Company.

Toledo serves as headquarters for three of the Prestolite companies—Prestolite Motor, Electronics and Battery as well as Prestolite International Company. Toledo personnel are engaged in administration,

marketing and engineering positions serving the company's national and international markets.

Prestolite Motor manufactures DC fractional HP motors, traction motors, pump and cranking motors and alternators, as well as hydraulic and mechanical lifts. It has plants at Bay City, Michigan; Syracuse, New York; Wagoner, Oklahoma; and Cheltenham, England.

Prestolite Electronics products include tune-up parts, coils, electronic engine controls, military and electronic ignition systems, overvoltage controls, spark plugs, switches and regulators manufactured at its plants at Decatur, Alabama; Elberton and Macon, Georgia; Florence, Kentucky; Mansfield, Ohio; and Cambridge, Ontario.

Prestolite Battery makes batteries for automotive, truck, marine, farm, aviation and recreational vehicles at plants in Manchester, Iowa; Niagara Falls, New York; Reading, Pennsylvania; Vincennes, Indiana; Visalia, California; Maple, Ontario; and Drummondville, Quebec.

In addition, Prestolite products, licensed by Prestolite International, are manufactured in 34 plants in 23 countries outside the United States and Canada and U.S.-produced products are sold worldwide.

Prestolite operates one of the finest and most modern research centers in its field at Toledo. Utilization of the technical skills and facilities in engineering research and production is achieved through a high degree of specialization and integration.

The company has a rich heritage in the automotive fields and is now devoting a considerable share of research and development toward applying the extensive background of technical and production experience to fill needs in other industries.

Special emphasis has been placed on establishing leadership position in special original equipment markets such as farm equipment, material handling, marine, aircraft and truck as well as related aftermarkets. Today Prestolite is a supplier to all of these industries.

Prestolite history in research and development is long and fruitful. The company developed the first battery requiring water only three times a year; it perfected the first resistor spark plug, transistorized ignition system, powertip spark plug and underwater ignition. It introduced the Oasis, the first water-activated battery, in 1971 and the following years announced

the Liberator, a maintenance free battery which does not require addition of water during its normal life. In 1981 Prestolite introduced the Firepower battery, the world's most powerful automotive battery designed for diesel automobiles.

The company employs more than 500 Toledoans at its headquarters at 511 Hamilton Street.

Aerial view of the Prestolite Company headquarters at Toledo, Ohio (above). C.O. Miniger, founder of the Electric Autolite Company (below).

Progressive spirit and leadership spark a century of health care

At half past seven on the morning of July 17, 1884, a baby boy was born. This was the first birth recorded at The Retreat: A Home for Friendless Girls, which more than half a century later became Riverside Hospital. The Retreat had been organized by a group of prominent Toledo women to "promote moral purity by offering a temporary home to erring women who manifest a desire to return to a life of virtue, and procuring employment whereby they may earn their living."

They rented a house for $18 a month, furnishing and equipping it with their own possessions and often coming in to wash dishes and make beds themselves. They secured the help of the mayor, the City Board of Health, and the Police Department, and by the end of the first year were able to report a number of successful rehabilitations.

Medical care for these pregnant women and their newborns was provided by one of the first women doctors of the time and later by the Northwestern Ohio Medical College. For 1893 the secretary reported 41 admissions, 34 births, twelve adoptions, homes secured for ten girls, with thirteen others returned to their families. A typical annual drug bill was $12.

By 1895 the Retreat had developed into "A Maternity and Foundlings Home," both a "home for foundlings and a hospital for the care, treatment, and accouchement of pregnant women." The increased need for medical care was met by establishing a nurses' training program. The period of training was at first four months, but was soon extended to a year. By 1902 it offered certificates in "obstetrical nursing and the care of children." Pediatrics was a term not yet in use.

By 1910 the home became Maternity and Children's Hospital, reflecting its widening purpose as a hospital specializing in full health care for all women and children. The founding members, who long ago had pledged 40¢ a month to pay the rent, now raised money for a new 75-bed fireproof building—to this day a wing of the hospital. Modern children's and obstetrics departments were added, making the hospital a desirable teaching unit for the medical college.

World War I drained both funds and staff. There was no hospital insurance or Social Security, but the tireless board persuaded the city of Toledo to make payments for charity patients: $1.43 a day for adults, $1 for "up patients," and 75¢ for infants.

By the time the name was changed again in 1928, Women's and Children's Hospital had initiated a breast milk station and a pioneering out-patient clinic, which offered specialized medical care in obstetrics, gynecology and pediatrics to those who could not afford a hospital stay. The cases ranged from orthopedic problems caused by polio or tuberculosis to pelvic surgery.

During the Depression, the clinic was so overworked and the budget was so reduced, that the hospital was forced to abandon its specialties, although at that time it was one of the few institutions in the nation to offer a combined residency in pediatrics, obstetrics and gynecology. To keep the hospital going, the director and the dietitian made daily trips to markets and bakeries for food, while board members gave coal and money for payroll and equipment. Still, the hospital opened one of the early cancer clinics, with new deep therapy X-ray.

The first male patient was admitted by special permission for an emergency operation in 1930. The board later designated Riverside, as it had been named in 1945, a general, acute-care hospital.

The present-day, 270-bed hospital continues its early commitment to family and maternity. Designated a District Perinatal Center in 1980, Riverside offers specialized staff and technology and a variety of outreach programs for parents, siblings and grandparents. The hospital has a full range of ancillary services, including a computerized tomography scanner which began operation in 1982. The $2.3 million Center for Health Promotion opened in 1982 offers a series of programs, classes and health and fitness exams to encourage community members to become involved in their own health.

Riverside's progressive spirit, innovative leadership, community involvement and dedicated staff and volunteers are a continuing force. Improving the quality of life in the community remains its goal.

211

In the early 1900s, Riverside Hospital, then Maternity and Children's Hospital, specialized in the care of women and children.

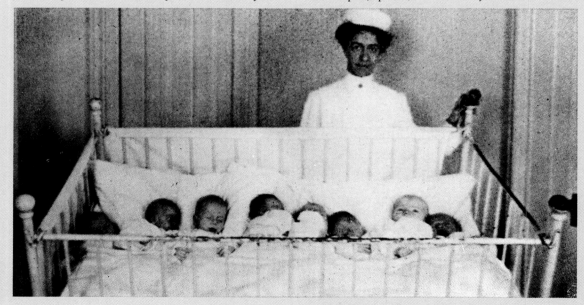

Blending innovative management with skilled craftsmanship

There were visible signs of prosperity in Northwest Ohio in the mid-1950s. But while progress was evident, some businessmen may have questioned seriously the common sense shown by three young and relatively inexperienced men who were determined to form their own construction company. One of the three was working on road construction and had some carpentry experience, another was fresh from duty as an Air Force pilot and the third was teaching high school math and physics—hardly qualifications for entering the construction business.

Nevertheless, Frederick Rudolph (the carpenter), his brother Philip (the pilot) and their cousin Allan Libbe (the teacher) stuck to their decision and, in the spring of 1955, Rudolph/Libbe/Inc. was formed. The company's first project was a room addition to the home of a family friend. Curiously enough, the company's first client later became one of its first employees.

Rudolph/Libbe has enjoyed steady growth since those formative days. The firm, which consistently ranks in the prestigious *Engineering News Record* 400 Largest Contractors list, has developed into one of the largest and most diversified construction firms in the Midwest. In addition to its general construction activity, Rudolph/Libbe has become very active in design and build construction as well as construction management. In the mid-1970s it also became involved in property development, opening its own Center for Business and Industry near its offices on the outskirts of Toledo. The firm participates as well in numerous other commercial office and warehouse-manufacturing center projects. In a corollary move to these activities, Rudolph/Libbe introduced fast-track site-cast tilt-up concrete construction in the area and has utilized this construction technique for many projects. One of these—the Adminstration Emergency Response Center at Toledo Edison's Davis-Besse Nuclear Power Station—was recognized as one of the nation's outstanding engineering achievements when it was completed in 1981.

Rudolph/Libbe has helped change the face of Toledo. In downtown Toledo it built the impressive headquarters for the Toledo Trust Company, the multi-story Port Lawrence parking structure across from Levis Square, the new headquarters and training center for the Marine Engineers Beneficial Association, the Lucas County Corrections Center, the Regional Criminal Justice Center and the Community Services Building.

The firm has also been active in the growth of the area's health care facilities. It built the new St. Luke's Hospital in Maumee in 1972 and handled a major expansion seven years later. It also worked on several major expansion projects at Parkview Hospital, Riverside Hospital and Flower Hospital.

One of the largest hospital projects the firm ever handled was construction of the 258-bed Teaching Hospital at the Medical College of Ohio. This building, erected in 1980, is among several major projects which Rudolph/Libbe built on the Medical College campus.

Rudolph/Libbe has also been visible on other college campuses in the area. It built the College Hall at Michael J. Owens Technical College as well as the school's Student Activities and Diesel buildings. At the University of Toledo, Rudolph/Libbe built the 17-story Parks Tower, the Theatre-Music Building and the Ritter Planetarium. The planetarium, built in 1968, was Rudolph/Libbe's first major construction project.

The firm has built several important commercial structures in the community, including the office complex for Blue Cross of Northwest Ohio. Another major commercial project was the total renovation of a World War I vintage factory structure into the highly efficient Business and Technology Center which Control Data Corporation established in Toledo.

On the industrial side, Rudolph/Libbe has been one of the area's busiest contractors. The firm built the enormous 264,000-square-foot coil-coating facility of Pre-Finish Metals, Inc. in just twelve months. It also handled a major expansion at Ford Motor Company's Maumee Stamping Plant.

In the 1970s Rudolph/Libbe became active in the government subsidized multi-family housing area and has renovated or put up more than 1,400 dwelling units in Northwest Ohio. Many of these units are occupied by retired people.

During its short history, Rudolph/Libbe completed a number of unusual projects, including the re-creation of Fort Meigs in Perrysburg. In this project, the firm built an authentic replica of the large eighteenth-century military installation using twentieth-century tools.

Still young, the firm has come a long way since its early days when the three founders also represented the company's total work force. At peak times Rudolph/Libbe employs several hundred people and points proudly to the fact that most of the general construction trades are included on its regular payroll. The firm's confidence in its employee force is symbolized by the introduction of several innovative employee programs, including a service award program and an employee suggestion program.

The 258-bed Teaching Hospital at the Medical College of Ohio, erected in 1980, is one of several major projects built by Rudolph/Libbe/Inc. on the Medical College campus.

Meeting the challenge of change

The roots of St. Luke's Hospital can actually be traced to the opening of a small clinic at the corner of Robinwood Avenue and Virginia Street in 1898. This clinic was a forerunner of the Robinwood Hospital erected in 1906 at 2517 Robinwood Avenue. Toledo had a population of 140,000 at the time and Robinwood Hospital, with a bed capacity of 50, became the fourth health care facility in the city. The hospital's primary objective, then as now, was to provide quality health care to the community.

Within a year of its founding, a history of change began at the hospital. In 1907 Robinwood School of Nursing graduated its first class. Ten years later, a home for students and faculty of the nursing school was built north of the hospital. As a result, the hospital's bed capacity was increased to 75.

In 1925, the Federated Lutheran Benevolent Society of Toledo purchased Robinwood Hospital for $175,000. The hospital underwent a dramatic change and was reorganized as a not-for-profit Christian institution. The goal of the hospital to provide quality health care gained new meaning—health care from a Christian perspective.

In 1928, just before the stock market crash, improvements on the structure were begun. A new wing, which increased bed capacity to 105, included an electric elevator, a surgery, a maternity delivery room and a laboratory.

During the 1930s, the hospital faced challenges and difficulties along with the rest of the nation. Anxious for the hospital facilities to remain available to the community, employees accepted reduced salaries for many months. Those who lived on the premises were paid only 40 percent of their wages, while those who lived away received 50 percent. Nurses, for example, received $23 a month for a ten to twelve hour work day that included scrubbing floors on hands and knees, preparing meals, boiling laundry and even sleeping at the bedside of critically ill patients. Meals were provided by the hospital to help offset the lowered salaries.

In 1938, the Blue Cross group plan was launched in Toledo and employees of the Robinwood Hospital became the first member group.

As the nation recovered, so did St. Luke's, and the 1940s began with a financial campaign conducted among members of the Lutheran churches to liquidate the hospital's $43,000 debt. Three years later, through rigid economy and careful financial planning, the hospital began preparing for the challenge of more changes.

Construction began on a new wing at the corner of Robinwood and Delaware Avenues in 1950. A city-wide campaign held the year before raised the funds to pay for the $770,000 program which increased the bed complement to 155 and extensively remodeled all the hospital's departments. At the project dedication on April 15, 1951, the institution was renamed St. Luke's Hospital. The new name emphasized the hospital's identity as a Christian institution.

Recognizing the growing demand for expanded services and facilities, St. Luke's faced its greatest challenge in the '60s and began to seek a new location. The potential in South Toledo and nearby suburbs led St. Luke's to its present 46-acre site on Monclova Road in Maumee. Groundbreaking was held on August 30, 1970, for the new $12 million, 206-bed hospital. The first patients were admitted to the new St. Luke's two years later.

St. Luke's spent the remainder of the '70s going beyond the care of the medically ill and injured to a more comprehensive program which stressed the promotion of health. As hospital costs increased and procedures improved, outpatient care grew as an important aspect of St. Luke's services. These services became an integral part of Phase II, the first major expansion and renovation program at the Maumee hospital. Groundbreaking was held on March 1, 1979, for the $14 million project which increased the hospital's size by 50 percent.

The '80s began with formation of the St. Luke's Hospital Foundation and the celebration of St. Luke's Diamond Jubilee at the dedication of Phase II on May 17, 1981. Late in 1981, the hospital began planning for Phase III, a project which included 80 beds and the addition of pediatrics to the hospital's services.

St. Luke's Hospital now looks forward to future growth and the challenge of changing health care needs.

St. Luke's Hospital, Maumee, Ohio.

Pioneering health care in the Toledo area

Toledo in the 1850s was a rapidly developing town in the middle of what was termed the Black Swamp. Work was plentiful on the railroads and canals, but the unyielding hardship of disease, too few doctors and no hospitals made life difficult. So when four Sisters of Charity of Montreal, the Grey Nuns, arrived in 1855 to establish the first hospital in Toledo, their task was prodigious—but their energy was inspired.

Within weeks of their arrival the sisters were established in a home where they operated both an orphanage and a hospital. A bazaar sponsored by concerned women of Toledo generated $669 to further their work. This began the tradition of innovative, progressive care supported by an appreciative community.

Acreage was acquired along Cherry Street and buildings constructed for use as a hospital and an orphanage. It was not until 1876, however, that the first comprehensive brick structure was built and became St. Vincent Hospital. (This building was used until the 1960s when it was leveled to make room for the construction of two nine-story wings.) Although there was only one doctor treating patients at St. Vincent during the first few years, by 1876 there were 24 physicians who officially organized the medical staff.

Physical changes were evident within the hospital during the next two decades. The addition of telephones, elevators,

electricity and natural gas all helped make patient care more efficient and the hospital more comfortable.

To ensure an appropriate number of well-trained individuals to assist in the provision of patient care, the Grey Nuns established a school of nursing in 1896. Although the size of the first graduating class in 1898 was only two students, over the years thousands have graduated, contributing their expertise in dozens of hospitals across the United States.

The turn of the century witnessed the beginning of numerous departments and services. When viewed in light of the sophisticated technology of today, images of these departments may be amusing because of their starkness and simplicity, but in their own time they were the best and most sophisticated available.

The Pathology department was established in 1906 and the Maternity department in 1908. Medical seminars were also begun, the forerunners of today's Continuing Medical Education department. Although the very first X-ray in Northwest Ohio was taken at St. Vincent in 1896, it was not until 1919 that the Radiology department was officially organized. Two years later the Emergency department was formally inaugurated although patients had been treated on an emergency basis since the early months of the hospital.

As services provided at the hospital continued to increase, so, too, did the

physical dimensions. In 1905, the hospital's golden jubilee year, a new wing was added to the hospital providing additional space for patients and services. Twenty years later another wing was dedicated, increasing the total bed capacity to 370.

A memorable event with long-lasting importance occurred in 1935 when the St. Vincent Hospital Guild formally organized. Although the Toledo community had always supported the hospital's work of—establishing a St. Vincent Sewing Society and the men's St. Vincent Hospital Society during the late 1800s,—the Guild holds a special place in the heart of St. Vincent. Through the years the Guild has served the hospital in numerous beneficial efforts, raising thousands of dollars to help purchase equipment, spon-

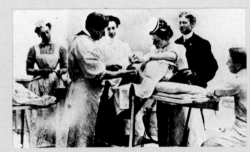

Although far removed from open heart or plastic surgery of today, surgery in the 1890s at St. Vincent was nevertheless progressively modern (above). The children's solarium in 1925 provided a bright, warm location for the Grey Nuns and staff to deliver their special kind of care (below).

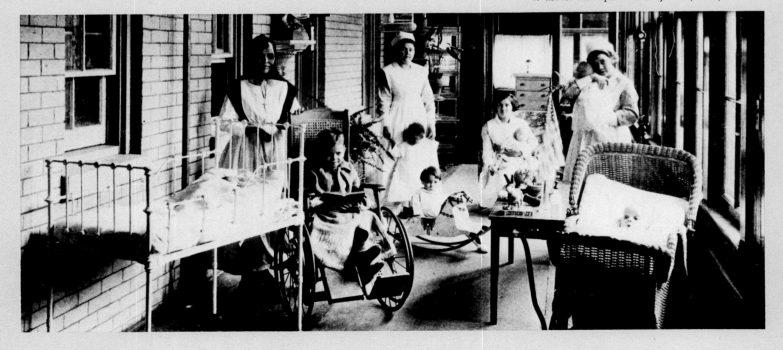

sor programs and provide additional services to countless individuals.

The Depression was not a time of major growth, but the presence of the Grey Nuns was appreciated on a different level as they provided free meals daily to many of those prostrated by the economy. The generosity and heartfelt concern of the Sisters of Charity of Montreal is always felt at St. Vincent. The hospital's philosophy reminds all that:

"The hospital strives to provide high-quality holistic patient care to meet the physical, emotional and spiritual needs of those it serves. St. Vincent serves all people in a spirit of Christian charity, regardless of race, creed, age, sex, national origin or financial status."

Following World War II, the hospital's growth, again required larger facilities, and the A-wing was dedicated in 1950, raising the bed capacity to 500.

In 1951 the ever increasing workload of the Grey Nuns forced them to withdraw from the administration of the orphanage they had begun simultaneously with the hospital in 1855. The Franciscan Sisters of Tiffin have operated St. Anthony's Villa ever since.

St. Vincent's centennial in 1955 was indeed joyous; the same year also witnessed the establishment of the Nuclear Medicine department and the completion of remodeling work to the Chapel of the Immaculate Conception.

St. Vincent steadfastly continued its century-long heritage of providing new services with superb quality care. Despite the feeling during the 1960s and 1970s of being hurtled along by technology, St. Vincent always managed to humanize the sophisticated services, remembering that its first commitment is always to the patient.

Initiating new services to continually enhance the level of health care, not only for Toledo, but all of Northwest Ohio and Southeast Michigan, St. Vincent emerged as a major medical referral center in the 1960s. Among the programs and services begun in these years were the Regional Burn Care and Reconstructive Center, Alcoholism and Chemical Dependency Rehabilitation Service, cardiovascular surgery, hemodialysis, psychiatric unit, retina unit and various intensive care units, including neonatal, pediatric, neuroscience, cardiovascular and peripheral vascular. Several of St. Vincent's programs are the only ones in the region, such as the Northwest Ohio

Reye's Syndrome Treatment Center, the Community Dialysis Center and the Northwest Ohio Spinal Deformity Center. The Life Flight emergency air medical service is the first of its kind in the state. When the 32-bed cardiac care unit opened in 1965, it was the largest monitor-equipped cardiac care unit in the nation.

With the construction in 1965 of two additional wings, raising bed capacity to 625, St. Vincent formally changed its name to St. Vincent Hospital and Medical Center (although it will always affectionately be known to many as St. V's.) The new wings included surgical suites for all types of surgical specialties, such as open heart, plastic surgery (including reimplantation of amputated limbs and digits), advanced orthopedic surgery and others.

Although the continued expansion of services has brought the total bed count to 729, St. Vincent remains a hospital serving its neighbors. This commitment was enhanced through increased ambulatory services in the 1970s and the dedication of the Marguerite d'Youville Ambulatory Care Center in 1979, named in honor of the foundress of the Grey Nuns.

While specialty medicine characterizes St. Vincent, programs such as pastoral care, social services, continuing patient care and patient representatives are also important to the patient's recovery.

The St. Vincent Hospital and Medical Center Foundation, incorporated in 1974, benefits the patients, medical and nursing

Demolition of the area's first major hospital (above), constructed in 1876, accommodated the expansion of the growing major medical center in 1966. Always at the forefront of innovative medical care to the region (below), St. Vincent initiated the Life Flight emergency air medical service in 1979.

staffs, employees and the general community through sponsorship of programs and through the purchase of equipment.

St. Vincent is also an important teaching institution, affiliated in residencies in emergency medicine, plastic surgery, radiology, orthopedics, pediatrics, obstetrics-gynecology, medicine, surgery, urology and psychiatry. Daily continuing medical education conferences help keep physicians informed of the latest advances in medicine, specialty seminars are held once a month for regional medical and nursing personnel.

The guiding care and concern of the Grey Nuns still permeates all medical advances, and the sisters, medical staff and St. Vincent employees remain aware that they are helping their fellow man. While St. Vincent will historically remain Toledo's first hospital, it has been described as the innovative leader in health services for the region.

From the ground up—growing into the future

Colonel Nathaniel Haughton entered business just after the Civil War. He made frequent calls on such customers as the Toledo Steam Engine Works, a small foundry and machine shop located on Huron Street near Lafayette, which manufactured steam engines, mill gearing, potash kettles and car castings. When Haughton learned that one of the partners was willing to sell his interest, he obtained the necessary $6,000 investment, and in 1868 joined in a three-way partnership. Within a year he purchased a second interest, and the firm became known as Haughton and Kneisser. The Haughton enterprise had begun.

By 1885, as a natural progression from the production of hoists and winches, the firm began the manufacture of elevators. The first Haughton elevators were hand-powered using ropes or cranks—but steam soon replaced muscle as the driving force.

In 1890 Colonel Haughton bought out George Kneisser and renamed the firm N. Haughton Foundry and Machine Company, and in 1897 the firm became known as the Haughton Elevator and Machine Company, Inc.

By 1916 the company had outgrown the existing facilities on Huron Street. Since Toledo was a rapidly expanding city, the plant was moved to Spencer Street where a modern factory and office were erected. Within three years the plant would include a major addition to house a growing business.

In 1936 the firm name was changed to the Haughton Elevator Corporation. Three years later Haughton instituted research and design for a new product,

"moving stairs," which escalated annual sales to $2,033,369.

In the early 1940s the company diversified to fill government contracts stemming from World War II. The April 1942 issue of the *Hera Herald,* an internal publication, stated, "Our factory has been taking in a large volume of special machine work in an effort to do all in our power to advance the war effort." A few of these special efforts included the design and manufacture of a turntable for testing bombers at Ford's Willow Run plant, the development of air gas turbines for the Navy and the fabrication of propeller shaft thrust couplings for escort ships.

In 1951, acquisition of the Elevator Maintenance Company, Ltd. in Los Angeles provided Haughton with a base of operations in the Western states.

Recognizing that electronics would play a principal role in vertical transportation technology, Haughton officials voted in 1957 to merge with the Toledo Scale Company—a Toledo-based firm which pioneered in the application of electronics.

In 1965 Haughton purchased Richmond Fireproof Door, the manufacturer of Peelle escalators. The Richmond, Indiana, plant was closed nine years later, and its escalator division moved to the Toledo facility.

Another major step was taken in 1967 when Haughton, along with Toledo Scale, joined with Reliance Electric Company of Cleveland, Ohio, a major developer and manufacturer of automated material handling systems.

In 1969 Haughton expanded and

opened an electro-mechanical assembly plant in Sidney, Ohio, and in 1972 the plant moved to new quarters on Vandemark Road in Sidney.

The service department moved in 1973 to Opportunity Drive in Toledo. This department—now the National Service Center—provides service to customers around the United States.

In 1976 Haughton purchased Elevator Sales and Service Company of Miami, Florida, and Associated Elevator Company, Inc. in Houston, Texas. In 1978 the company purchased International Energy Management Corporation, headquartered in Indianapolis.

In 1979 the firm was purchased by Schindler Holding, Ltd.—a worldwide manufacturer and marketer of elevators, escalators, automatic material handling systems and railway coaches. Headquartered in Lucerne, Switzerland, Schindler has major manufacturing facilities located in 25 countries, and is represented in more than 100 countries through wholly owned operations, affiliated companies and unconsolidated subsidiaries.

In 1981 Schindler Haughton's SW Escalator—the ultimate in escalator technology—was introduced. To make room for the escalator, Schindler Haughton leased 50,000 square feet of warehouse space on Airport Highway.

The expansion of the '70s complete, Schindler Haughton and its more than 2,000 employees located in 92 cities nationwide, look forward to continued technological leadership in the marketplace and to expansion in the United States and abroad.

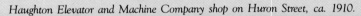

Haughton Elevator and Machine Company shop on Huron Street, ca. 1910.

... And how it grew!

In 1948, five independent food store operators agreed to merge into a voluntary chain. Wally Iott, Paul Pope, Frank Ulrich, Tom Swinghammer and Joe Altschuller.

It seemed the sensible thing to do in those days—to join forces for strength in buying and advertising. The new chain operated as "Food Town." Each member of the group brought with him the knowledge and experience necessary to manage a small business. Together they were to become a big business.

This small group of five stores continued to grow; by 1956 it was a chain of eight stores. The group decided to incorporate and selected the operating name of "Seaway Food Town, Inc." for the conglomerate. A headquarters office was also established in a remodeled store at 1514 S. Detroit Ave., Toledo, OH.

Each of the original five men brought his own expertise into the organization. They were more than working partners, they were friends. This friendship endured over the years—through retirements and deaths, through enormous growth and expansion and through raising the sons and bringing them into the business. Now, only two members of the original five remain. Paul Pope, retired from day-to-day operations and serves as a member of the board. Wallace D. (Wally) Iott, has been president of the company since it's inception and chairman of the board since Food Town, in April 1962, went public by filing a registration statement with the Securities & Exchange Commission covering a public offering of 125,056 shares of common stock.

In June of the same year, the company purchased a combined office and warehouse in Maumee, Ohio. There were only seventeen stores at that time and the warehouse was larger than was

needed. It has since been enlarged to double the original size. Another warehouse has been built in the same complex, and additional land and buildings have been purchased adjacent to the original office and warehouse.

The company has diversified in several directions with a wholly owned bakery; a 50 percent interest in a dairy; a food service division, a wholesale division servicing other supermarkets and a general merchandise division. The warehouse that was once too large is now too small to accommodate the growth, and the company has been forced to make use of satellite warehouses to take care of the overflow.

When the company was first formed, all of the stores were within a radius of 15

miles. Over the years a steady rate of growth has expanded operations to a 150-mile radius. The one pickup truck that very easily serviced the original five stores has grown to a fleet of 85 pieces of rolling stock and a garage to keep them rolling.

As a result of Wally Iott's preference to promote people from within the company, several of the current vice presidents were carryout boys at the beginning of their careers with Seaway Food Town.

The food industry is a fast-paced, highly competitive business. The profits are the smallest of all industries and the hours are the longest, but it is also an industry of opportunity and challenge. Seaway Food Town has accepted the challenge.

W.D. (Wally) Iott during his freshman year in 1930, on his first job (right). Wally Iott's first Food Town Store (below).

217

Family owned for over 100 years and four generations

More than a century ago a 17-year-old German immigrant named Valentine Seeger left Pfungstadt, Germany, to begin a new life in Toledo. He began an apprenticeship as a machinist that took him seven years to complete.

In 1881, at the age of 26, Valentine Seeger began his own business as a machinist and brass finisher on the third floor of 92 South St. Clair Street in Toledo. Today, Seeger Metals and Plastics, Inc. is observing more than 100 years in business with the fourth generation of Seeger family actively involved. The third floor walk-up is now a 30,000-square-foot warehouse at 1315 East Manhattan Boulevard.

As with many new businesses, the initial years were a struggle. Word of Seeger's work apparently spread, because the next year he advertised in the Toledo City Directory that he was operating a shop for "brass goods and fine work." He added "castings" to the ad a few years later and in 1888 moved to 15 North St. Clair Street, where the family eventually purchased the building.

The operation expanded as it added new items to its product line. By 1891, he was also listing brass goods, copper and brass tubing, brass sheet and babbitt metal. The Seeger company still follows the original philosophy, adding new items as market conditions and requirements change.

The name was changed to The Toledo Brass and Iron Works in 1897.

Seeger attended the Pan American Exposition in St. Louis in 1901. He had an ulterior motive for visiting the exposition. He wanted to learn about a new metal called aluminum. He liked what he saw and returned with samples of aluminum castings.

By 1907, The Seeger firm had grown enough to move to new quarters at 19-21 North St. Clair and add another new product, brass rods. Things moved so well that a contractor was hired in 1908 to build an up-to-date nonferrous foundry for the operation on St. Clair Street.

The company made a line of brass pipe fittings that were sold to the National Supply Company and also gained fame by assisting inventors with their mechanical requirements. The inventors liked to do business with the Seeger family because it could be trusted to keep their secrets. The company helped a Detroit dentist develop an anesthetic unit and received royalties on it for years. Sprinkling sys-

1909 home of Seeger Metals and Plastics Inc., then the Toledo Brass and Iron Works (above). Present 30,000-square-foot warehouse and office (below).

tems also were coming into use, for which the Seegers developed a low-melting-point metal.

During World War I, Seeger's son, Valentine Jr., took over as manager of the business, which continued to boom during the 1920s. By the early 1930s, however, the Depression was being severely felt and business had fallen to a dangerous level.

Valentine Seeger III took over the business from his father in 1936 and incorporated it as The Seeger Brass Company. Business was bad, the senior Seeger, now 71 and retired, was aided by a line of credit from the American Brass Company which also provided valuable assistance and advice.

When World War II began, the business was solvent, but Valentine III, a reserve officer, was called to active duty, and his mother, Dorothy Seeger, assumed managment. She did everything possible to work with small businesses, helping scores of small firms stay in business as they switched into war-related areas. Many never forgot the favors.

Valentine III returned from military

service in 1945. He continued the company's policy of adding new lines and services. Growth was steady but not dynamic.

In 1950, property next door to company headquarters at 23 North St. Clair Street was purchased and a new office and warehouse added to three structures that had been in use since 1881. Through the years new products such as stainless steel, aluminum and several different bronze alloys were added to the original brass and copper line. After 95 years in the same location, The Seeger Company purchased the warehouse at 1315 East Manhattan Boulevard.

Bruce Seeger, great-grandson of the founder and son of Valentine Seeger III, became president in 1977. Douglas Wiemer, a son-in-law, is executive vice president. He added the industrial plastics section which by last year was contributing about eighteen percent of gross sales.

As part of its 100th anniversary the name was changed to Seeger Metals and Plastics, Inc., a move designed to better reflect the company's present products and services.

Serving Northwest Ohio for over 70 years

No history of Northwest Ohio would be complete without an account of the Religious Sisters of Mercy who have served the area people since 1913 by sponsoring and staffing hospitals, schools of nursing, elementary and high schools, homes for the aged, catechetical programs, a commercial school and residences for young ladies.

The Sisters of Mercy were founded in Dublin, Ireland, over 150 years ago by Catherine McAuley, a woman dedicated to working with the poor, sick and uneducated. As others joined her, the work of the Sisters of Mercy quickly spread throughout Ireland and in England. In 1843, two years after Catherine McAuley's death, Frances Warde established the first convent of the Institute of Mercy in the United States. Today, the 20,000 members serve worldwide.

Ohio's first Sisters of Mercy came from Kinsale, Ireland, to Cincinnati in 1858. The Sisters of Mercy in Northwest Ohio trace their origin to a group that began a foundation in Brooklyn, New York, in 1855. One of the members, Mother Mary Joseph Lynch, set out in 1873 for Grand Rapids, Michigan, to establish a new house of the Institute.

Early in 1912, the late Archbishop Joseph Schrembs, then Bishop of Toledo, appealed to the Bishop of Grand Rapids for Sisters of Mercy to provide hospital care and teaching services for the Toledo area. Mother Mary Bernardine McMullen, Mother Mary Anthony McMullen and Mother Mary deChantal Lyons established the first Mercy Community in the Toledo diocese at Tiffin, Ohio, and immediately began plans to erect a much-needed hospital there. The 35-bed Tiffin Mercy Hospital was formally blessed in 1913 and has grown to a general medical facility of nearly 100 beds.

In 1917, Bishop Schrembs requested that the Sisters administer a hospital to be built in Toledo. While it was under construction Mother Bernardine used the Reynolds home located at 2205 Madison Avenue as a hospital, ministering particularly to influenza victims. The 101-bed Mercy Hospital was dedicated on June 21, 1918; the Mercy School of Nursing opened the same year. Today, Mercy Hospital is one of Toledo's most modern health care facilities.

Also in 1918, the Sisters of Mercy established St. Rita's Hospital in Lima, which has grown to a 455-bed facility.

The Sisters established St. Charles

Hospital in 1953 to serve the people of Toledo's East Side. Its short-term psychiatric care unit was the first of its kind in a general hospital in Toledo. The 342-bed St. Charles plays a major role in serving the health care needs of eastern metropolitan Toledo.

In 1915, the Sisters opened St. Philomena Home for Working Girls in Toledo, which operated until 1923.

The Sisters' contributions to elementary education throughout Northwest Ohio have been numerous. In 1914, the Sisters opened St. Ann School in Fremont and in 1915, St. Thomas Aquinas School in Toledo. In 1922 St. Mary School was opened in Kirby, Ohio, followed by the opening of Holy Angels School in Sandusky in 1923 and St. Peter School in Archbold in 1924. Others include Toledo's St. Vincent dePaul School, 1928; St. Catherine School, 1931; St. Peter School in Upper Sandusky, 1943; St. Mary Parish Catechetical School in Vermilion and Ascension School in Cleveland, 1949; St. Mary School in Mansfield, 1950; and St. Clement School in Toledo, 1953.

In secondary education, the Sisters provided staff for Toledo's Central Catholic High School from 1941 to 1981. McAuley High School, featuring a college preparatory program for girls, opened in 1958.

Our Lady of the Pines in Fremont, Ohio, served as the motherhouse from 1926 to 1936 when the Toledo Sisters joined the Sisters of Mercy of the Union, with province headquarters in Cincinnati. In 1970, the St. Bernardine Home retirement residence was opened on the grounds of the former motherhouse.

The Sisters of Mercy proudly opened St. Charles Hospital in 1953 for all area residents (above), in particular those of Oregon and Toledo's East Side. Sisters of Mercy played a major part in the education of elementary and secondary students in Toledo and throughout Northwest Ohio (below).

The work of the Sisters of Mercy in Northwest Ohio currently includes services such as health care, education, parish and campus ministry, social work, and art and music instruction. The Sisters of Mercy are constantly seeking to serve God by helping the people of Northwest Ohio through traditional as well as new ministries. Future projects include urgent care and industrial medicine centers, housing and supportive care for the elderly and more.

Northwest Ohio will continue to benefit from the commitment of the Sisters of Mercy which began in the area over 70 years ago.

Serving Toledo for more than a century

The Standard Oil Company (Ohio), popularly known as Sohio, has been part of the Toledo story since 1878, when it established a "bulk station" in the city. The installation consisted of a warehouse and a stable to shelter the horses which hauled tank wagons of kerosine and other petroleum products for delivery to customers.

Sohio's involvement in Toledo has burgeoned since then. In 1919 the company broke ground for a petroleum refinery in what is now the suburb of Oregon—today's modern 120,000 barrels-per-day-capacity plant and one of three refineries now operated by Sohio. Sohio's marketing network in the Toledo area now includes some 68 service stations. Altogether, Sohio employs more than 1,300 people in the area.

The Standard Oil Company is the original "Standard Oil" founded in 1870 by John D. Rockefeller in Cleveland, where it still maintains its headquarters. The firm quickly grew into the largest oil company in the United States, with operations worldwide.

In 1882 the Standard Oil trust was created to manage the business of The Standard Oil Company and its affiliated corporations. The original Standard Oil Company lost its dominant position and became merely one of a number of companies in the trust.

In 1899 all assets controlled by the trustees were transferred to Standard Oil Company (New Jersey) as a holding company. Twelve years later, the U.S. Supreme Court ordered Standard Oil

Company (New Jersey) to divest itself of its holdings in 33 companies. The decision resulted in the formation of 34 independent companies, eight bearing the name "Standard Oil". Sohio emerged as one of the smaller companies, owning one refinery (in Cleveland), a string of bulk stations, a fleet of tank wagons and marketing operations in an area confined to Ohio.

The advent of the internal combustion engine made gasoline the most important product of the industry. Sohio grew and became the leading retail petroleum marketer in Ohio, with major refineries at Toledo and Lima.

Sohio gradually acquired oil properties and conducted oil exploration and development in the United States. It joined in constructing pipelines to bring oil to Ohio and established a highly efficient pipeline system for distributing petroleum products from its refineries throughout the state. In 1956 Sohio expanded its marketing outside Ohio under the Boron brand. However, the company's own production of crude oil continued to be far short of its refining requirements.

In 1954 the company entered the chemicals business. Discovery in Sohio's research laboratories of a revolutionary process to produce acrylonitrile, a basic chemical used in textiles and plastics, expanded the chemicals operations. Most of the world's acrylonitrile now is produced using Sohio's process.

In 1964 Sohio joined in experimental ventures to develop oil shale. The company entered the coal business in 1968

with the acquisition of Old Ben Coal Company of Chicago and leased uranium lands in New Mexico the same year.

In 1970 Sohio signed an agreement with The British Petroleum Company p.l.c. of London, England. Under its terms, Sohio acquired valuable oil leases on the North Slope of Alaska, two refineries, and marketing properties on the U.S. East Coast. British Petroleum received stock in Sohio that since has grown to approximately 53-percent common stock interest.

Sohio owns approximately 50 percent of the oil in Alaska's Prudhoe Bay Field, which is estimated to hold 32 percent of U.S. total proven reserves. The company joined in building the trans-Alaska pipeline to bring this oil to U.S. markets and owns approximately 33 percent of that pipeline.

In 1981 Sohio acquired Kennecott Corporation, the largest U.S. copper producer, and a leading U.S. producer of gold, silver, molybdenum, lead and zinc.

Nonminerals operations acquired by Sohio in the Kennecott merger supply one-fourth of the worldwide titanium dioxide raw materials market and one-third of the ductile iron market. The merger also made Sohio the world's largest producer of abrasives and a major manufacturer of wear- and corrosion-resistant materials.

In its first 100 years, Sohio grew to a company with roughly $1 billion in assets. Since then, it has grown to $15.7 billion in assets—the fifteenth largest industrial corporation in the nation in terms of assets.

Sohio is proud to be part of the Toledo story for more than 100 years and looks forward to contributing to and sharing in the Toledo community's development in the years ahead.

Tankwagons like this (left), in photo taken during the 1890s, were used to deliver kerosine to Sohio customers in Toledo in the early days. The 1958 photo shows operators in the Central Control House or "Nerve Center" of the new Integrated Unit of Sohio's Toledo Refinery which was completed that year (below).

A proud past

It all began back in 1912, when stories spread of how distress signals from the stricken *Titanic* were picked up on shore through the magic of Marconi's wireless device. The stories fired the imagination of a 13-year-old Toledo boy. With cat's whisker crystals and spark coils from scrapped Model-Ts, the boy soon had his own ham radio station operating in the attic of his parents' home. It was the start of a lifelong love affair with the art, the science and the business of broadcasting.

His name was George Butler Storer.

Commitments to the family business, the Standard Steel Tube Company of Toledo, kept young Storer from following up his interest in radio. In 1927, he became involved in another of the family's enterprises, the Fort Industry Oil Company. Indirectly, it was to become the foundation for the Storer Broadcasting Company.

Storer looked for a new twist that would put Fort Industry Oil a step ahead of its competition. He hit upon the idea of building his gas stations adjacent to railroad sidings, where they could be supplied from passing tank cars. The company would save trucking charges, Storer reasoned—a savings which could be passed along to customers. The idea

worked, and soon Fort Industry Oil had thirteen outlets in Toledo and Cleveland.

The petroleum industry at the time was controlled largely by the major distributors who frowned upon the smaller operations like Fort Industry—as Storer discovered when he tried to buy advertising space in local newspapers. The major distributors threatened to withdraw *their* advertising if the papers sold space to Fort Industry. Storer looked elsewhere for an advertising forum. What he found combined an old interest with a growing new medium—radio.

WTAL was a crackling mite of a station—all 50 watts of it—and was more than willing to accept advertising for Storer's gas stations. In fact, by the end of 1927 Storer was running so much advertising on WTAL that he deemed it cheaper to buy the station outright than to continue to finance it as its major client.

Storer's trade name for the gasoline his stations sold, Speedene, was incorporated into the call letters of his new acquisition, and WSPD was born. He soon boosted the station's power to 250 watts and, as a favor to his friend William S. Paley, became the eighth station in the

country to affiliate with the fledgling Columbia Broadcasting System. Through the guidance of J. Harold Ryan, Storer's brother-in-law, Fort Industry's broadcast division grew rapidly, acquiring WGHP in Detroit; WWVA in Wheeling; CKLW, WMMN in Fairmont, West Virginia; WLOK in Lima and WHIZ in Zanesville—all in the span of ten years.

In 1931, Storer sold the petroleum arm of the business to Standard Oil of Ohio to concentrate his full energies on the business of broadcasting.

The nation's first independent group broadcaster, Storer was instrumental in the formation of network policies and programming, especially at CBS. During the war years, he served on the Broadcaster's Victory Council and as a lieutenant commander in the Navy.

After the war, Storer envisioned a booming economy. Once the FCC lifted its ban on television station construction, the company boldly began work on three stations in Toledo, Atlanta and Detroit—a feat unduplicated by any independent broadcaster. On July 17, 1948, the WSPD-TV test pattern first appeared on the 500 or so television sets in the Toledo area, most of them located in bars and hotel lobbies. At that time, since WSPD-TV was "the only game in town," the station's program manager could "cherrypick" the lineups of all the networks for the best programming. So, for a while, Channel 13 was an affiliate of CBS, NBC, ABC and the now all-but-forgotten DuMont network. Storer Television continued to grow, building stations in Cleveland, Milwaukee, Boston and San Diego.

To generate capital for expansion of its Cable Communications Division, Storer Broadcasting Company sold its radio stations, including WSPD in Toledo. The call letters were sold along with the station, so WSPD-TV became WTVG and stayed "13 Strong" as ever.

The desire to serve the community has always been strong at Channel 13. WTVG was the first to present color programs to Toledo; first with live microwave news capability; first with five-color Weatheradar. WTVG was also the first commercial broadcaster in Toledo with a satellite earth station and has already added a second one.

The desire, the *drive* to serve has always been with Channel 13. It's what makes the station 13 STRONG—and getting stronger every day!

Frank Venner reporting the news in the early 1960s.

221

Sun's first refinery... nearing a century of operation

Oil production was booming in Ohio in 1886, and Toledo was rapidly becoming a refining and distribution center for oil products. Two Pennsylvanians, Joseph N. Pew and Edward O. Emerson, had been active in the natural gas business in Titusville, Pennsylvania. Intrigued by the possibilities of the oil industry, they set out to pursue a partnership in the oil business.

Their first venture was the acquisition of oil leases in Ohio. Three years later, they laid pipeline to transport their crude and incorporated as the Sun Oil Line Company, making the first use of the name soon to be used in connection with their various enterprises—Sun Oil Company headquarters were in Pittsburgh, Pennsylvania.

On December 10, 1884, with Merriam and Morgan Paraffine Company of Cleveland, Sun Oil purchased the failing Crystal Oil Company's refinery on the Toledo city line for $22,200, thus forming the Diamond Oil Company. The property covered fourteen acres and included four batch stills. Principal products were kerosene, gas oil and fuel oil. The work force totaled five men, who in the first year processed 58,000 barrels of crude.

Merriam and Morgan failed in 1895. Pew and Emerson bought out their interest and the refinery became part of the Sun Oil Company. Toledo was soon advertising illuminating oil, naphtha, black oil and grease. Kerosene, the number one product, was distributed throughout Ohio, Indiana, Michigan and as far west as Wisconsin.

Fourteen acres became 44 and additions and changes had only begun. By 1905 the refinery had gained worldwide recognition for its top quality industrial lubricating oils.

As the motor car replaced the horse and buggy, demand for additional petroleum products grew, and the company entered the motor products field. The "Sunoco Diamond and Arrow" came to be the company's marketing logo for Sunoco motor oil and gasoline.

The manufacture of fuel components for war planes came with World War I. The first fractionating towers of the modern bubble type were built in 1922. This innovation merited petroleum headlines and enabled the refinery to operate its stills continuously. Crude processing capacity soared.

Much of the refinery was rebuilt in 1928. Included among the changes was a

Four-footed friends and helpers. Sun horses of bygone days were used to transport refined products.

continuous distillation topping unit which is said to have contained the largest tower erected at any refinery at that time—90 feet high by fifteen feet in diameter.

Sun Oil Company moved its headquarters to Philadelphia, Pennsylvania, in 1929. By that time the company was operating a second refinery, had purchased oil producing fields in the South and had acquired a shipbuilding business.

The Toledo Refinery began the production of aviation gasoline base stock soon after the Japenese struck Pearl Harbor in 1941. The demand for rubber also stemmed from the war, and a plant was soon built for the production of butadiene, a chief component of synthetic rubber.

The world's first houdriflow "catalytic cracker" was erected at the facility in 1950, making it possible to extract more gasoline from every barrel of crude. Years later, a hydrocracking unit was built to convert kerosene and other stocks into much-needed gasoline for millions of motorists.

Sun Oil Company merged with Sunray DX of Tulsa, Oklahoma, in 1968. This added refineries in the South to the Sun family that already included four refineries in Ohio, Pennsylvania, Puerto Rico and Canada. In 1976, Sun Oil Company became Sun Company, reflect-

ing company involvement in more than just oil. The Toledo Refinery became part of Sun Petroleum Products Company, one of fourteen major operating units.

Today, Toledo Refining Inc. is part of Sun Refining and Marketing Company, a division of Sun Company, headquartered in Radnor, Pennsylvania. Operating around the clock, the refinery employs approximately 620 people in over 100 different occupations. The property covers 600 acres, including a tank farm storage area and the Hocking Valley Dock and Marine Terminal on the Maumee River.

The refinery can process up to 120 thousand barrels of crude daily. Major products produced at Toledo are gasoline and heating oil. Benzene, toluene and xylene are processed at the refinery's newest plant, constructed in 1977. Also produced are liquid petroleum gas, kerosene, tetramer, mineral spirits, residual fuels and asphalts.

As in any industry, energy and environmental conservation are a major concern. Since 1973, the Toledo Refinery has studied over 300 energy projects resulting in savings equal to nearly 35 percent of 1973 energy consumption. All systems have been designed with a concern for pollution, and procedures are followed to assure compliance with pollution control regulations.

Locally owned, controlled by average citizens from areas served

Townspeople who walked through the door of Sylvania Savings Bank for the first time on December 3, 1900 had every reason to be proud of their new bank. While its furnishings and fixtures were hardly plush by today's standards, it had everything banks were supposed to have—it was manned by trusted fellow citizens and had an impressive $30,000 in assets.

The handful of shareholders were committed to a principle that has continued to this day. Simply, that ownership should be kept in the control of average citizens, rather than a few wealthy individuals or families.

The 24 shareholders consisted of a high school teacher, some farmers, a harness shop operator, veterinarian, physician, dry goods store proprietor, druggist, shoe store owner, undertaker and the president of the Sylvania Telephone Company. The new bank was located just down the street from another one that was operated by a hardware dealer at the rear of his store.

In the minutes of the first shareholders' meeting, it was noted that a banker from Blissfield, Michigan, was hired as secretary-treasurer "at a salary of $600 per year guaranteed and all left in undivided profits up to $150 each year, after paying a four percent dividend."

In just seven years, the fledgling bank was already showing signs of the steady growth that was to characterize its history up to the present day. Board members decided that an expansion was in order and approved plans for a two-story brick building, complete with plumbing and electricity. It was built at a cost of $10,270 at the corner of Main and Maplewood streets in Sylvania.

By 1909, board members were being paid for attending meetings, and the proud little bank paid a 20 percent dividend.

In those days the Toledo & Western electric trolley ran from Toledo, through Sylvania and on to Adrian. The board's minutes had to be re-read at one of its meetings for the benefit of a director "who arrived on a later car than other members of the board."

The bank's first bookkeeping machine was purchased in 1930. Everyone on the board was in favor of the investment, although one director voted against buying a standard to place it on. He also frowned on purchasing ledger or statement sheets for the machine.

It may well have been such conservatism, however, that enabled Sylvania Savings Bank to successfully weather the Depression, which began in 1931. Those were difficult days for bankers everywhere, but the bank emerged sound and solvent, even though a number of Toledo area banks closed their doors.

Farmers & Merchants Bank Company was absorbed in 1940. Since its building was larger and better suited to carry on the combined operations, the building at Main and Maplewood was sold.

Combined assets at the time of the merger were $1,800,000. During the World War II years that followed, Sylvania Savings Bank grew to about four times that size.

The big news of 1967 was the acquisition of the Community Savings and Loan Association. A bond of common ownership between the two financial institutions had existed for some years. Four Sylvania Savings Bank directors were also on the board of Community Savings. Around 90 percent of the shareholders of Community Savings owned stock in Sylvania Savings as well. Both boards agreed to merge for greater efficiency and better service for the depositors and borrowers of both institutions.

Today, under the direction of Stanley R. Hesselbart, board chairman and chief executive officer, Sylvania Savings Bank has over $240 million in assets and ten offices. It is still locally owned by average citizens, as envisioned by its founders. The majority of them live and work in the areas served by the bank. Most importantly, they are in a position to see that its policies and resources work in the best interests of the community.

This fortified teller cage in Sylvania Savings Bank (above) was the last word in bank security during the Pretty Boy Floyd era. It featured armored glass 2" thick and a row of steel spikes that prevented would-be robbers from climbing over the top. Touching the wires along the top edge of the cage set off an alarm. The Sylvania Savings Bank main office (below) on the corner of Monroe and Main streets in 1954.

223

Pacesetters in high temperature heat processing

The history of Surface Division, Midland-Ross Corporation began almost concurrently in three places nearly 80 years ago. During the early 1900s, independent experiments with combustion of fuel gases were conducted by Dr. William Arthur Bone in London, England, and Dr. Charles Edward Lucke in New York. Each determined that mixing air with fuel gas in the correct proportion, before ignition, produced a much hotter, less wasteful combustion. Pursuing this theory, it was found that if combustion occurred through a refractory bed, the combustion rate increased greatly as refractory temperature rose. During this process the surface of the refractory bed became incandescent, radiating heat more intensely than the combustion itself. Bone and Lucke used the term "surface combustion" to describe the phenomena.

Bone and Lucke were granted patents by their governments. Lucke assigned his patent to the Gas and Oil Combustion Company, while Bone assigned his to Radiant Heating Ltd. These companies merged in 1915 forming Surface Combustion, Inc.

Industrial development continued after an exclusive license under the "surface combustion" patent was granted to two engineers, Linzee Blagden and Clement Peterkin, who organized the Surface Combustion Company with factory operations in New York City.

About the same time, Henry L. Doherty, then president of the Denver Gas and Electric Company, promoted the gas industry as a fuel supplier for the vast heating requirements of industry. The promotion eventually led to Doherty's formation of the Improved Appliance Company, which developed appliances for use in commercial and industrial operations.

During 1920, owners and managers of the Surface Combustion Company realized that increased operations, greater financial support and improved leadership were necessary if the company were to survive and expand. To aid their growth, owners of Surface Combustion Company, knowing of the aggressive research and commercial activities in the industrial gas field, offered Surface Combustion to Doherty for purchase. Thus, in 1924 Doherty bought controlling interest of the Surface Combustion Company and made it a subsidiary of Combustion Utilities Corporation. That was followed by the purchase of Webster Engineering in 1928, Mantle Engineering in 1929, Chapman Stein Company and the Gas Furnace Division of Columbus Heating and Ventilating in 1931.

Surface Combustion outgrew its facilities in New York and Ohio, and in August 1927, all operations were moved to the present location at 2375 Dorr Street in Toledo, Ohio. Research and development activities were increased to accelerate development of Surface Combustion products and processes. During these years of expansion, the company designed and marketed new products and improved others. It built a reputation as a reliable manufacturer of high-quality equipment, which was indispensable to success in American business.

In the domestic field, Surface Combustion introduced Janitrol conversion burners, forced air conditioners, gravity furnaces and unit heaters—all with radical new improvements in burners, heat exchangers and design. In the industrial field, Surface Combustion developed carburizing furnaces, radiant tubes, glass lehrs, soaking pits, walking beam furnaces and other equipment until all requirements of industry could be satisfied. By 1940, Surface Combustion had three manufacturing plants, more than 30 district sales offices, an agent distribution organization and widespread dealer representation.

During World War II, Surface Combustion furnaces were used in many industries to manufacture an array of military equipment and material including radar and even the atomic bomb. Space heating units were installed by the thousands in army camps and government buildings. Surface Combustion's most impressive contribution to the war was an aircraft heater used in nearly 60,000 allied fighting planes.

The Janitrol Aircraft Division (now the Janitrol Aero Division of Midland-Ross), Janitrol Heating and Air Conditioning Division and the Industrial Division were the three major groups operated by Surface Combustion during 1959. Products included industrial heating equipment and support equipment for aircraft and missiles.

On November 9, 1959, Surface Combustion was acquired by Midland-Ross Corporation of Cleveland, Ohio. Less than five years earlier, virtually all of Midland-Ross' sales were to the automotive market. With the acquisition of Surface Combustion, automotive business was reduced to less than 40 percent of Midland-Ross' sales volume. After purchasing Surface, Midland-Ross had nearly 6,000 employees, fourteen plants and more than two million square feet of manufacturing space. Midland-Ross considered the acquisition of Surface Combustion a key move in its long-range diversification program.

Surface concentrated its efforts on new techniques for high-temperature heat processing. Equipment currently marketed by Surface for vacuum processing, pyrolizing and nitriding stemmed from these efforts.

During the early 1970s, manufacturers began to view the type and amount of energy consumed as important considerations in purchasing equipment. In response, Surface designed equipment

Walking beam furnace (below). Surface Division of Midland-Ross, Toledo, Ohio (bottom). Vacuum furnace (top right). Surface plant and employees (bottom right).

which gave manufacturers the option to operate on either gas, oil or electrical energy. Designs also were modified to reduce fuel consumption and allow operators to select one of two fuel types. Electrified radiant tube heating, developed in 1976, allowed manufacturers to operate on either gas or electrical energy. With the continuing demand for and development of electrical heating caused by the shortage of fossil fuels, it became apparent that the name Surface Combustion Division implied gas heating products only. This resulted in Midland-Ross changing the name to Surface Division, thus eliminating "combustion" and false implication.

The Midland-Ross acquisition of the Robotron Corporation in May 1977 enhanced Surface's capability of offering industrial heating equipment using electrical power. Robotron's induction heating, electronic control for resistance welding and generator products enabled Surface to respond to the industry's need for reliable, low-maintenance induction equipment.

Solid and liquid waste disposal systems developed by Surface are gaining acceptance from manufacturers needing to destroy waste materials generated during production. These unique systems return energy safely to the manufacturing environment while destroying waste materials. A major breakthrough in this area was the successful incineration of Kepone, a toxic insecticide which had contaminated the land, water and even people in the community where it was produced. Under close scrutiny by Environmental Protec-

tion Agency officials, Surface proved that dangerous wastes can be safely disposed of without endangering the environment. Waste disposal systems employ rich fume reactors, operating at temperatures between 2500°F. and 3000°F., to destroy toxic organic compounds while oxidizing volatiles. Energy is then released to a boiler or other heat recovery device following stoichiometric combustion.

Surface waste disposal systems reduce waste to innocuous ash containing salts, heavy metals and fixed carbon fractions. Processed materials are a fraction of the original weight and volume of waste material, thereby minimizing disposal expense. Final residues often are used for landfill or resource recovery.

The Surface Research and Development laboratories became the cornerstone for the Midland-Ross Thermal Systems Technical Center, which supports Surface and other Midland-Ross divisions in the development of new processes and equipment. An example is the Ionitriding™ process and equipment recently introduced to the market which can lower processing costs and eliminate pollution problems. Ion nitriding occurs when metallic surfaces are diffused with nitrogen, forming ion nitrides, resulting in wear and corrosion-resistant metallic surfaces.

The Surface Ionitriding™ process, licensed by Klochner Ionen, negatively charges the work piece with direct current while surrounding it with ionized nitrogen. During the Ionitriding process, a plasma discharge causes the work piece to glow.

Compared with other case hardening methods, Ionitriding appeals to manufacturers because it requires less energy, operates at lower temperatures, does not require use of toxic gas, allows precise control, maintains structural stability of work, produces work with minimal surface roughness and can be safely performed.

Surface is recognized as an outstanding manufacturer of gas-fired and electrical high-temperature processing equipment for industrial and other purposes. Its engineering, research and development capabilities are second to that of no other company in the field. This factor, combined with sound business management and good judgment in expansion policies, has enabled the division to rise to a dominant position in a dynamic, highly competitive business.

225

Ideas with Power

TELEDYNE CAE, a world leader in developing and manufacturing small gas turbine engines, has been growing with Toledo for over a quarter of a century. It is now a part of Teledyne Industries, Inc., and its family of widely diversified companies.

In the field of aerospace turbine power, the name Teledyne CAE continues to stand for excellence, perpetuating the tradition of its predecessor, Continental Motors Corporation, renowned for automotive, aeronautical, military and industrial engines since the turn of the century.

Teledyne CAE, formerly Continental Aviation and Engineering (CAE), was founded in 1940 as a majority-owned subsidiary of Continental Motors to conduct research and development activities relating to aircraft power plants. Already the foremost manufacturer of 40- to 250-horsepower aircraft piston engines, Continental Motors Corporation expanded its product line and made important additions to it during World War II, including a jet engine pioneering program.

Shortly after World War II, CAE's jet engine development began as part of a government contract, and since 1951 has devoted itself to the design, development and production of gas turbine engines in the small thrust and horsepower class.

Manufacturing operations were moved to Toledo from Detroit in 1955. In 1969 Teledyne Industries, Inc., purchased Ryan Aeronautical Corporation which had gained controlling interest in Continental Motors in 1965. CAE joined the Teledyne family of companies and became Teledyne CAE. In 1970 the company headquarters and all remaining Detroit operations were moved to Toledo.

The company's Laskey Road facility consists of over 375,000 square feet of covered floor space built on a 79-acre site. The Defense Plant Corporation originally built the facility which was assigned in 1942 to the Liquid Cooled Division of Aviation Corporation to design and build engines for Navy aircraft. Packard Motor Car Company took over the facility in 1943 and built Rolls Royce piston engines for the Air Force until the end of World War II, then worked on developing turbojet and turbofan engines until 1949. Thereafter, Frederic Flader, Inc., and A. O. Smith both occupied the premises manufacturing electronic instruments and B-47 landing gears.

In 1955 Continental Aviation & Engineering was assigned the production facility to fabricate jet components and assemble compressors and turbojet engines.

Full occupancy of the facilities commenced in 1957 when the environment laboratories were also taken over by Continental.

Today, anything a gas turbine will do under normal operating conditions can be duplicated under controlled test conditions in Teledyne's laboratories. Engineers are able to evaluate either individual components or develop and qualify full-scale engines in eleven sea-level test cells, 30 component test rigs and two altitude chambers which are capable of testing engines at altitudes from sea-level to 90,000 feet and at speeds up to Mach two (twice the speed of sound).

The manufacturing area houses the most modern, automated machinery that the industry offers for the fabrication of gas turbine engine components. Numerically controlled lathes, electron beam welders and other highly specialized equipment combined with the highly skilled people who run them have contributed significantly to Teledyne CAE's reputation for building low-cost, high-quality engines.

Teledyne CAE is able to take an engine concept from initial design, through development and testing of all components and full engine prototypes, into full-scale production — all with in-house staff and facilities. Capable and experienced engineering and manufacturing specialists employ the latest technologies using extensive advance computer programs, analytical modeling continuously refined with test data and highly sophisticated manufacturing and testing techniques.

Over the past 30 years Teledyne CAE has manufactured and delivered worldwide more than 12,000 small gas turbine engines for a wide variety of challenging applications from aircraft to missiles. Even while building for today, extensive and comprehensive gas turbine engine research programs ensure that Teledyne CAE will meet tomorrow's needs.

Under the leadership of President James L. Murray, Teledyne CAE's management has created a positive environment where initiative is encouraged, imaginations flourish and ideas are transformed into hardware. Teledyne CAE's unqualified success in the small gas turbine engine business is a direct reflection upon the quality people who are industry innovators, generating "ideas with power" in the pursuit of technological and manufacturing excellence.

From drafting board to full scale production.

Business builds a city

Today's Chamber of Commerce in Toledo with its 3,300 members, nearly $1 million budget and paid staff of 28 is a far cry numerically from its namesake predecessor organization founded in 1894, but many of the goals and functions—primarily fostering a good business climate and promoting the community—are identical.

The first organization in Toledo with a marked resemblance to the present chamber was the Citizens Board of Trade, incorporated in 1888. It expired in 1892 and was replaced in 1893 by the Toledo Manufacturers Association. Both concerned themselves with taxation, railroad shipping, smoke nuisance and fire prevention.

John S. Craig, owner of a shipbuilding company, became first president of the newly organized Chamber of Commerce in 1894. Merging with the manufacturers association, the chamber promoted new water mains, roads, harbor improvements and industrial development.

A year later, the Chamber had 392 members and rented quarters for $500 for 12 months. Some 175,000 pieces of mail were sent across the nation in two years advertising the city. Dues were $10 a year, the office was open six days a week and any employee accepting a tip was subject to immediate dismissal.

In 1899, the Business Men's Chamber of Commerce headed by C.E.B. Lamson took over and the chamber became a strong municipal government lobbying force. Industrial growth in the city was rampant with some 1,050 factories. The new 30-mile Toledo Terminal Railroad opened new "cheap land" on the outskirts for development.

Several young businessmen created the Business Men's Commerce Club in 1908 with pool and card tables and a dining room. A popular social innovation, it grew to 808 members within a year and in 1911 merged with the Business Men's Chamber of Commerce to form the Toledo Commerce Club. John D. Biggers was secretary, later to become president of the Libbey-Owens-Ford Glass Co.

A weekly magazine was started, city planning was advocated and the club grew quickly with some 35 committees ranging from mosquito control to Civic Center development. In 1920, the name was changed back to Toledo Chamber of Commerce. Membership exceeded 3,000, among the largest in the United States.

In June 1925, the entire fifth floor of the Richardson Building was transformed into the ultimate chamber of commerce of its day—nationally famous—with 28,000 square feet, 5,000 of it in the kitchen alone. There was an elegant lounge, a main dining room seating up to 900, fourteen offices and a variety of plush amenities. The ads said "Good Food, Reasonable Prices, Famous Cooks." It played to banquets, dances, bridge parties and some 60 organizations who met there.

In following years, work plans by referendum were adopted and the chamber became active in airport development and export promotion. On one occasion, the organization raised $257,000 in 33 hours to procure a site for Transcontinental Airport. City-manager government was promoted. The Miami and Erie Canal was replaced by a boulevard and the chamber labored for the new High Level Bridge, Civic Auditorium and sewage disposal plant.

Development promotion followed economic recovery after the Depression and was interupted by World War II, during which the chamber labored for defense production and good military relations. In 1949, the organization invested $125,000 in its own building at 217 Huron Street. It became an advocate for St. Lawrence Seaway port development in spite of internal strife based on its historic support of the local rail industry.

In 1957, the name was changed to Toledo *Area* Chamber of Commerce to reflect multi-county metro growth. During the '60s, the chamber was a powerful factor in expressway construction, air service and market promotion.

The chamber took the lead in creation of a public transit authority, bringing Toledo Express Airport under port authority management, and created a convention bureau division under contract to city and county government.

In 1981, Arthur C. Kochendorfer retired after 36 years with the agency, 26 of them as chief paid executive. He was replaced by then-City Manager J. Michael Porter. While Toledo was enduring deep national recession, particularly in its automotive industry, a quarter of a billion dollars was pumped into downtown redevelopment and the chamber reorganized its staff to stress new industry attraction and existing industry retention.

Toledo Chamber secretaries in the '60s wore interchangeable white or navy blue suits as uniforms. Although they voted for the scheme, everybody got tired of it after a year, and the practice ceased.

227

A newspaper that has maintained a courageous, independent, editorial policy

More than a year before the tiny settlement at the mouth of the Maumee River received its charter as the city of Toledo, The *Blade* published its first issue. That was December 19, 1835.

Today The *Blade*, publishing daily and Sunday, is the oldest continuous business in the city.

The *Blade* was founded by a group of business and professional men who were active in the Whig Party and desired representation in the newspaper world as well as to promote the growth of the new community, and decided that the best way to accomplish that was to start a newspaper.

In the first editorial in the first issue the publishers wrote: "We should prefer to keep our Blade always in its scabbard and hope not to be compelled to use it often in the offensive." But they added: "We hope it will always leap from its scabbard whenever the rights of individuals or of the community shall be infringed."

Those words still form the basis for the editorial policy of The *Blade* which aggressively maintains its role as a watchdog of what happens in the city and its neighboring areas and impartially reports those happenings to its readers.

In May 1846, The *Blade* added a tri-weekly edition, and in April 1848, because of the continued growth of the city plus the development of a means of transmitting news by telegraph, started a daily edition.

Many prominent Toledo residents were associated with The *Blade* in those early years, but the most famous of the nineteenth-century editors and publishers was David Ross Locke, who wrote under the name of "Petroleum V. Nasby." Under his guidance, The *Blade* became a nationally known publication, and its weekly edition, which some have called the forerunner of the national news magazines, was read by hundreds of thousands of Americans from coast to coast.

After Locke's death in 1888, his son, Robinson, took over operation of The *Blade*. He devoted more attention to the daily *Blade* and raised it to a pre-eminent position in Toledo and the surrounding area. The weekly *Blade* was discontinued in 1924.

In 1926 The *Blade* was purchased from the Locke estate by Paul Block, who was publisher until his death in 1941. The *Blade* is now published by Paul Block, Jr. His brother, William, is co-publisher.

Another well-known *Blade* editor was Grove Patterson, who was associated with the newspaper from 1910 until his death in 1956. He was a founder and twice president of the American Society of Newspaper Editors, honorary president of the Society of Professional Journalists and the recipient of honors from the governments of Poland and Spain.

The *Blade* has always been a newspaper dedicated to bringing its readers a large amount of international and national news as well as a complete report of local and suburban activities. It is the smallest newspaper in the country to have its own full-time European correspondent. Fernand Auberjonois, based in London, devotes his time to writing interpretive and analytical articles on foreign developments usually not obtainable from regular news services.

The *Blade* also operates bureaus in Washington, D.C.;and Columbus and Bowling Green, Ohio.

For years The *Blade* has been the leader in pushing for the renovation of downtown Toledo; Paul Block Jr. served as chairman of the Toledo Development Committee during the time the downtown plan was formulated.

Block also served as first chairman of the Toledo-Lucas County Port Authority which directed the development of the Toledo port, enabling it to take advantage of the St. Lawrence Seaway traffic. He was also the first chairman of the board of the Medical College of Ohio when it was founded in Toledo in 1965.

The *Blade* has won its share of journalistic acclaim, including awards from the American and Ohio Bar Associations, state and national press associations and the prestigious Grady Award of the American Chemical Society. The paper has been selected by the Society of Professional Journalists as an Historic Site in Journalism, listing the accomplishments of The *Blade* and Editor Locke.

The *Blade* has consistently maintained an independent editorial policy on political questions and endorsements, refusing to align itself with any party or special interest, and has made determined efforts to insure that political news is presented to its readers without bias.

The *Blade* staff includes many specialists in the fields of government, politics, business, education, art, music and religion, and the newspaper has compiled an outstanding record in dealing with some of the great issues of our times—civil rights, atomic energy, water conservancy, gun control and international relations, to name but a few.

News Department personnel of The Blade *work with the latest in electronic editing equipment (above). The building which houses The* Blade *on Superior Street in downtown Toledo was opened in 1927 (below).*

Supplying energy to keep Toledo moving forward

For nearly a century, Toledo Edison Company has supplied the energy to keep Toledo on the move—first for the streetcars and later for the manufacture of automobile parts.

It all began at Water Street Station, the first generating plant in Toledo to utilize Thomas Edison's three-wire system of electricity distribution. One of four predecessors to today's Toledo Edison Company, Toledo Consolidated Electric Company, built Water Street Station in 1895. It received an exclusive Toledo license for the system as well as permission to use the inventor's name in the corporate title more than 30 years later.

Toledo Edison's predecessor, the Toledo Railways and Light Company, was incorporated in 1901 to bring together the street railways and most other electric business. This is considered to be Toledo Edison's real beginning. "Rail-Light," as it was popularly known, served 3,120 customers located mainly in Toledo.

Cities Service Company bought "Rail-Light" in 1912, and its president, Henry L. Doherty, began to reorganize and revitalize the utility. The production facilities then consisted of four electric plants and one artificial gas plant. One of Doherty's first decisions was to install a new 12,500-kilowatt turbine at Water Street Station.

Plans were announced in 1916 for a new generating plant, Acme Station, as major industrial customers such as Willys, Auto-Lite, Champion Spark Plug, Toledo Scale and Libbey Glass required greater quantities of electricity.

In 1921, when it was decided to separate the electric and gas business from the railway business, the utility's name was changed to the Toledo Edison Company. The company expanded from a local Toledo utility to one serving most of northwestern Ohio and acquired several small municipal systems, as well as some privately owned companies.

Toledo Edison became primarily an electric utility in 1928, retaining only the small gas distribution systems which served Defiance and Delta. That same year, Toledo Edison began its steam-heating system for downtown Toledo.

In the 1930s, Toledo Edison management maintained a strong holding action against the Depression. Efforts were made to make operations as efficient as possible and to minimize layoffs. The demand for electricity grew very slowly as Toledo industry suffered from a series of labor disputes and strikes. By 1938, however, business was improving. Electric output—a good barometer of the economy—reached its highest level of the decade. Plans were drawn and work begun on a new 60,000-kilowatt unit for Acme Station.

The new generator went on line in 1941, only a few months before the Japanese attack on Pearl Harbor. It provided the extra margin of capacity needed to operate the area's war plants during the next five years.

Cities Service remained the parent organization of Toledo Edison until May 1950, when Toledo Edison became an independent, investor-owned electric utility.

Additional generating capacity was added at the Acme Station in East Toledo during the 1950s, and the Bay Shore Station, on Bay Shore Road, was built to meet increased consumer demand. In the 1960s, capacity was further expanded at Bay Shore, which consistently has been rated one of the nation's most efficient fossil-fired plants.

In 1977, Davis-Besse Nuclear Power Station went into operation. Ohio's first commercial nuclear generating unit is jointly owned by Cleveland Electric Illuminating Company and Toledo Edison, the operator of the unit.

Electric lighting in the early days was limited largely to the new mansions of what is now the Old West End. Electricity prices in Toledo were in the range of twelve cents per kilowatt hour at the turn of the century when twelve cents represented an hour's hard work for many people. Yet the price per kilowatt-hour of electricity paid by today's average householder is only slightly more than half of that amount. Much of the difference lies in the efficiency of modern generating plants.

Today, Toledo Edison provides electric service to about 750,000 people in a 2,500-square-mile area of northwestern Ohio. Employment is provided for some 2,300 highly trained people who are primarily interested in offering the best service possible to company customers.

Water Street Station (above) was the first generating plant in Toledo to utilize Thomas Edison's three-wire system of electricity distribution. Located in downtown Toledo, it was built by one of four predecessors of today's Toledo Edison Company. In 1916, O. T. Rankin and Kenny Peterson drove a Seagrave truck (below), an earlier version of the present-day "bucket" truck. Workers had to crank the truck platform into position for streetlighting repairs.

229

The making of a major medical center

In 1874, Toledo as a municipal corporation was just 38 years old and already had a population of 40,000. The first movements from agriculture to industrial development were being felt in Northwest Ohio.

A group of church women sensed a need in the growing city to minister to the sick and aged among the immigrants, newcomers and indigents who had no homes, families or financial means. Led by Mrs. Thomas Daniels, the Women's Christian Association purchased property at 171 Union Street and opened The City Hospital of Toledo. This event marked the beginning of what is now one of the largest health-care institutions in the United States.

The white frame house on Union Street was purchased from Elizabeth B. Norris. With room for eight patients at a time, 42 people received care during the hospital's first fifteen months. The cost was $7 per week for those who were able to pay, and expenses for that period totaled $1,146.67. Operations were performed in patients' rooms with primitive anesthesia, hot water and cotton bandages.

Many of those who supported the hospital in those early days were pioneer Toledo families active in mercantile, transportation, banking, lumber, grain and other businesses.

Two physicians, S.S. Lungren and Symmes H. Bergen, constituted the first medical staff. Day-to-day operating tasks were carried out by the women of the Christian Association. Physicians and board members donated their time, and the only paid employees were a warden and a matron. Even though the hospital raised its own vegetables to cut costs, donations were also solicited from gardeners, farmers and merchants. Lumber dealers and tradesmen donated materials for repairs and maintenance.

In 1876 the first nurse was hired. The name of the hospital was changed to the Protestant Hospital of Toledo, and its connections with the Women's Christian Association were dissolved. Under the auspices of the Toledo Homeopathic Medical Society, a new board was formed.

This was only the first of many changes. During its 108 years, The Toledo Hospital has had several homes and many modernizations and expansions.

In 1888 the Valentine H. Ketcham homestead at Bancroft and Cherry Streets was purchased, and the hospital opened new facilities there in 1892. Most of the funds for the new hospital came from the estate of William J. Finlay, a pioneer businessman and philanthropist.

In 1893 the name was changed to the Toledo Hospital Association and finally, in 1901, to The Toledo Hospital.

Also in 1893, the hospital opened a school of nursing at the original Ketcham homestead. (This building served as its headquarters until 1930.) From five student nurses enrolled at the outset, this diploma school has now graduated over 2,500 students.

The Cherry Street building accommodated 100 patients and was a four-story brick structure trimmed in stone, closely following the style of many large residences of the period. An annex was built in 1898 to house 50 private rooms and the hospital's first X-ray machine. A second annex was added in 1914.

Under its first superintendent, P.W. Behrens, the hospital won recognition as a standard hospital from the American College of Surgeons and as a training facility for interns from the American Medical Association.

By the late 1920s the hospital had again outgrown its facilities. Under the leadership of two prominent Toledo businessmen, William W. Knight, president of the board of trustees, and Frank Collins, chairman of the building committee, funds were raised and a new site was selected. The 22.5 acres the board purchased on North Cove Boulevard remain the present site of the main hospital.

The Chicago-based architectural firm of Schmidt, Garden & Erickson, specialists in hospital construction, was selected to prepare the plans. The building contract was awarded to A.L. Bentley & Sons Company, Toledo general contractors.

Construction of the 250-bed hospital began in February 1928 and was completed in January 1930. It was the largest structure of its kind in Toledo. Croxton House, a residence for nurses, and Johnson House, the power plant and laundry, were also built during this time.

Croxton House was named for Gertrude Bailey Croxton, whose bequest helped to build it, and Johnson House for Lyman R. Johnson, a handyman at the hospital for 27 years. Johnson had given $625 from his meager savings to the building fund and upon his death, left his remaining property to the hospital.

When the Great Depression began, the hospital still owed $500,000 on its new building. It was a full decade before this debt was eliminated and the administration and board took heroic measures to keep the institution moving forward during this period.

It was during the Depression, however, that research excelled at The Toledo Hospital with the development of colibactragen for the prevention of peritonitis in surgical cases. This discovery led in 1943 to the construction of an Institute of Medical Research on the hospital grounds. In later years, under the direction of Dr. Bernhard Steinberg, the institute was recognized for its leukemia research.

Since emerging from the Depression in sound financial condition, growth has been synonymous with The Toledo Hospital and services have remained at peak levels.

The Toledo Hospital today.

A five-story north wing was added in 1957. And in 1958, the original building underwent major modernization. The hospital could now accommodate more than 500 patients. Among important new services were cardiac care and postoperative facilities—in 1959, the first open heart surgery in the city was performed at The Toledo Hospital.

In 1966 further expansion enlarged hospital areas facing Oatis Avenue and added four stories to the new north wing. Between 1968 and 1973 additional floors were opened for medical surgical beds, intensive and coronary care and psychiatry. This brought the bed capacity to 700. A major fund-raising campaign financed expansion.

During the decades of change, the medical staff grew under the leadership of Drs. L.C. Grosh, Lewis Snead, John Stifel and many others. Full-time medical education directors were appointed for all departments. And in 1973, an affiliation agreement was signed with the Medical College of Ohio, making The Toledo Hospital a major teaching institution.

Administrators, too, have played a vital role. From the time of the first superintendent to the present, these men—John Ransom, George Wilson, Wilson Benfer and Bryan Rogers—have speeded growth and development.

Today, with 809 beds, The Toledo Hospital is a major economic force in Toledo, employing over 4,000 people and with a medical staff of 750. More than 31,000 patients are admitted each year and the emergency department is the busiest in the city.

The Toledo Hospital serves as the regional center for perinatal and pediatric care, including high-risk pregnancies, intensive care for newborns, cystic fibrosis, pediatric pulmonary diseases and hemophilia. Major services include the W.W. Knight Family Practice Center (established in 1974) alcoholism treatment for adults and adolescents, obstetrics (with over 4,000 births per year), physical medicine, open heart surgery, cancer treatment, kidney dialysis, outpatient surgery, cardiac and intensive care and education and health promotion.

Under the leadership of an enlightened and progressive board and administration, The Toledo Hospital has a master plan for the next decade to continue developing facilities and services to meet its obligation as a major regional center of Northwest Ohio.

The Cherry Street facility—the first to be built especially for the intended use as a hospital—was occupied by The Toledo Hospital from 1893 until January of 1930 (above). The Ketcham homestead at Bancroft and Cherry streets (below) was acquired by The Toledo Hospital in 1889 and used until a new hospital, built on the property, was completed in 1893. This building then became the home of The Toledo Hospital School of Nursing.

Pioneer bank remains strong and innovative community leader

The formation and growth of Toledo Trust is a story which closely parallels the growth of the City of Toledo. In 1868, Toledo, as an incorporated town, was just 31 years old when Toledo Trust's original predecessor bank, The Toledo Savings Institution, opened its doors with $100,000 of original capital. Richard Mott was the president and later served as Toledo's sixth mayor.

In 1875, The Toledo Savings Institution was consolidated with The Toledo Savings Bank and Trust Company which had its offices at the corner of Summit and Monroe streets on the exact site where the famous Fort Industry once stood—a pioneer fort well-remembered for its strength during the Indian Wars in the early 1800s. Much later, on December 31, 1923, the two banks were merged with the Summit Trust Company under the name of The Toledo Trust Company. The next ten years were marked by the merger of four additional banks, which brought the total assets of the bank in 1933 to an excess of $53 million. Headquarters for the bank were located at Madison and Summit Streets in a new 21-story office building—said to be the second tallest building in Ohio at the time it was built. It served as headquarters until 1981 when a new headquarters building was opened as part of the Sea-Gate riverfront redevelopment.

It is ironic that the site of the new headquarters building once was the location for the Merchants and Clerks Savings Bank whose president, Oliver S. Bond, was the great-grandfather of Toledo Trust president, George Haigh. The bank building at 338 Summit was considered the finest building on Summit Street in 1891. It's also historically significant that Bond was a member of the board of directors of Northern National Bank which merged with Toledo Trust in 1924. Bond, like Toledo Trust, was a pioneer in Toledo. He began his career with a firm which traded with Indians and was in the banking business with one bank for 52 years. As history would have it, Oliver Bond's great-grandson, George Haigh, would leave a successful career in industry to become president of Toledo Trust in 1976.

The late 1920s and the early '30s were difficult economic times, and banking institutions were severely tested. Toledo Trust met the test. Toledo was hardest hit in 1931 when five local banks closed their doors within several months. Hysteria

and panic were rampant as bank customers flocked to withdraw their money. Yet the policy at Toledo Trust, verbalized at the time by the president, Henry L. Thompson, was "Pay everyone who wants his money." Bank notes were piled high on Toledo Trust counters, and the bank remained open late at night to make sure everyone was served.

In neighboring Michigan, a bank holiday was declared which started another series of runs, and Toledo Trust was used by railroads and large industries attempting to do business as usual despite the strain. It has been reported that prior to the bank holiday in March 1933, Toledo Trust was the largest bank open between New York and Chicago.

The strength and stability is still recognized 50 years later, as Toledo Trust remains the largest bank in Northwest Ohio. It became the lead bank of a holding company formed in 1971—the first in Northwest Ohio to take advantage of increased opportunities for expansion. Under the leadership of George W. Haigh, president and chief executive officer of Toledo Trustcorp, the bank holding company has become a major financial service corporation.

Today, Toledo Trustcorp services a 30-county market area in Northwest Ohio with 58 offices. The acquisition of First Buckeye Bank of Mansfield, Ohio, expected by year-end 1982, will increase the branch network to 83 offices. Comprised of four regional banks, Toledo Trustcorp

A unique triangular office building was opened in late 1981 as part of Toledo's waterfront redevelopment (left). Toledo Trust's original predecessor bank, Toledo Savings Institution, at Summit and Monroe Street in 1886 (below).

combines local knowledge of the community with the expertise and resources of a large corporation to provide financial services for the future.

A description in an 1882 city directory explained that, "The business of the bank is entirely savings." Much has changed since that listing. Not only does Toledo Trustcorp offer checking accounts, safe deposit boxes, certificates of deposit, trust services, commercial and installment loans and other traditional bank services, but it offers travel services, investment management and international trade consulting as well.

Atlas Tours & Travel Service, Inc., one of the country's largest travel agencies, was purchased by Toledo Trust and offers comprehensive travel services for businesses and individuals. Another significant development for Toledo Trustcorp was the formation of SeaGate Capital Management Company, an independent investment management firm. Another unique service was added in 1981 when International Trade Consulting was organized to aid companies that could greatly benefit from international trade.

In its 114-year history, Toledo Trustcorp has changed with the city and the times. As a catalyst for downtown and neighborhood revitalization, Toledo Trustcorp is optimistic about the future of the bank and its community. The bank has spearheaded the nationally recognized Warren-Sherman neighborhood revitalization—a comprehensive plan to create jobs and provide shopping, housing, health care and recreation to the depressed area. By forming a threeway partnership with the public sector and the neighborhood residents and by designing loan packages to meet the needs of the residents, the neighborhood revitalization has become a model for urban enterprise.

In addition to building its own $15 million headquarters to promote the revitalization of the riverfront, the bank is working with developers to bring a Festival Marketplace to the shores of the Maumee River. The Marketplace is expected to bring five million visitors the first year and an estimated 1,100 new jobs. This project, together with the many other redevelopment efforts, is making Toledo "Ohio's Newest City." Toledo Trustcorp looks back with pride on its many accomplishments and looks forward to a strong future for the bank and its communities.

UT marks 110 years of community service

Jesup Wakeman Scott, his two sons and four others had virtually no community support when they incorporated the Toledo University of Arts and Trades in October 1872. When Scott died less than fourteen months later, the university was still a homeless and penniless institution without teachers or students.

Scott—lawyer, teacher, scientist and journalist—had given the university 160 acres of land on the old Airline Junction in South Toledo, near the present location of Nebraska Avenue and Parkside Boulevard.

Dubbed "Pyrotechnic Institute" because of fierce political battles between university directors and the Toledo school board during UT's first 55 years, UT was shut down in 1878 and again in 1906 because of lack of funds. Prior to 1909, the university had no presidents; most major policy decisions were made by the university board of directors or the Toledo Board of Education, and the public schools superintendent served as chief administrator.

The University of Toledo is vastly different from that "weak infant" of early years. Enrollment was 2,029 in 1928. It topped 21,000 in 1982 and continues to set enrollment records every fall, with students in 147 academic programs in eight colleges.

Once Toledo's neglected stepchild, UT now generates an estimated $370 million annually in economic activity in the Toledo metropolitan area and boasts nearly 40 facilities on two campuses encompassing nearly 380 acres in West Toledo.

When the Toledo University of Arts and Trades opened in 1875, 30 students enrolled in mechanical and architectural drawing classes. The first home was Raymond Hall, an old brick church located on Adams Street at the northern edge of downtown Toledo. Classes were held six days a week, and the first students were high school seniors and laborers who took manual training courses to earn high school and college diplomas simultaneously.

Unfortunately, operating funds were depleted in 1878 and the school closed.

Classes resumed after the university was incorporated as a municipal institution in 1884, and the Toledo Board of Education donated classroom space in the old Central High School for college curriculum use. Enrollment climbed gradually, exceeding 275 in 1900.

The manual training school offered a curriculum of architecture, woodworking, mechanical arts, cooking and dressmaking. Women students were first admitted in 1886. The school gained national exposure by presenting an exhibit of "the education of the eye and the hand" during the 1893 World's Fair in Chicago and was praised as one of the top two manual training schools in the country.

However, the school was linked so closely to the public school system that the board of directors was restrained from developing higher level programs for a large number of people. The university was reorganized into a polytechnic institute in 1900, but UT directors and Toledo School Board members continued to wrangle over control of the university. The school board had been given legal authority over UT as early as 1902, but directors nailed shut the doors on the polytechnic institute in an attempt to prevent the school board from taking control.

Some board members pulled off a successful raid on the campus in October 1906, and classes, which had been discontinued in September, were resumed.

The battle raged under eleven lawsuits for another five years until 1911. At that time, the UT directors were declared the rightful inheritors of the original Scott deed.

Jerome Raymond, a brilliant lecturer and "Puritan perfectionist," accepted the university presidency in 1909 after refusing it for four years. He quit eleven months later over disagreement in a leasing contract with the old Toledo Medical College which had become affiliated with the university in 1904. Nonetheless, newly organized colleges of law, arts and sciences and industrial science were housed in the medical college after 1909.

The medical school was nearly destroyed in a 1911 fire, and UT took refuge in the Meredith Building on Michigan Street and Jefferson Avenue six days after the fire. The medical school reopened after several months of repair, but the College of Law remained in the Meredith Building.

In 1914, the Toledo Medical College closed, and UT moved its entire operations to the old Illinois Elementary School—a Civil-War vintage, dilapidated building vacated by the Toledo School Board. The eight-room schoolhouse, located at the corner of Illinois and Eleventh streets, was transformed into a mini-campus by $7,000 spent on remodeling.

The university started a housing and training structure for auto mechanics for the U.S. Army in 1918 on the original Scott property on Nebraska Avenue, but the building was never used for that pur-

University Hall, 1982.

pose. The three-story edifice was refitted and renamed the Science Building in 1922, when most university operations were moved there. The site, nicknamed the "university farm" because of its rural location, included repair shops and barracks which were transformed into gymnasium facilities.

The unsightly location of the "downtown" campus and "university farm," (which was inaccessible by trolley car lines and centered in a rapidly growing industrial district), led the UT board to search for a permanent home in April 1928.

Dr. Henry J. Doermann, a former vice chancellor of the University of Puerto Rico, became president of the university in 1927 after two presidents died within 150 days in 1926. He immediately started plans for a new home for the beleaguered school.

The dynamic leadership of Dr. Doermann and the united efforts of faculty and students paid off in the 1928 general election. A $2.85 million bond issue for university construction was passed after nearly every Toledo home was canvassed by students and alumni encouraging support for "UT: Worth a Million Per Year."

Officials moved quickly to select a 114-acre farm site on Bancroft Street for the new home and ground was broken on a snowy March 3, 1930. In less than eleven months, 400 men with 598 rail carloads of material built the 205-foot tower and six-story University Hall and nearby Field House.

University Hall was dedicated in February 1931—a landmark for college education in Toledo's sprawling urban laboratory. Observers noted that the university's energy could now turn from fractious political debate to nurturing leadership and creativity.

UT weathered the Great Depression when administrators and faculty took pay cuts beginning in 1931, and worked weeks without pay in 1933 and 1935. The Depression-born Public Works Administration and Work Projects Administration provided the men and the wherewithal to build the Glass Bowl football stadium and an array of residence halls between 1935 and 1938.

The university was an important part of the World War II effort, opening its facilities 24 hours a day to train 14,500 men and women for war industry jobs. Fewer than 270 men remained as regular students in a total student body of under 1,200. Air Force cadets moved into the Field House, and there were civilian pilot and nurse training programs on campus.

UT looked beyond its local orientation to broader horizons during the 1950s. Campus groups campaigned successfully for national affiliation while the business and pharmacy colleges gained national accreditation. Growing pains moved the university to appeal, unsuccessfully at first, for state support, but faculty, administrators and students again banded together in 1959 to persuade Toledo voters to approve tax levies generating $2.5 million annually. UT's financial situation was so stable that student fees were not increased from 1959 to 1963.

State status was finally granted in 1967 as Dr. William S. Carlson continued to lead the university during a fourteen year period of rapid growth. During his tenure, the Graduate School was expanded with nine doctoral programs, a full-time law school program was instituted and the $7.3 million Community and Technical College complex was built on the farmland that Jesup Scott and his wife Susan had given to the university in 1872. More than $45 million in capital improvements were completed during Dr. Carlson's tenure, including the Ritter Planetarium and Observatory, the Bowman-Oddy Laboratories and a sixteen-story, 700-bed dormitory.

Dr. Glen R. Driscoll became the eleventh president of The University of Toledo coincident with its centennial year—1972. The following year, with trustees and community leaders, he initiated a "Decade of Development" campaign to raise $10.5 million for the continued enhancement of the university with scholarship, library and equipment assistance, as well as physical construction.

Between 1967 and 1980 new facilities were added at the rate of one each year. Direct outgrowths of the Centennial Fund Campaign, the initial stage of the "Decade of Development," were the Continuing Education Center and Centennial Hall, which brought 1.5 million persons to concerts and athletic events through its first five seasons.

With the assistance of a substantial private gift, President Driscoll and the board of trustees planned the construction start of the new College of Business Administration building, as well as an addition in 1982 to the Engineering-Science building at a total cost of more than $8 million.

The University's academic and physical expansion and enthusiastic community support seem proof enough that Toledo's "once neglected infant" has become a mature and vital educational force in Northwest Ohio.

235

Toledo University of Arts and Trades, UT's name at its founding in 1872, placed students at drafting boards.

Heritage spans 80 years of noted art collection

The Toledo Museum of Art ranks among the foremost art museums in the United States because of its internationally recognized collections, noted programs in adult and children's art education and its broad base of community support, including a remarkable degree of volunteer participation. Unlike other museums, it maintains a diversified music program, and for over 60 years has acted as the art department of The University of Toledo. But like most American museums, it is a private, nonprofit charitable foundation almost entirely funded from gifts, endowment income and annual memberships.

The leader in founding the museum in 1901 was Edward Drummond Libbey (1854-1925), who had established Toledo's glass industry in 1888. His gifts made possible the first two parts of the present building in 1912 and 1926. His bequest provided for the two wings built in 1933 and is the principal continuing source of art purchase funds. In the last 30 years interior unfinished spaces have been completed and others have been extensively remodeled. In the summer of 1982, reconstruction of much of the museum's center was completed to provide new facilities, including a main stairway, a gallery for special exhibitions, an entrance from Grove Place, a bookstore, a sales-rental gallery, various service and security facilities and a loading dock.

The art collections range in time from ancient Egypt, Greece and Rome through the Middle Ages and the Renaissance to the arts of our own time in Europe and America. In many fields, the Toledo collections are of international importance, widely recognized for their high quality and comprehensiveness. The Greek vases are among the finest groups of this art form in America. Medieval art in enamels, ivory, silver, tapestry, bronze, stone and wood is centered around the Cloister, composed of three fourteenth-century arcades from southwestern France. The Great Gallery contains European paintings from the fifteenth to eighteenth centuries, including masterpieces such as the *Adoration of the Child* (1492) by the Florentine Pietro de Cosimo, *The Agony in the Garden* by El Greco, *The Crowning of Saint Catherine* by Rubens and Rembrandt's *Man in a Fur-Lined Coat.* Nearby are Toledo's famous groups of seventeenth-eighteenth century French, Spanish, Italian, Dutch, Flemish and British painting, sculpture and furniture. A series of special galleries devoted to the arts of gold and silver, jewelry, vessels of semiprecious stones, enameling, porcelain and faience surround a richly decorated room of about 1640 from the Loire Valley in France. Nineteenth- and early twentieth-century Europe are represented by well-known works by Turner, Constable, Courbet, Millet, Degas, Pissarro, Renoir, Monet, Gauguin, Van Gogh, Picasso and Bonnard. The collection of American works includes such famous paintings as *The Architect's Dream* by Thomas Cole and *The Open Air Breakfast* by W. M. Chase; the collection's impressive range extends from the eighteenth century to the 1980s. The museum's important collections of prints, photography and the art of the book have special galleries devoted to works of art on paper. The arts of Africa and the Far East are represented by small but distinguished groups. The museum's glass collection is known worldwide. It is unique among general art museums in being presented as an impressive small museum in itself which shows the art of glass from its earliest productions in about 2000 B.C. to the American studio glass movements of the last twenty years which originated at the Toledo Museum.

Concert in the Great Gallery (above). The Toledo Museum of Art's Monroe Street entrance (below).

More than 50 years of moving & storage with many pluses in other services

Foresight and service are two ingredients in the overall operation of Willis Day Management, Inc. which have ingratiated the firm with its ever-growing legion of customers.

Willis Day Management, Inc. is the parent company of several Willis Day enterprises—Willis Day Storage Co., Willis Day Moving & Storage Co., Willis Day Materials Handling, Willis Day Freight Systems, Willis Day Machinery Moving & Rigging and Century 21 Willis Day Realty.

Willis Day Storage Co. was founded in 1919 by Willis Day Jr., the father of three sons—Willis F. III, Thomas R. and P. Richard—who became associated with the business in the mid-1940s. Guided by their father, the sons soon had key operational posts in the business and assumed management upon his death. Their combined efforts have been responsible for growth of the existing firm and expansion into allied business operations.

The original moving and storage business founded by Willis Jr. continues to be the cornerstone of the Willis Day enterprises and centers around residential, commercial and office moves. Willis Day is Toledo's exclusive Mayflower agent and one of Mayflower's original agents.

To broaden the Willis Day service base, a machinery moving and rigging business was established to provide an additional service for industrial clients who demand moves which minimize downtime to their operations. The scheduling efficiencies and professional skills provided by Willis Day personnel are the plus factors sought by many in the industrial field. Two recent moves handled by Willis Day Moving & Storage exemplify the flexibility of the organization. Two Toledo television stations, both affiliated with national networks, required careful coordination to assure the continuous telecasting without any interruptions. The moves were made without any alteration of telecast schedules; both stations signed off at regular hours in the early a.m. and resumed programming from new studios and facilities at regular sign-on later in the morning. While speed and care were of the essence, the delicate electronic equipment involved in the move had to be transported at a slow pace to assure its operation when installed in the new quarters of each station.

From the original building on Monroe Street which housed offices and warehousing space, the Willis Day firm now

The Willis Day Dearborn Avenue warehouse is adjacent to the Detroit-Toledo Expressway (Interstate 280)—ideally situated, as are other Willis Day facilities, to expedite shipping and receiving (above). This Willis Day Storage Co. building is located in downtown Toledo (right). It houses offices, shops and warehousing space. Nearby are two more large warehousing centers.

has nine huge warehousing centers in Northwest Ohio. In addition, Willis Day Materials Handling, a sales-service organization for all types of materials handling equipment, operates from 927 Dearborn Avenue adjacent to one of the Willis Day Storage Company's large warehousing centers. Its services have proved invaluable to many warehousing clients who can quickly obtain equipment or the service they need.

Another natural and allied growth was the establishment of Willis Day Freight Systems. Recognizing the need of warehousing clients to move goods to outlets throughout Ohio, the freight service provides consolidation of products at the warehouse with shipping by one line on a regular schedule, resulting in savings for warehouse clients as well as assured rapid delivery.

Among the outstanding achievements accomplished by the Day firm was the establishment of Willis Day Industrial Park on an 880-acre abandoned U.S. Army Ordnance Depot. Regarded as a "white elephant" by many, the Day brothers envisioned a modern business/industrial complex on the site. With their knowledge of real estate, warehousing, creative salesmanship and a broad recognition by potential tenants for the facility, they transformed the depot into a modern business/industrial park.

Through the years, many of the Day

brothers', transactions have involved real estate. A natural consideration was the establishment of a realty firm—Century 21 Willis Day Realty. Headquartered at 420 Louisiana Avenue, Perrysburg, the firm handles commercial and residential realty transactions.

Another sector of Willis Day operations handles packing and crating of products for domestic as well as worldwide shipping.

The respect and warm friendships developed by the three Day brothers have been earned through service, courteousness and common sense applied to business operations. The attitude of "It Can Be Done" is noteworthy throughout the organization.

The continuance of the firm and its progressive policies are being assured with the entry into the operations by a third generation of Days. They are instilled with the same fervor, vision and knowledge which have gained Willis Day an international reputation for service when and where it counts.

237

A friend Toledo depends on

In the pivotal year of 1921, America and Toledo were recovering from World War I and ushering in a new era that history would remember as the Roaring '20s. It was hardly heard as a roar, but the tiny ten-watt signal coming from a storeroom in the old Navarre Hotel on April 15th was Ohio's first commercial radio station, WTAL. At that time WTAL was owned by the Toledo Radio and Electric Company which moved the station to the Waldorf Hotel in 1925 and, a year later, relocated in the Recreation Building on Superior Street and increased power to a booming 50 watts!

Meanwhile, the horse and buggy had been replaced by the automobile and Toledoans were chugging along on Speedene gasoline. Speedene's popularity skyrocketed as a result of an advertising campaign on WTAL by the Fort Industry Oil Company. The Storer family, owners of the oil company, were so impressed with radio as an advertising medium that they decided it would be smart to own the station.

They purchased WTAL in 1927; the next year George B. Storer changed the call letters to WSPD in honor of Speedene, and the Fort Industry Company was born. Many Toledoans continue to refer to WSPD as "Speedy" radio.

WSPD's enthusiastic new owners entered the infant broadcast business with zest and a pioneering spirit. Within a year, WSPD moved into new custom-designed studios atop the Commodore Perry Hotel, became the Columbia Broadcasting System's eighth affiliate, increased power twice and launched a new era.

Toledo's recollections of WSPD's first dozen years could fill at least that many scrapbooks. Many remember hearing London's impressive Big Ben chime on WSPD in 1928; even more impressive was the fact that it was the first transatlantic broadcast in northwest Ohio. Many still fondly recall "Station WSPD Jamboree," "Singing Strings," "Kiddie Carnival Show," Martha Raye's comedy, Alice O'Connell's music and Jim Uebelhart's news. Live entertainment and community involvement made WSPD a good friend and companion of Toledo.

Friends of WSPD will never forget the day a bolt of lightning demolished WSPD's transmitting tower on Oregon Road. That was in 1936, the same year WSPD increased power to 5,000 watts and became an affiliate of the National

Broadcasting Company, as it is today. WSPD was growing.

In 1940, WSPD moved to new studios at 136 Huron Street, then in 1961, to the new building it still occupies today at 125 South Superior Street in downtown Toledo. WSPD continued to innovate with live sports coverage from the University of Toledo, remote broadcasts, entertainment, community features and news that would win many prestigious awards in the following years.

One of radio's highest awards was presented to WSPD in 1968. That year WSPD became the eighth recipient of the Broadcast Pioneer's coveted Mike Award which is given only to long-established radio stations that have consistently maintained an outstanding record of service to the public and to the broadcast industry. In 1979, WSPD Radio was purchased by WSPD, Incorporated, a group of veteran broadcasters, with Willard Schroeder, chairman, and James P. White, vice president/general manager.

WSPD Radio has grown up with Toledo, and many Toledoans have grown up with WSPD. Both have new aspirations to share in the future. WSPD today is northwest Ohio's only 5000 watt 24-hour, full-service, adult contemporary radio station with the region's most popular personalities. WSPD continues its pledge to community service, information and entertainment and looks forward to pioneering the next 60 years of radio at 1370 AM with you in Toledo.

An era to remember: live studio orchestras, singing stars. . . . WSPD pioneered radio entertainment (below). WSPD's pledge to community involvement continues as strong as it was in 1940, when WSPD personalities supported a community event via remote broadcast (above), a tradition that continues today.

Toledo's television pioneer—a partner in Toledo's future

Television—the great entertainer and informer. By the late 1950s, TV had already become an indispensable household item. Along with the automatic washer, electric coffee pot, freezer and hi-fi, television sprang up in homes across America in the '50s.

The infant medium had created overnight stars out of Milton Berle, Lucy and Ricky, Ed Wynn, Ozzie and Harriet, Ed Sullivan and Jackie Gleason. For the first time, families were able to watch news being made. Edward R. Murrow had brought the immediacy of television news stories to millions via his "See It Now" program on CBS.

In October 1958, television viewers in Toledo and all of Northwest Ohio witnessed the birth of WTOL-TV, Channel Eleven. Not only was Toledo Eleven's initial sign-on the start of CBS programming in Northwest Ohio, but it began an era of unceasing commitment to serving the public's needs.

WTOL-TV was founded by the Community Broadcasting Company comprised of three local attorneys—Frazier Reams Sr., Thomas Bretherton and Morton Neipp. The first location of Toledo Eleven's broadcasting studios was in the Hillcrest Hotel. From this modest facility, WTOL-TV introduced Toledoans to the beginning of community-oriented local programming.

While still occupying its original broadcasting studios in the Hillcrest, WTOL-TV began remodeling work on the News-Bee Building at 604 Jackson Street. The *News-Bee* was a daily newspaper that had gone out of business sometime earlier. While remodeling was underway, the structure at 604 Jackson served as the location for the Selective Service offices, the U.S. Coast Guard and Social Security.

In September 1961, WTOL-TV made its second home at 604 Jackson Street. Toledo Eleven was growing along with the burgeoning area that it was serving. With its move to larger facilities, WTOL-TV began a proud history of helping make Toledo a great place to live.

Toledo Eleven sponsored "WTOL Day At The Zoo" in the early 1960s. This popular event annually set attendance records with free admission, prizes, live shows and telecasts.

WTOL-TV was at the forefront in bringing Toledoans the most up-to-date and innovative coverage of local and world events. In September 1964, then-

news Director Joe Gillis and a photographer traveled to Moscow, U.S.S.R., to film a documentary on the U.S. ambassador to Russia, Foy Kohler who was a Toledo native. During their stay in Moscow, Nikita Khrushchev was deposed.

In 1964 and '65, crews were sent to England and France to film more than 100 eight-minute features depicting lifestyles, fashion and other topics.

In 1965, Community Broadcasting sold WTOL-TV to the Broadcast Company of the South, which later became Cosmos Broadcasting Corporation, current owners of Toledo Eleven.

The mid-'60s and early '70s were a time of great technological, political and social change in the world. Throughout Northwest Ohio, WTOL-TV continued to keep viewers informed and enlightened through an impressive string of technical and programming innovations.

The year 1966 saw WTOL-TV become the first Toledo station to provide viewers with locally produced color newsfilm. In 1968, a Toledo Eleven news crew traveled to Normandy, France, to film a series of reports on the status of affairs since the Normandy invasion of World War II.

Also in 1968, when presidential politics were heating up, then-candidate Hubert Humphrey made a Toledo stop at the studios of WTOL-TV for various interviews.

In 1970, a Toledo Eleven news crew was sent to Israel to film a series of reports on life in Israel, border clashes with Jordan and life on a kibbutz.

By the beginning of the '70s, Toledo's television viewers were becoming more sophisticated in their viewing habits and

expectations, and WTOL-TV remained the leader in up-to-date television presentations. WTOL-TV pioneered electronic news gathering with the first electronic camera/videotape capability in Toledo. The "Mini-Cam" was a new idea in the latest, fastest way to bring a story to viewers, and Toledoans saw news stories reported with these lightweight compact cameras first on Toledo Eleven.

This accomplishment was followed closely by WTOL-TV becoming the first station in Northwest Ohio to have live remote news telecasts. Now viewers didn't have to wait for news stories to come back to the studio to be presented on the air. They could witness breaking events as they happened and when they happened. From that time until the present, WTOL-TV still has the largest capability in Toledo for originating live remote broadcasts with three individual live units.

Just as color television had become a slow reality to viewers, color broadcasts were first aired on Toledo television on WTOL-TV. Toledo Eleven eventually became the first station in the area to have all color cameras and total color programming.

In November 1981, WTOL-TV renewed its commitment to Toledo and the re-birth of the downtown area by moving into its new facility at 730 North Summit Street, formerly the site of the Retail Clerks Union. The Summit Street facility gave Toledo Eleven 35,000 square feet of usable working space.

A pioneer in bringing Toledo the finest in visual communications—a partner in Toledo's bright future—that's WTOL-TV's commitment.

The original WTOL-TV studio located at 604 Jackson.

A turn-of-the-century street cleaner pauses for a cigarette in the 200 block of Summit Street.

240

Today, Toledo is a city of contrasts—
of factory workers and corporate bankers,
hot dogs and haute cuisine,
art museums and oil terminals,
staid old-money mansions and industrial parks.
Comedians make fun of it,
but even Toledoans laugh at the jokes.
If the city has never become
*   the major Western metropolis,*
those who live there do not mind.
For they have found it is a good city,
a place where lake breezes always
*   blow around every house,*
and variety is just around the corner.

241

Bibliography

The research for this publication relied heavily upon the resources of the Local History and Genealogy Department of the Toledo-Lucas County Public Library. In addition to the published sources found in the collection, the authors made extensive use of the newspaper clipping files and scrapbooks of the department. Readers interested in more detailed information about the topics discussed in this Toledo history can visit the Local History Department.

Books and articles

Anderson, Elaine. "Pauline Steinum, Dynamic Immigrant." In *Women in Ohio History,* edited by Marta Whitlock. Columbus: The Ohio Historical Society, 1976.

———. "William Kraus and the Jewish Community." *Northwest Ohio Quarterly* 49 (1977): 127–163.

Barclay, Morgan J. "Changing Images of Toledo's Polish Community, 1870–1920." *Northwest Ohio Quarterly* 44 (1972): 64.

———. "Images of Toledo's German Community, 1850–1890." *Northwest Ohio Quarterly* 45 (1973): 133–143.

———. "Reform in Toledo: The Political Career of Samuel M. Jones." *Northwest Ohio Quarterly* 50 (1978): 79–89.

Barclay, Morgan J., and Strong, Jean W. *The Samuel Milton Jones Papers: An Inventory to the Microfilm Edition.* Columbus: Ohio Historical Society, 1978.

Bauman, Robert F. "Claims vs. Realities: The Anglo-Iroquois Partnership." *Northwest Ohio Quarterly* 32 (1960): 87–101.

———. "Iroquois 'Empire'." *Northwest Ohio Quarterly* 32 (1960): 138–172.

———. "Ottawa Fleets and Iroquois Frustration." *Northwest Ohio Quarterly* 33 (1960–61): 7–40.

Brenner, Robert H. "The Civic Revival in Ohio—Artist in Politics: Brand Whitlock." *American Journal of Economics and Sociology* 9 (1949–50): 477–482.

———. "The Civic Revival in Ohio—Police, Penal and Parole Policies in Cleveland and Toledo." *American Journal of Economics and Sociology* 14 (1954–55): 387–398.

Cary, Lorin Lee. *Guide to Research in the History of Toledo, Ohio.* Toledo, Ohio: University of Toledo, 1977.

Clapp, Tom. "Toledo Industrial Peace Board." (Parts I–IV), *Northwest Ohio Quarterly* 40–42 (1968–70): 50–67, 25–41, 70–86, 19–28.

Crunden, Robert M. *A Hero in Spite of Himself: Brand Whitlock in Art, Politics, and War.* New York: Alfred A. Knopf, 1969.

Davis, Harold E. "Elisha Whittlesey and Maumee Land Speculation, 1834–1840." *Northwest Ohio Quarterly* 15 (1943): 139–158.

Downes, Randolph C. *Canal Days.* Toledo, Ohio: The Historical Society of Northwestern Ohio, 1949.

———. *The Conquest.* Toledo, Ohio: The Historical Society of Northwestern Ohio, 1948.

———. *Industrial Beginnings.* Toledo, Ohio: The Historical Society of Northwestern Ohio, 1954.

———. *Lake Port.* Toledo, Ohio: The Historical Society of Northwestern Ohio, 1951.

———, ed. "The Migration of Zophar Case from Cleveland to Vandalia, 1829–1830." *Northwest Ohio Quarterly* 24 (1952): 83–91.

———. "Toledo's History—A Birdseye View." *Northwest Ohio Quarterly* 34 (1962): 71–81.

Fauster, Carl U. *Libbey Glass Since 1818: Pictorial History & Collector's Guide.* Toledo, Ohio: Antique and Historical Glass Foundation, 1979.

Fine, Sidney. "The Toledo Chevrolet Strike of 1935." *Ohio Historical Quarterly* 67 (1958): 326–356.

Foley, Sara. *Early Times.* n. p., n. d.

Folger, Fred. "Trilby—An Early History, 1835–1919." *Northwest Ohio Quarterly* 50 (1978): 43–55.

Frederick, Peter J. *Knights of the Golden Rule: The Intellectual as Christian Social Reformer in the 1890s.* Lexington: University Press of Kentucky, c1976.

Glaab, Charles N. "Jesup W. Scott and A West of Cities." *Ohio History* 73 (1964): 3–12.

Gutyon, Priscilla L. "John Hunt." (Parts I–IV), *Northwest Ohio Quarterly* 52–53, (1980–81): 179–190, 214–226, 254–258, 50–66.

Harrison, John M. *The Man Who Made Nasby, David Ross Locke.* Chapel Hill, North Carolina: University of North Carolina Press, 1969.

Hurd, Thaddeus B. "Fifty Years of Toledo Architecture, A Survey of the Recent Past." *Northwest Ohio Quarterly* 24 (1952): 68–82.

Johannesen, Eric. and Dickes, Allen. *Look Again: Landmark Architecture in Downtown Toledo and Old West End.* Pittsburgh: Ober Park Associates, 1973.

Johnson, Wendell F. *Toledo's Non-Partisan Movement.* Toledo, Ohio: The H. J. Chittenden Company, 1922.

Jones, Samuel M. *The New Right: A Plea for Fair Play Through a More Just Social Order.* New York: Eastern Book Concern, 1899.

Keller, Kathryn M. "Scene: Toledo-Time 1837." *Northwest Ohio Quarterly* 34 (1962): 52–70.

Killits, John Milton. *Toledo and Lucas County Ohio.* 3 Vols. Chicago: S. J. Clarke Co., 1923.

Kime, Wayne R. "Pierre M. Irving and The Toledo Blade." *Northwest Ohio Quarterly* 47 (1975): 131–151.

———. "Pierre M. Irving in Toledo, 1836–1838: Ten Letters." *Northwest Ohio Quarterly* 51 (1979): 35–68.

Knopf, Richard C. "Fort Miamis: The International Background." *Ohio State Archaeological and Historical Quarterly* 61 (1952): 146–166.

Ligibel, Ted J. "Toledo Minus Port Lawrence Equals Vistula—A Retrospective Look at Toledo's Oldest Remaining Neighborhood." *Northwest Ohio Quarterly* 46 (1974): 123–130.

Machen, Edwin A. and Downes, Randolph C. "William Henry Machen: Pioneer Local Colorist of Northwestern Ohio." *Northwest Ohio Quarterly* 20 (1948): 59–81.

Macklin, Barbara June. *Structural Stability and Culture Change in a Mexican-American Community.* New York: Arno Press, 1976.

Mayfield, Harold. "The Changing Toledo Region—A Naturalist's Point of View." *Northwest Ohio Quarterly* 34 (1962): 83–104.

Mohler, Edward Francis. "Vignette of a Pioneer The Reverend Edward Hannin." *Northwest Ohio Quarterly* 14 (1942): 70–82.

Perry, Harriet Collins. "The Life History of Harriet Whitney Collins." *Northwest Ohio Quarterly* 31 (1959): 143–155.

Quaife, M. M. "From Marietta to Detroit in 1814." *Northwest Ohio Quarterly* 14 (1942): 135–155.

Rich, David. "The Toledo Mechanics Association: The City's First Labor Union." *Northwest Ohio Quarterly* 46 (1973–74): 25–31.

Rodabaugh, James H. "Samuel M. Jones—Evangel of Equality." *Northwest Ohio Quarterly* 15 (1943): 17–46.

Scott, Jesup Wakeman. *A Presentation of Causes Tending to Fit the Position of the Future Great City of the World in the Central Plain.* Toledo, Ohio: Blade Printing Company, 1876. (2nd edition, revised.)

Scoville, Warren C. *Revolution in Glassmaking.* Cambridge, Mass.: Harvard University Press, 1948.

Scribner, Harvey. *Memoirs of Lucas County and the City of Toledo.* 2 Vols. Madison, Wis.: Western Historical Association, 1910.

Simonis, Louis A. *Maumee River 1835.* Defiance, Ohio: Defiance County Historical Society, 1979.

Smith, Delores. "Northwestern Ohio's Cholera Years, 1849–1864." *Northwest Ohio Quarterly* 47 (1975): 60–69.

Staelin, Carl Gustav. *Toledo Highlights.* Toledo, Ohio: Rotary Club of Toledo, 1966.

Stinchcombe, Jean L. *Reform and Reaction: City Politics in Toledo.* Belmont, California: Wadsworth Publishing Company, 1968.

Tager, Jack. *The Intellectual As Urban Reformer: Brand Whitlock and the Progressive Movement.* Cleveland: Case-Western University Press, 1968.

"Toledo's Old West End." *Museum News* 10 (1967): 55–75.

Towe, Harold T. *The Legal Basis for Municipal Functions in Toledo.* Fostoria, Ohio: Gray Printing Company, 1940.

Van Tassel, Charles Sumner, ed. *Historical Toledo and Northwestern Ohio.* Toledo, Ohio: n. p., 1901.

Waggoner, Clark, ed. *History of the City of Toledo and Lucas County, Ohio.* New York: Munsell & Company, 1888.

Warner, Hoyt Landon. *Progressivism in Ohio 1897–1970.* Columbus, Ohio: Ohio State University Press, 1964.

Wendler, Marilyn V. "Anti-Slavery Sentiment and the Underground Railroad in the Lower Maumee Valley." *Northwest Ohio Quarterly* 52 (1980): 193–208.

Whitlock, Brand. *Forty Years of It.* New York: Appleton and Company, 1914.

Williams, Lee. "Newcomers to the City: A Study of Black Population Growth in Toledo, Ohio, 1910–1930." *Ohio History* 89 (1980): 5–24.

Wittke, Carl. "The Ohio-Michigan Boundary Dispute Reexamined." *Ohio Archaeological and Historical Quarterly* 45 (1936): 299–319.

Wolfe, Don. *Frazier Reams: His Life and Time.* n. p., n. p., 1978.

Wright, Isaac. *The East Side. Past and Present.* Toledo, Ohio: Hadley and Hadley Printers, 1894.

Wright, Richard J., ed. *The John Hunt Memoirs Early Years of the Maumee Basin, 1812–1835.* Maumee, Ohio: Maumee Valley Historical Society, 1978.

A lack of published material on twentieth century Toledo remains critical. The authors' main sources of information included master's theses, doctoral dissertations, research papers and public documents.

Documents and unpublished sources

Anderson, Elaine. "The Humorist and the City." Seminar Paper, University of Toledo, 1969.

_____. "The Jews of Toledo, 1845–1895." Ph.D. dissertation, University of Toledo, 1974.

Ballert, Albert G. "The Primary Function of Toledo, Ohio," Ph.D. dissertation, University of Chicago, 1947.

Barclay, Morgan J. "The Toledo Museum of Art and the Urban Community." Master's thesis, University of Toledo, 1972.

Bartha, Stephen J. "A History of Immigrant Groups In Toledo." Master's thesis, University of Toledo, 1945.

Barton-Aschman Associates, Incorporated. *Toledo CBD Master Plan City of Toledo, Ohio.* Evanston, Illinois: Barton-Aschman Associates, 1977.

Bates, Dennis L. "Canal and Courthouse Urban Images Along the Maumee River, 1833–1837." Seminar Paper, University of Toledo, 1969.

Brown, Larry W. "The City of Toledo Ohio During the Civil War." Seminar Paper, University of Toledo, 1977.

Burke, Kathy. "The Toledo Police Department: Its Growth and Development to 1873." Seminar Paper, University of Toledo, 1973.

_____. "Toledo Police Board Controversy, 1902." Seminar Paper, University of Toledo, 1973.

Chelminski, David Gwidon. "The Ethnicity of the Poles in Toledo, c. 1830–1886." Master's thesis, University of Toledo, 1978.

_____. "Population Figures and Contemporary Attention Allowed for the Ethnic Groups in Toledo, Ohio and Its Vicinity Through 1945." Seminar Paper, University of Toledo, 1978.

_____. "Strikebreakers, Slavs and Violence in the 1919 Willys-Overland Labor Dispute." Seminar Paper, University of Toledo, 1977.

Davis, Charles P. "Toledo's Natural Gas Years: A Study of Urban Self-Delusion." Seminar Paper, University of Toledo, 1969.

Dickes, Allen Leroy. "The Development of the Port of Toledo, 1946–1966." Master's thesis, University of Toledo, 1970.

_____. "Toledo Business Promotion, 1870–1900." Seminar Paper, University of Toledo, 1969.

Ford, Harvey S. "The Life and Times of Golden Rule Jones." Ph.D. dissertation, University of Michigan, 1953.

Grefe, Hugh W. "Clark Waggoner's World: The Nineteenth-Century Journalist as Urban Promoter." Master's thesis, University of Toledo, 1981.

Hanson, Jo Ann. "Urbanization in Toledo: An Historical Review." Typescript, n. p., 1974.

Leckie, Shirley A. "Parks, Planning and Progressivism in Toledo, Ohio: 1890–1929." Ph.D. dissertation, University of Toledo, 1981.

Ligibel, Ted and Szuberla, Guy. "Toledo's Tomorrows: An Exhibition of Architectural Drawings and Documents." Exhibition Guide, University of Toledo, 1982.

Monks, Anne. "City Planning in the 1920's: Harland Bartholomew's Master Plan for Toledo." Seminar Paper, University of Toledo, 1977.

Mosier, Tana. "Brand Whitlock Homes: The Land, the People, and the Project." Master's thesis, University of Toledo, 1981.

Reese, William J. "William Backus Guitteau and Educational Reform in Toledo During the Progressive Era." Master's thesis, Bowling Green State University, 1975.

Reuling, William J. "Samuel Golden Rule Jones and the City-Family Ideal." Seminar Paper, University of Toledo, 1971.

Rich, David. "Panic in Toledo." Seminar Paper, University of Toledo, 1971.

_____. "Toledo: City of Optimism." Seminar Paper, University of Toledo, 1971.

_____. "Urban Promotion: A View of Toledo in the Nineteenth Century." Master's thesis, University of Toledo, 1972.

Scherer, Emil J. "Edward Drummond Libbey: Citizen of the Community." Seminar Paper, University of Toledo, n. d.

Skalski, Anne. "The Trolley Park, 1895–1927." Seminar Paper, University of Toledo, 1973.

Sobczak, John N. "The Inadequacies of Localism: The Collapse of Relief in Toledo, 1929–1939." Master's thesis, Bowling Green State University, 1975.

Toledo Economic Planning Council. *Overall Economic Development Plan: City of Toledo.* Toledo, Ohio: Toledo Economic Planning Council, n. d.

Wendler, Marilyn. "A History of Organized Development at the Foot of the Rapids (Maumee City), 1815–1850." Seminar Paper, University of Toledo, n. d.

_____. "Maumee City: A Study of Urban Development in the Early Nineteenth Century." Master's thesis, University of Toledo, 1977.

Williams, Leroy T. "Black Toledo: Afro-Americans in Toledo, Ohio, 1890–1920." Ph.D. dissertation, University of Toledo, 1977.

Index

Numerals in italics indicate an illustration of the subject.

A

Abbot, Francis Ellingwood: 86.
Acme Power Plant: *160.*
Acme Sucker Rod Company: 84.
Adams, Hyman: 148.
Adams streetcar line: *101.*
Addams, Jane: 85.
Adrian, Mich.: 24, 28, 37, 156.
Akron, Ohio: 158.
American Association: 37, 123.
American Bicycle Company: 50.
American Federation of Teachers (AFT): 167.
American Hotel: 37.
"American League of the Friends of New Germany": 75.
American Legion: 122.
American Motors: 60, 177.
American Protective Association: 84.
American Turner Club: 75.
Ameryka (Polish periodical): 64.
Ameryka-Echo (see also *Ameryka, Echo*): 64.
Anderson, George W.: 80, 84.
Angelo Hotel: 39.
Anshei Sfard (Jewish temple): *70.*
Anthony Wayne Bridge (see High Level Bridge).
Anthony Wayne Trail: 136, *138.*
AP Parts: 60.
Armory, National Guard: 68, *115.*
Arrow (steamer): *43.*
Arthur Young & Co.: 169.
Ash-Consaul Bridge: 128.
Ashley block: 92.
Ashley, James M., Jr.: 84.
Auburndale: 95.
Auditorium, The (theater): 126.
Austerlitz: 20.
Austro-Hungarian Empire: 64.
"Auto Parts Capital of the World": 60.

B

Babe (Toledo Zoo elephant): *143.*
Baker Brothers: 154.
Balkans: 64, 71.
Ball, George F.: 34.
Ballot Box (Suffrage periodical): 86.
"Barbarians": 75.
Barber House: *179.*
Bartholomew, Harland: 118.
Bartholomew Plan: 118, 125, 156.
Bartley, Rudolph A.: 71, *74* (home).
Battle of Fallen Timbers: 20.
Battle of Lake Erie: 21.
Bavaria (Bavarians): 71, 75, 77.
Bay View Park: 118, 123.
Beach, Helen W.: 84.
Beachey, Lincoln: 112.
Beatty Park: 118.
Beecher, Henry Ward: 34.
Beecher, William Henry: 34.
Bel Geddes, Norman: 156.
Bell, Louise: 148.
Bell & Powell's store: 54.
Benedict, Clarence: 138.
Berdan, John: 39, 41.
"Big Lucas": 156.
Birckhead Place: 113.
Birmingham, Ohio: 64, 68, 71, 80, 177.

"Black Metropolis" (Chicago): 78.
Black Panthers: 167.
Black Swamp: 16, 18, 22, 29, 160.
Blade Building: *32, 124-25, 180.*
Blatt, Norman: 148.
Bliss Auto Sales: *60-61.*
Block, Paul R., Jr.: 156.
Bon-Aire Supper Club: 149.
"Bonfire Committee": 34.
Boody, Azariah: 39.
Boody House: *38,* 39.
Boody House restaurant: *170.*
B&O Railroad docks: *136.*
Bowen, Badger C.: 113, 118.
Boy Scout reservation: 138.
Brand & Lenk Wine Company: 71.
Brewer, Teresa: *172.*
British (see English).
Broadway Pumping Station: *96-97.*
Bronson Place: 113.
Broom Drill Square: *106-07.*
Brown, Joe E.: 68, *125.*
Brown, John: *79.*
Brunswick Recording Orchestra: 125.
Brussels, Belgium: 94.
Bulgaria (Bulgarians): 68, 71, 73, 80.
Bund, the (*Volkesbund*): 75.
Burnham, Daniel H.: 119.
Burritt, Elihu: 26.
Burt's Theater: 126.

C

Calvary Cemetery: 36.
Campion, Father (Catholic priest): 32.
Canada (Canadians): 20, 64, 78, 148.
Canal Boulevard (see also Anthony Wayne Trail): 136.
Cannon Cleaners: *144.*
"Capital of Bulgars in America": 71.
Capital Theater: 126.
Capital Tire and Rubber: *142.*
Case, Zophar: 16.
Census, U.S.: 29, 64, 78.
Central Grove Park: 103.
Chamber of Commerce: 156.
Champion Spark Plug: 60.
Champlain (freighter): 128.
Chateau La France (nightclub): 80.
Cherry Pickers: 64.
Cherry Street Bridge: 86, 118, *128-29, 130.*
Cherry streetcar line: 113.
Cherry-Summit district: 113.
Chicago Columbian Exposition, 1893: *54-55,* 59.
Chicago Fire of 1871: 33.
Chicago, Ill.: 27, 38, 39, 41, 44, 52, 68, 78, 80, 113, 119, 126, 148, 149, 158, 160, 176.
Chicago World's Fair, 1893 (see Chicago Columbian Exposition).
Chicken Charlie's (nightclub): 80.
Cholera, Asiatic: 37.
Christ (Christians): 84, 85, 86.
Christian Socialism: 85.
Cincinnati, Ohio: 20, 23, 27, 29, 52, 68, 71, 75, 163.
Citizens' Emergency Fund Committee: 143.
Citizens Federation of Toledo: 86.
City Brewing and Malting Company: 71.
City Journal (Toledo): 80.
City Park: 71, *102,* 103.

City of Toledo (steamer): *43,* 86.
Civic Mall sculpture: *164.*
Civil War: 44, 45, 75, 78, 79, 84, 87, 110, 113.
Civil Works Administration (CWA): 136, 138.
Clapp and Jones fire engine: *33.*
Clark, George Rogers: 18.
Cleveland, Ohio: 16, 22, 29, 41, 47, 48, 52, 68, 71, 78, 80, 88, 101, 162, 163, 172.
Clinton, DeWitt: 23.
Close, E. H., Company: 113.
Colburn, Irving M.: 56.
Collins, Harriet Whitney: 22.
Collins, Sanford Langworthy: 22.
Collins Park: 71, 103, 118.
Colony Shopping Center: 162, *167.*
Columbia (S.C.) *Telescope*: 26.
Columbus, Ohio: 85, 149, 158.
Commodore Perry Hotel: 39, 119, 120.
Communism (Communist party): 71, *145* (circular).
Community Traction Company: 100-01.
Congress, U.S.: 27.
Connellsville coal: 47.
"Corn City": 44, 50.
Corning Glass Works: 54.
Corsair (fighter planes): 154.
Cottrill, Charles A.: *80.*
Courthouse (see Lucas County Courthouse).
Courthouse Mall: 103.
"Coventry of America": 50.
Crosby Express (barge): 86.
Croton Company No. 2: 33.
Czechs: 71.

D

Dallas, Jack: 112.
Dana Corporation: 60, *158.*
Davey Crockett No. 2: 33.
Davis Business College: *256.*
Dayton, Ohio: 23, 78.
De Bow's Review: 26.
Defiance, Ohio: 23.
Democrats (Democratic party): 27, 33, 85, 87, 88, 167.
Dempsey, Jack: *123.*
Depression: 39, 56, 60, 71, 80, 98, 113, 118, 119, 125, 136, *137,* 138, 142, 143, 148, 149, 154, 156, 163.
de Seversky, Major Alexander: 156.
Detroit, Mich.: 18, 20, 37, 41, 60, 68, 78, 80, 101, 148, 158, 167, 172, 176, 177.
Deutsche Gesellochaft: 75.
De Veaux: 113.
DeVilbiss, Allen: 58, 59.
DeVilbiss, Allen, Jr.: 58, 59.
DeVilbiss High School: 136.
DeVilbiss Manufacturing Company: 58, 59, 154.
Dictionary of English and Polish Languages (Anthony Paryski): 68.
DiSalle, Michael V., Bridge: 128.
Dix, Richard: 125.
Dixon, Charles N.: 78.
Dodge, Helen: 40.
Doehler, Herman: 59.
Dogpatch: 160.
Don Carlos, Professor (see also Knabenshue, A. Roy): 112.
Dorr-Detroit district: 95, 167.

Dorr Street fairgrounds: 113.
Dorr Street streetcar: *10-11.*
Doyle, Judge John Hardy, home: *72-73.*
Duluth, Minn.: 44, 158.
Dunbar, Paul Laurence: 78, 79.

E

East Marengo: 20.
East Saint Louis, Mo.: 112.
East Side (Toledo): 73.
East Toledo: 37, 64, *65,* 68, 71, 78, 80, 84, 95, 101, 113, 118, 138, 160, 162, 177.
Eaton, Frederick: 119.
Echo, The (see also *Ameryka, Ameryka-Echo*): 64.
Edison General Electric: 54.
Edler, Fred J.: 61.
Electric Auto-Lite Company: 60, 134, 143, *144-45, 146-47,* 154.
Elks Carnival: *111.*
Empire, The (theater): 126.
Engel, Christopher: 148.
Engine Company No. 3: 33.
Engine House No. 2: *33.*
English, Joseph: 148.
England (English): 4, 18, 20, 21, 37, 50, 64, 80.
Episcopalians: 34.
Erie Canal: 23.
Erie Indians: 18.
Erie & Kalamazoo Railroad: 24, 28, 37.
Erin Engine Company No. 2: 33.
Ermer, Carl: 177.
Esquire Theater: 163.
Eulalia, Princess, of Spain: 59.
Europe (Europeans): 16, 18, 23, 64, 68, 94, 143, 154.

F

Fairbanks scale: 78.
Fairmont Park: 113.
Falcon bicycle: 50.
Fallen Timbers Monument: 15.
Fallis, Edward O.: 74, 113, 117, 119.
Farmers Market: 168, 177.
Fassett Street Bridge: 9, 128, *131.*
Federal Building: 158, 173.
Federal Court and Customs Building: 118.
Federal Emergency Relief Administration (FERA): 136, 138.
Fifteenth Amendment: 87.
Findlay, Ohio: 52, 54.
Findlay (Ohio) *Jeffersonian*: 87.
Firemen's Ball: 34.
First Congregational Church: 34, 37.
First Congregationalists: 34.
Fish and Game Commission, U.S.: 36.
Florence (later Huron), Ohio: 26.
Florida (tug): *42-43.*
Folger, Jacob, Packing Company: 47.
Foraker, Senator Joseph: 84, 88.
Ford auto: *61.*
Ford, Edward, Plate Glass Company: 57, 95.
Ford, Henry: 59, 60.
Forest Cemetery: 32.
Fort Industry: 20, *23.*
Fort Industry Industrial Park: 158.
Fort Industry Square: *170,* 172.

Fort Meigs: *4, 20,* 37.
Fort Meigs Celebration (1840): 34.
Fort Meigs Hotel: 39.
Fort Miami (Fort Miamis): 18; 20.
Fort Wayne, Ind.: 16, 23, 24, 29.
Forty Years of It (Brand Whitlock): 93.
Fourth Ward Old Timers Club: 125.
France (French): 18, 36, 64, 68, 73.
Franklin-Bancroft area: 167.
Franklin No. 2: 33.
Franklin Park Mall: 162, 163, *171.*
Fremont, Ohio: 22.
French and Indian War: 18.
French-Canadians: 68.
Frogtown: *12* (mosaic), 37.
Future Great City of the World, The (Jesup Scott): 27, 50.

G

Gayvan, Georgia: 59.
Gendron bicycle: 48, *49.*
Gendron, Peter: 48, *49.*
General Foundry and Machine Shop: *30.*
George, Henry: 27.
German-American Alliance: 77.
German-American Festival (GAF): 77, 168.
German-American insurance agency: 77.
German Hall: 75, 77.
Germania No. 4: 33.
German Jews: 68.
Germany (Germans): 33, 34, 62, 64, 68, 71, 73, 75, 77, 85, 86.
Gladden, Washington: 85.
"Glass Center of the World": 53, 54.
Golden Rose (nightclub): 148.
Golden Rule, the: 84.
Golden Rule Hall: 85.
Golden Rule Park: 82, 85.
Golden Rule Playground: *85.*
Grand Army of the Republic (GAR): *79,* 110.
"Grand Gas Celebration": 52.
Grange, "Red": 123.
Grant, President Ulysses S.: 87.
Great Britain (see England).
Great Depression (see Depression).
"Great Inland Empire": 47.
Great Lakes: 23, 24, 26, 29, 41, 43, 44.
"Great Natural Gas Bubble": 52.
Great Plains: 44.
Greece (Greeks): 64, 71, *168.*
Greek Festival: 168.
Grey Nuns (Sisters of Charity): 32.
Gwiazda (Polish periodical): 64.

H

Halfway Creek: 22.
Hamilton, Mayor James K.: 52.
Hampton Park: 113.
Hanna, Marcus: 84.
Hannin, Father Edward: 68, 69.
Harding, Warren G., Memorial Bridge: 125.
Harlem (New York): 78, 80.
Harrison, William Henry: 20, 34.
Haughton, Colonel Nathaniel: 30.
Haughton Elevator Company: 31.
Hayes, Alfred A.: 148.
Hayes, President Rutherford B.: 52.
Hazdi, Dimitri: 176.

Heatherdowns: 163.
High Level Bridge: 8-9, 125, 128, *130-31,* 176.
Hillcrest Hotel: 39.
Holiday Inn: 39, 158.
Holland: 36.
Holtgrieve, B.H., and Son grocery: *52.*
"Holy Toledo!": 68.
Holy Trinity Church: 64.
Hopkins, Major O. J.: 23.
Howard, Colonel Dresden W.H.: 28.
Howells, William Dean: 80.
Howlett's, Miss, school: 34.
Hungary (Hungarians): 64, 68, 71, 73.
Hunt's Merchant's Magazine: 26.
Huron, Ohio: 26.
Hussars: 64.

I

Illinois: 40, 57.
Illinois River: 40.
Illinois River valley: 18.
Independent party: 92, 93.
Independent Relief Hook and Ladder Company: 33.
Index (religious publication): 86.
Indiana: 23, 24.
Indianapolis, Ind.: 59.
International Institute: *75.*
International Postal Union: 36.
Interstate 75: 166.
Inverness Golf Club: 123.
Iowa: 18.
Ireland (Irish): 33, 64, 68, 69, 71, 73, 75.
Ironville (manufacturing district): 95.
Iroquois Indians: 18.
Irving, Ebenezer: 39.
Irving, Pierre M.: 39, 41.
Irving, Washington: 39.
Island House: 38, 39, 86.
Italy (Italians): 64, 71, 73.

J

Jackson, Andrew: 27.
Jacksonville, Ill.: 39.
Jay's Treaty: 20.
Jeep, Willys: 60, *154-55.*
Jermain Park: 118.
Jermain, Sylvanus P.: 88, 103.
Jews (Jewish): 70, 71, 75, 86.
Jones, Mayor Samuel: 80, 84, 85, 86, 88, 92, 94, 95, 101, 103.
Jovial Club: 99.
Jukes, Reverend Mark: 37.

K

Kaiser, Henry J.: 60.
Kalamazoo, Mich.: 24.
Keith's (theater): 126.
Kelsey, Joel W.: 33.
Kennedy, Jackie: 148, 149, 150, *151.*
Kennedy, President John F.: 128.
King Mathias Sick and Benevolent Society: 64.
Knabenshue, A. Roy: 112.
Knabenshue, S.S. (father): 112.
Knights of Labor: 64.
Kocharoff, Alexander: 71.
Koch, Edward W.E., family home: *65.*
Kraus and Smith bank: 71.
Kraus, William: 71.

Kroger (food store): *157.*
Krueger, Bernie: 125.

L

Labor-Management Citizens' Committee: 143.
Lafayette, Ind.: 23.
Lagrange-Manhattan district: 95.
Lake Erie: 16, 20, 23, 24, 27, 37, 40, *42-43,* 97, *178.*
Lake Erie Park and Casino: 98, 99.
Lake Shore Michigan and Southern Railroad bridge: 9.
Lamson Brothers Store: *120-21, 122,* 162.
La Rose, Rose: 163.
Lasalle and Koch Building: 119.
Lasalle stores: 119, 120.
La Tabernella (nightclub): 80.
Lawford, Geoffrey: 156.
Lebanon (Lebanese): 71.
Leeper-Geddes House: *179.*
Legal Tender (canal boat): 29.
Lenk, Peter: 71.
Lenk's Hill: 71, 80, 138.
Lenk's Park: 71.
Levis Square Park: 158, 173.
Lewis, Charles L.: 34.
Libbey, Edward Drummond: *53, 54,* 57, 113, 118.
Libbey Glass Company: 53, *54-55,* 59.
Libbey House: *179.*
Libbey-Owens-Ford Company: 57, 148, 154.
Libbey-Owens Sheet Glass Company: 57.
Licavoli gang: 148, 149, 150, 151.
Licavoli, Thomas "Yonnie": 148, 149, *150.*
Life Magazine: 156.
Lima, Ohio: 84.
Lincoln, President Abraham: 86, 87.
Lion Stores: 119, 120, 122.
Locke, David Ross: 86, 87.
Lorraine Hotel: 39.
Lower Town: 71.
Lozier and Yost Bicycle Works: 50.
Lubitsky, Abe: 148.
Lucas City: 24.
Lucas County: 29, 86, 93, 136, 138.
Lucas County Courthouse: 12, *114-15,* 165.
Lucas County Equal Suffrage League: 88.
Lucas County Guards: 37.
Lucas County Jail: 149.
Lucas County Plan Commission: 118.
Lucas County Selective Service Board: 154.

M

McGrady, Edward F.: 143.
Machen, Agatha (mother): 36.
Machen, Augustine (father): 36.
Machen, Constant (brother): 36.
Machen, William Henry: 17, 18, 36.
Major, Mayor Guy: 84.
Majors and Minors: Poems (Paul Laurence Dunbar): 80.
Manewski, Miss ("Miss Toledo" winner): *122.*
Manhattan Advertiser: 32.
Manhattan, Ohio: 20, 24, 27, 29, 32, 95.

Marengo: 20, 27, 29.
Marleau's, David, hardware: *77.*
Martin, Glenn L.: 112.
Marx, Guido: 71.
Masonic auditorium: *170.*
Masonic Lodge: 163.
Masonic Temple: 163.
Mason, Judge H.D.: 37.
Mason, Stevens T.: 24.
Mathias, Louis: 75.
Maumee Bay: 24, 99.
Maumee City Express: 17.
Maumee Land and Railroad Company: 24.
Maumee, Ohio: 20, 24, 26, 27, 29, 95, 158, 160, 162, 177.
Maumee River: 16, 17, 18, 20, 22, 23, 24, 26, 29, 37, 38, 40, 43, 52, 64, 68, 86, 93, 118, 125, 128, 158, 169.
Maumee Valley: 4, 5, 16, 18, 19, 20, 23, 26, 27, 28, 29, 34, 95.
Maumee Valley Historical Society: 174.
Medical College of Ohio at Toledo: *170-71.*
Memorial Hall: 84.
Mensing, Charles: 99, *102.*
Merchants National Bank: *184.*
Miami and Erie Canal: 27, 29, 38, 95, 138.
Miami Indians: 18, 20.
Miami of the Lake: 18.
Miami of the Lake (newspaper): 26, 35.
Michigan (state): 99, 101, *100-01,* 158.
Michigan Territory: 16, 24, 27.
Middle Bass Island: 43.
Middlegrounds: 38, 86, 95.
Mid-States grain elevators: *161.*
Milburn Wagon Works: 48, 50, 95, 138.
Miles, William: *79.*
Miller, Dick: *177.*
Milwaukee, Wis.: 52, 71, 167.
Minneapolis, Minn.: 44.
Mississippi River: 41, 44.
Missouri River: 40.
"Miss Toledo" competition: *122.*
Monroe, Mich.: 24, 101.
Mott, Richard: 25, 86.
Mozart Society: 40.
Mud Creek: 39.
Mulhenny, John: 33.
Mudhen, Theodore Theodolphus: 37.
Mud Hens, Toledo: 37, 123, *177.*
Musicverein: 75.

N

Nasby Building (see also Security Building): 78, *118,* 119.
Nasby, Petroleum V.: 86, 87.
Nassr, Anthony M.: 112.
National Bank Building: 119.
National Guard: 143, *146-47.*
National Malleable Castings Company: 71.
National Open championships: 123.
National Woman's Suffrage Association: 86.
Navarre Hotel: 113.
Navarre Park: 68, 118.
Navarre, Peter: *18,* 36, 68.
Navarre Triangle: 68.

Nazis: 75.
Near East: 64, 71.
Neptune Hose Company: 33.
New Deal: 118, 134, 136, 138, 143, 148.
New England Glass Company: 54.
New York (city): 22, 23, 38, 39, 40, 54, 68, 78, 80, 87, 126, 160, 172.
New York (state): 23, 34, 84.
New York Central Railroad: 46-47.
New York World's Fair of 1939: 156.
North Cape Marina: 178.
North Dakota: 123.
North End (Vistula): 73.
Northtown Mall: 167.

O

Oak Openings: 28.
Oak Shade Hall: 77.
Oak Shade Park: 77.
Ohio Board of Canal Commissioners: 27.
Ohio Building: 165.
Ohio Canal: 40.
Ohio Citizens Building: 158.
Ohio River: 40.
Ohio Savings and Trust Company: 119, 120, 134, 135.
"Ohio's Newest City": 180.
Ohio Staats-Zeitung: 75.
Old Newsboys' Association: 134.
Old Orchard: 113.
Old Reliable (Milburn wagon): 48.
Olds, C.R., Grocery Store: 78.
Old South End: 65, 73.
Old West End: 71, 73, 74, 101, 113, 160, 176, 179.
Oliver House: 38, 39.
Olmstead, Frederick Law, Jr.: 113.
One Lake Erie Center: 120, 165.
Oregon, Ohio: 20, 77, 160, 162, 163, 177.
Orleans: 20.
Osthaus, Edmund: 34.
Ottawa Hills: 113, 158, 160, 177.
Ottawa Indians: 16, 18, 28.
Ottawa Park: 88, 103, 118.
Ottawa River: 113.
Overland auto: 59.
Owens Bottle Machine Company: 57.
Owens-Corning Fiberglas: 59.
Owens-Corning Fiberglas Tower: 158, 170.
Owens-Illinois: 57, 59, 134, 158, 162, 169.
Owens-Illinois (O-I) Building: 119, 161, 172.
Owens, Michael J.: 54, 56, 59.

P

Painesville, Ohio: 22.
Palace Theater: 126.
Panic of 1819: 20.
Panic of 1873: 48, 71.
Panic of 1893: 36.
Paramount Theater: 125, 126, 148.
Parke Street: 113.
Park Lane Hotel: 39.
Park Side: 113.
Paryski, Anthony A.: 64.

Peace of Paris of 1763: 18.
People's Theater: 126, 127.
Perry, Commander Oliver Hazard: 20, 21.
Perrysburg Journal: 86.
Perrysburg, Ohio: 18, 20, 22, 24, 27, 29, 37, 78, 95, 160, 177.
Philadelphia, Pa.: 75, 156.
Phillips-Sylvania district: 95.
Pinewood: 64, 80, 138.
Playdium Theater: 165.
Plaza Hotel: 169.
Pluto Oil Company: 36.
Point Place: 99, 177.
Poland (Polish, Poles): 64, 68, 71, 73, 75.
"Polanders": 75.
Pontiac, Chief: 19.
Poor Relief, Division of: 143.
Pope, Albert A.: 59, 60.
Pope-Hartford auto: 59.
Pope Motor Car Company: 59, 95.
Pope-Toledo auto: 59.
Portage River: 22.
Port Lawrence Company: 20.
Port Lawrence, Ohio: 20, 22, 23, 24, 26, 29.
Presbyterian-Congregational building: 34.
Presbyterians: 34.
Presque Isle Park: 98, 99.
Progressive movement (Progressives): 68, 84, 85, 86, 88, 90-91, 92, 93, 94, 95, 101, 113.
Prohibition: 80, 113, 148, 149, 151.
Promenade Park: 172.
Propylaea (sculpture): 176.
"Pruskies": 75.
Public Works Administration (PWA): 97, 138.
Put-in-Bay: 20, 26, 43.
Pythian Castle: 118.

Q

Quakers: 25, 85, 86.

R

Rakestraw, L.M.: 112.
Rauls, Audrey: 151.
Ravine Park: 118.
Reams, Frazier: 150, 151.
Republicans (Republican party): 84, 88.
Richardson, Alpa: 174.
Rickard, Tex.: 123.
Riverside Park: 103, 118.
Riverview I: 158, 160, 162.
Rivoli (theater): 126.
Rockefeller, John D.: 48.
Rodemich Brothers grocery: 2-3, 76-77, 78.
Rogers, George L.: 149.
Rogers, Isaiah: 38.
Romeis, Jacob: 71.
Roosevelt, Eleanor: 156.
Roosevelt, President Franklin D.: 143.
Rosary Cathedral: 164.
Rossford Army Depot: 158.
Rossford, Ohio: 57, 95.
Russia (Russians): 64, 71.

S

Saarinen, Eliel: 119.
Saengerbund: 75.
Safety Building: 169.
Saint Adelbert's Church: 71.
Saint Francis de Sales Catholic Church: 32, 34, 36.
Saint Hedwig's Church: 64.
Saint Lawrence Seaway: 43, 156.
Saint Louis' Church: 64.
Saint Louis, Mo.: 27, 52, 71, 177.
Saint Louis World's Fair of 1904: 59, 112.
Saint Patrick's Church: 64, 68.
Saint Vincent Hospital: 32.
Sampson, Caswell: 79.
Sandusky, Ohio: 22, 43.
San Francisco, Cal.: 112, 176.
Schonnacker's, Michael, Hall: 75.
Schypaski (Szperski), John and Joseph: 75.
Scott, Frank: 26.
Scott High School: 122, 123.
Scott, Jesup Wakeman: 24, 26, 29, 32, 39, 41, 156, 172, 180.
Scott, Jesup W., family: 86, 176.
SeaGate Center: 161, 169, 172, 176.
Second National Bank Building: 119.
Secor Hotel: 39.
Security Building (see also Nasby Building): 78, 119.
Security-Home Trust: 134.
Segur, Rosa L.: 86.
Senate, U.S.: 34.
Serbian Beneficial Union: 64.
Sharpshooters: 64.
Sheets, George: 71.
Sisters of Charity (Grey Nuns): 32.
Slovenian Beneficial Union: 64.
Smead, Benjamin Franklin: 32.
Smith Bridge Company: 56-57.
Smith, Dr. Calvin: 37.
Smith, Grace E.: 142, 163.
Smith, Robert W.: 56-57.
Smith's Cafeteria: 142, 163.
Smyth, Anson: 34.
Snow, Dr. John: 37.
"Soaphouse Pete's" public bathhouse: 113.
Social Gospel movement: 85.
Social Service Federation: 136.
Soldiers Memorial Building: 116.
South (Southerners): 64.
South Bend, Ind.: 48.
South Carolina: 26.
South Carolina Female College: 26.
South Toledo: 95, 101, 113, 118, 177.
Spafford, Jarvis: 22, 37.
Spanish-American War: 48, 115.
Specie Circular: 27.
Spencer, John: 79.
Spencer Township: 80.
Spicer Manufacturing: 60, 158.
Spieker Terrace: 138.
Spitzer, A.L.: 112.
Spitzer Building: 112, 118, 119.
Springfield Roadster: 50.
Standard Oil "trust": 48.
State Department, U.S.: 36.
State Theater: 126.

Station No. 7 (fire company): 33.
Steedman, General James Blair: 45, 50-51, 113.
Steinem, Gloria: 88.
Steinem, Pauline: 88.
Stengel, Charles Dillon "Casey": 123.
Steriff's Ohio Smoke Shop: 68.
Stevens, George W.: 34.
Stickney, Benjamin F.: 23, 24, 26, 32.
Stickney, One: 24.
Stickney School: 66-67.
Stickney, Two: 24.
Stine, David L.: 115.
Storer Broadcasting: 119.
Stowe, Harriet Beecher: 34.
Stranahan Building: 170-71.
Stranahan-Rothschild House: 179.
Studio Club: 148.
Suffrage movement: 25.
Sulkin, Jacob "Firetop": 148, 150, 151.
Sullivan, Louis: 119.
Summit-Cherry Market: 99.
Sumner, Charles: 87.
Sunday, Billy: 68.
Sun Oil Company: 160.
Superior Street Station: 101.
Supreme Court, U.S.: 80.
Swabians: 75, 77.
"Swabs": 75.
"Swamponia—A Tragedy in One Act" (T. T. Mudhen): 37.
Swan Creek: 20, 38, 95.
Swan Creek Metropark: 158.
Swayne Field: 123.
Swiss-Germans: 75, 77.
Sylvania Academy: 34.
Sylvania, Ohio: 28, 160, 163, 177.
Sylvania Township: 160.
Syria (Syrians): 71.
Szperski (Schypaski), John and Joseph: 75.

T

Taft, Charles P.: 143.
Tatum, Art: 80.
Taylor, Graham: 85.
Tchernayoff, General: 75.
Tecumseh, Chief: 19.
Ten Mile Creek: 16-17, 36.
Terre Haute, Ind.: 59, 172.
Teutonia Männerchor: 75, 77.
Teutonic Fire Guards: 33.
Thacher, Addison Q.: 136.
Third Baptist Church: 78.
Third Reich: 75.
Thomas, Danny: 68.
Tiedtke store: 120, 122, 125.
Tillinghast House: 179.
Timiney, Captain George: 148.
Titus, Israel (postmaster): 37.
Tobey, Dr. Henry: 78.
Toledo, The (theater): 126.
Toledo Academy of Fine Arts: 34.
Toledoan's Creed: 55.
Toledo Beach: 98, 99.
Toledo Blade: 26, 32, 34, 37, 39, 40, 52, 54, 75, 80, 86, 87, 92, 156.
Toledo City Mission: 136.

Toledo City Plan Commission: 95, 113, 118.
"Toledo Day" 1931: 125.
Toledo Edison Building: 158, 161, 162, 163.
Toledo Express (German-Language newspaper): 64.
Toledo Express Airport: 163.
Toledofest (Festival): 169, 174.
Toledo Gazette: 32.
Toledo Handbook, 1912: 55.
Toledo High School: 32.
Toledo Hospital: 117.
Toledo House: 33.
Toledo Humane Society: 86.
Toledo-Lucas County Plan Commission: 118, 156.
Toledo-Lucas County Port Authority: 156.
Toledo Lyceum: 40.
Toledo Manual Training School: 89.
Toledo Metropolitan Housing Authority: 138.
Toledo Metropolitan Park Board: 118.
Toledo Museum of Art: 34, 113, 164, 176.
Toledo Naval Armory: 136.
Toledo Newsboys Association: 81.
Toledo, Norwalk and Cleveland Railroad: 38.
"Toledo Number One" (airship): 112.
"Toledo Plan" for industrial peace: 143.
Toledo Public Library: 115, 148.
Toledo Rail and Light Company: 92, 101.
Toledo Scale: 58, 59, 78, 154, 156.
Toledo School Board: 88.
Toledo, Spain: 23, 68.
Toledo State Hospital: 78, 116-17.
Toledo steam auto: 50.
Toledo Symphony Orchestra: 172.
"Toledo the Future Great City of the Midwest": 180.
Toledo Tigers: 172.
Toledo Times: 93.

"Toledo Tomorrow" exhibit: 156.
Toledo Transmission Plant of Chevrolet Motor Company: 143.
Toledo Trust: 134.
Toledo Trust Building: 119, 172.
Toledo University of Arts and Trades: 26.
Toledo War of 1835: 24.
Toledo Zoo: 103, 122, 136, 138, 143, 156, 168, 176.
Toledo Zoological Society: 138.
Town Hall Theater: 163.
Treaty of Greenville: 20.
Tremainsville, Ohio: 32, 95.
Trianon Ballroom: 125.
Trinity Episcopal Church: 34.
Tubular Axle Company: 48.
Tunget (oil) Well: 84.
Turkey Foot Rock: 14.
Turner Hall: 75, 77.
Turners, the: 75, 77.
Turnervereine: 75.
Turn of the Balance, The (Brand Whitlock): 94.
Twelve Mile Tract (Twelve Mile Square Reserve): 20.

U

Underground Railway: 78.
Union School: 34.
Union Station: 95, 156.
Union Terminal: 156.
Universalist Unitarians: 34, 86.
University Hall: 143.
University of Toledo: 26, 86, 167, 176, 177 (basketball team).
Urbaytis, Frank: 149.
Urbaytis, Joe: 148, 149.
Utah: 20, 37.

V

Valentine Theater: 126.
Vandalia, Ill.: 16.
Vincennes, Ind.: 18.
Vistula Meadows: 113, 143, 163.
Vistula, Ohio: 23, 24, 26, 29, 71, 73, 172.

Vita-Temple: 126, 127.
V-J Day: 157.
Volkesbund (the Bund): 75.

W

Wabash and Erie Canal: 23, 27, 29.
Wabash Grain Elevator Number Four: 44.
Wabash Railroad: 39.
Wabash River valley: 18, 23.
Wabash Roundhouse: 138.
Wachter, Harry: 113.
Waggoner, Clark: 41.
Waite High School: 123, 136.
Wakeman, Jessup: 26.
Walbridge Park: 103.
Walding, William J.: 41.
Waldorf Hotel: 39.
Wall, Fire Chief: 93.
War of 1812: 16, 18, 19, 20, 23.
Warren African Methodist Episcopal Church: 78.
Waterfront Railway: 168.
Waterville, Ohio: 29. 162.
Waverly Electric auto: 59.
Wayne, General Anthony: 20.
Webster, Daniel: 34, 37.
Weiler, Charles, Homes: 138.
Wells-Bowen Company: 113.
West End Community Welfare Club: 136.
Westmoreland: 113, 177.
West Toledo: 73, 77, 101, 143.
Wheeler Opera House: 107, 126.
Wheeling & Lake Erie Railroad Bridge: 86.
Wheeling, W.Va.: 54.
Whigs: 26, 33, 34.
White City Park: 98, 99.
White, Governor George: 143.
Whitlock, Brand: 59, 84, 86, 88, 92, 94, 95, 101, 113, 118, 180.
Whitlock, Brand, Homes: 138.
Whitney, Harriet, Vocational School: 22.
Whittlesey, Elisha: 26.
Wildwood Metropark: 183.

Wildwood Preserve: 158.
Willard, Jess: 123.
Williams, Sarah R.L.: 86.
Williams, Uyless: 154.
Willis Day Warehousing Company: 158.
Willys, John North: 59, 60.
Willys-Knight auto: 59.
Willys-Overland Company: 59, 71, 95, 134, 154, 156.
Willys Park: 103, 118.
Wisconsin: 18.
Wolcott House: 174.
Woodbridge, William: 16.
Woodville (shopping mall): 162.
Wooster, Ohio: 20.
Works Progress Administration (WPA): 24, 128, 132-33, 138, 140-41, 143, 148, 154, 158.
World War I: 64, 71, 77, 80, 93.
World War II: 60, 75, 77, 138, 154-57.
Wright brothers: 112.
Wright, Samuel: 37.
WSPD Radio: 80, 119.

Y

Yale Bicycle Company: 59.
Yaranowsky, "Chalky Red": 148.
Yaryan, Homer T.: 59.
YMCA Building, Jefferson Avenue: 138.
Yost, Joseph L.: 50.
Young Ladies Literary Institute and Boarding School of the Sisters of Notre Dame: 34.
Young Men's Association: 40.
Young Men's Christian Association: 85.
Youngstown, Ohio: 47.
Yugoslavia (Yugoslavs): 64.
Yuma (steamer): 128, 129.

Z

Zion Reform Church: 70.

Photo Credits

Publishers' Acknowledgments

The editors and publishers are indebted to a number of people and organizations who, over the many months of preparation and production, believed as we did that Toledo area citizens and visitors should have an entertaining and pictorially interesting history book.

Our special thanks, of course, to authors Morgan Barclay and Charles N. Glaab. Haz and Sue Keyser provided a sensitive eye, a steady shutter and strong support. For that we are grateful.

To the entire Maumee Valley Historical Society, its officers and volunteer leadership, a hearty thanks. Special gratitude goes to Anne Marie Ballmer who shepherded the project from early considerations to conclusion.

Mike Porter and the staff of the Toledo Area Chamber of Commerce lent considerable support and enthusiasm. Thanks, also, to Kent Galvin, Robin Orwig and Wanda Langenderfer of the Chamber.

Edwin Dodd, chairman of Owens-Illinois, along with Jack Pacquette, were particularly helpful and for their support we are indebted.

In addition, our thanks to Dr. Frederick J. Folger III for his contribution as historical consultant.

The staff of Continental Heritage Press deserves considerable credit for the success of *Toledo: Gateway to the Great Lakes,* especially Mickey Thompson, BJ Mallinger, Laura Murphree, Tim Colwell, Karen Keim, Joel Turner, Marie Salsbury, Ginny Katz and Tony Flatt. Our special acknowledgment to Rick Robinson, Nina LeMaire, Nancy Myers, Ann McGill and Pat Plunkett.

Authors' Acknowledgments

This volume could not have been completed without the help of many people. Toledo-Lucas County Public Library Director Ardath Danford and Assistant Director Clyde Scoles gave administrative support to the project. Local history department staff members Donna Christian, Jane Habib, Tana Mosier and Matthew Onion provided valuable suggestions. Clerical assistance from Mary E. Glaab, Martha A. Glaab, June Kutzly, Pat Neikirk and Sandra Kujawa helped the project proceed smoothly.

Photographic printing by the Toledo Photo Arts Club and by Matthew Onion added to the quality of the volume. Kathy Trimble and Mary Reddington of the *Toledo Blade* library gathered visuals and the American Turners provided valuable information.

The Maumee Valley Historical Society and its Publications Committee worked diligently on the planning of the project. Cynthia Barclay offered her research and editing talents and Fred Folger read the manuscript. We wish especially to acknowledge graduate research papers, theses and dissertations. The authors accept joint responsibility for the entire book.

Charles N. Glaab
Morgan J. Barclay

Students at Davis Business College, one of Toledo's oldest businesses, around 1895.

Concept and design by
Continental Heritage Press, Inc., Tulsa.
Printed and bound by Walsworth Publishing Company.
Type is Cheltenham and Bodoni.
Text Sheets are Warren Flo. Endleaves are Eagle A.
Cover is Holliston Kingston Linen.